International
Library of the
Philosophy of
Education

Plato,
utilitarianism
and education

International
Library of the
Philosophy of
Education

General Editor

R. S. Peters

Professor of Philosophy of Education
Institute of Education
University of London

Plato, utilitarianism and education

Robin Barrow

Department of Education
University of Leicester

Routledge & Kegan Paul

London and Boston

First published in 1975
by Routledge & Kegan Paul Ltd
Broadway House, 68–74 Carter Lane,
London EC4V 5EL and
9 Park Street, Boston, Mass. 02108, USA
Set in Baskerville 10 on 11 point
and printed in Great Britain by
Ebenezer Baylis and Son Ltd
The Trinity Press, Worcester, and London

ISBN 0 7100 8044 1

Contents

Contents

General editor's note

There is a growing interest in philosophy of education amongst students of philosophy as well as amongst those who are more specifically and practically concerned with educational problems. Philosophers, of course, from the time of Plato onwards, have taken an interest in education and have dealt with education in the context of wider concerns about knowledge and the good life. But it is only quite recently in this country that philosophy of education has come to be conceived of as a specific branch of philosophy like the philosophy of science or political philosophy.

To call philosophy of education a specific branch of philosophy is not, however, to suggest that it is a distinct branch in the sense that it could exist apart from established branches of philosophy such as epistemology, ethics, and philosophy of mind. It would be more appropriate to conceive of it as drawing on established branches of philosophy and bringing them together in ways which are relevant to educational issues. In this respect the analogy with political philosophy would be a good one. Thus use can often be made of work that already exists in philosophy. In tackling, for instance, issues such as the rights of parents and children, punishment in schools, and the authority of the teacher, it is possible to draw on and develop work already done by philosophers on 'rights', 'punishment', and 'authority'. In other cases, however, no systematic work exists in the relevant branches of philosophy—e.g. on concepts such as 'education', 'teaching', 'learning', 'indoctrination'. So philosophers of education have had to break new ground—in these cases in the philosophy of mind. Work on educational issues can also bring to life and throw new light on long-standing problems in philosophy. Concentration, for instance, on the particular predicament of children can throw new light on problems of punishment and responsibility. G. E. Moore's old worries about what sorts of things are good in themselves can be brought to life by urgent questions about the justification of the curriculum in schools.

There is a danger in philosophy of education, as in any other applied field, of polarization to one of two extremes. The work could be practically relevant but philosophically feeble; or it could be philosophically sophisticated but remote from practical problems. The aim of the International Library of the Philosophy of Education

General editor's note

is to build up a body of fundamental work in this area which is both practically relevant and philosophically competent. For unless it achieves both types of objective it will fail to satisfy those for whom it is intended and fall short of the conception of philosophy of education which the International Library is meant to embody.

To date there has been too little attention paid by philosophers of education to the contribution made to the subject by philosophers of the past. Robin Barrow's book on Plato is therefore a welcome addition to the International Library; for his treatment of Plato is consistent with its aims in that he attempts to show the relevance of Plato's thought to contemporary problems.

The way in which Barrow demonstrates Plato's relevance, however, makes his book extremely controversial. For he holds not only that Plato has been unconvincingly criticized by liberal-democratic philosophers such as Russell, Popper, and Crossman, but also that his basic thesis about society and education is still tenable. Barrow believes that Plato's basic concern was rightly with human happiness and that the claims of freedom both in society and in education must be subordinated to this. He pursues the consequences of this for education in particular and maintains that the much lauded current educational ideal of autonomy needs re-assessment.

There will be many who will dispute whether Barrow does justice to Plato's critics, whether it is really appropriate to regard Plato as a utilitarian, and whether Barrow's own defence of happiness as the ultimate moral principle is tenable. But he argues his case clearly and persuasively, and, on many points he certainly has a case to answer. It is hoped that, at very least, his book will lead many to have a fresh look at what Plato actually said; for many hold a stereotype of Plato's views on education which is not based on any close familiarity with his work. It is also hoped that it will lead to a re-examination of some current educational ideals which are just taken for granted.

R.S.P.

Preface

Essentially I am concerned only with Plato's *Republic* as a source for his political, ethical and educational theory. References to other dialogues include the name of the dialogue in question, e.g. *Gorgias* 490 B. All Platonic references without the name of a dialogue included are to the *Republic*, e.g. 421 E.

I should like to take this opportunity to thank F. W. Garforth and R. K. Elliott for various helpful comments that they have made on an earlier draft of the text. I owe an even greater debt of gratitude to R. S. Peters and Pat White. To the latter in particular I am indebted not only for a wealth of detailed and constructive criticism, but also for continued encouragement and support over a period of time that has come to seem like a lifetime.

Robin Barrow

Introduction   I

1 Plato's critics

The view that I shall put forward is that utilitarianism is the only
acceptable ethical theory and that this was recognised by Plato
in the *Republic*. What is particularly important about Plato is his
ability to take a comprehensive view of the logical consequences for
society of his ethical standpoint, and hence his ability to consider
education in the context of ethical, social and political considerations
rather than in isolation. Stated simply his ethical and political
philosophy is based upon the principle that all men are equally
entitled to happiness and that consequently provision should be
made for the happiness of all men in the ideal state. This ultimate
moral principle has the immediate consequence for education that
its prime object should be to produce adults who may successfully
contribute to the happiness of the whole community, while themselves enjoying happiness within that community. This in turn
leads to the view that the claims of freedom must be subordinated
to the claims of happiness and consequently (if the argument is
accepted) that various terms currently lauded in educational
circles that are essentially regarded as desirable under the aegis of
freedom, such as 'autonomy' and 'self-development', have to be
reassessed as educational objectives.

Plato, of course, does not formally and clearly enunciate a
utilitarian ethic, which is why it is necessary to argue that he is in
fact committed to one. On the other hand he alone of those who
might reasonably be regarded as utilitarians has a real grasp of what
consistent adherence to utilitarianism would involve; he alone
unblushingly spells out the implications of utilitarianism. But
whether we blush or not, if a case can be made for the claim that the
Republic is consistently grounded on utilitarianism and that it is
right that it should be, as I shall try to argue, it follows that a great
deal of current educational theory and practice is fundamentally
unacceptable.

Perhaps the single most important factor that has contributed
to a widespread failure at the present time to see both the nature
of Plato's contribution to educational theory and the significance of
that contribution, has been the nature of recent Platonic criticism.
The critics of Plato with whom I am primarily concerned are:
K. R. Popper, Bertrand Russell and R. H. S. Crossman. These

three men I shall dub the liberal-democrats. It is important to stress at this point that in using the term 'liberal-democrats' in this book, as I frequently do for convenience, I do so only as a shorthand reference to these three writers. My criticisms of liberal-democratic philosophy are not intended to apply necessarily to all who might regard themselves (or be regarded) as liberal-democrats, but only to the particular brand of liberal-democratic theory to be found in the work of Russell, Popper and Crossman, and to any others whom the shoe may fit. Occasionally I cite passages from other philosophers which seem to betray a liberal-democratic stance (in my limited sense), but then I am concerned with the implications of the passage in question, rather than the overall philosophical viewpoint of the author in question.

The liberal-democrats explicitly claim that they are champions of 'our civilisation'[1] and 'our ideals',[2] by which they mean the ideals of the Free West as opposed to those of any planned society. To them, given this premiss, Plato, of course, is not simply mistaken here or inconsistent there. He is dangerous. His work is 'a savage . . . attack upon liberal ideas'[3] according to Crossman, but, according to Popper, 'Crossman himself is not free from that tendency' to idealise Plato 'which he so clearly exposes'.[4] Russell describes the *Republic* as 'repulsive' and regards the fact that it 'should have been admired, on its political side, by decent people' as 'perhaps the most astonishing example of literary snobbery in all history'.[5]

I shall try to argue that Plato is not some subtle reactionary who has just been detected in his evil game by a few percipient champions of humanity; every correct observation made about the *Republic* by Popper and Crossman, and there are many, is, and has always been, fully apparent to any who bothered to read it. Plato knew what he was doing and he did it openly: he was challenging the philosophy of men such as Popper and Crossman. And he did this because he believed that the open society was doomed to promote inequality, unhappiness and injustice. He also knew why the open society chose to pay such a price: because it clung in an inconsistent manner to an ill-defined ideal of freedom. The *Republic* is the great challenge to 'our civilisation'. And that challenge is not met by revealing the fact that it is a challenge.

Russell, one of the most prolific of writers, in fact wrote very little on the *Republic*, and we are concerned only with his summary and comment on it in his *History of Western Philosophy*, and with the essay 'Philosophy and politics'.[6] The former is considerably less strident in tone and provides a technically accurate summary of the content of the *Republic*, but its main contribution to the Platonic debate is that it illustrates the great danger in assuming that the *Republic* can be meaningfully summarised without distortion. For instance, Russell writes: 'Plato begins by deciding that the citizens are to be divided into three classes: the common people, the soldiers and the Guardians. The last alone are to have political power'.[7] This is not a false statement, but, in such truncated form, it is bound to give the impression that Plato begins by observing an actual city, ('the' citizens), and immediately draws a distinction between those who are of the common people and those who are not. (Crossman, more specifically, claims that Plato held 'the presumption that wise men are not often found among the working classes').[8] But both writers are ignoring the fact that Plato is defining the group which may be called the common people or the working class by reference to their lack of wisdom. He does not say 'the common people are not wise', but 'those who are not wise shall be called the common people'. To say the least, this point is obscured by Russell's brevity.

Likewise when he comments that Plato's definition of justice 'makes it possible to have inequalities of power and privilege without injustice',[9] a number of important questions are raised: ought people to have equal power? What is equal power? Could everybody have equal power? Alas, the questions are not answered.

Even in this earlier work, Russell is prone to dismiss by means of emotive phraseology ('in spite of all the fine talk, skill in war and enough to eat is all that will be achieved'),[10] but this technique becomes almost the only manner of argument by the time that 'Philosophy and politics' was written. In the *History of Western Philosophy* all the complexities of the *Republic* had perforce been summarised in ten pages; now they are summarised in two words: 'totalitarian tract'. It is taken for granted that the term is pejorative, and Russell then attempts to identify Plato's totalitarianism, if such it be, with that of Hitler and Lenin, who are referred to as disciples of Plato who provided 'a practical exegesis' of his 'reactionary tendencies'.[11] The very lack of distinction between Hitler and Lenin, even if one happens to dislike both, is philosophically disturbing.

Although Crossman rather surprisingly claims, in the introduction to the 1963 edition of *Plato Today*, to have 'proved Plato wrong', the text of the book still shows no evidence of an attempt to 'prove' anything, which is in fact one of the reasons that *Plato Today* is considerably more satisfying than Popper's *Open Society*; the other reason is that it lacks the emotive tones of both Russell and Popper. Crossman gives no indication that he intends to do more than explain that Plato did not share 'our ideals', and consider what Plato might have said in respect of various aspects of the modern world. It does not appear that even those ideals which might nominally be claimed to be shared by both Plato and our civilisation (such as 'equality') are supposed to come under examination: all Crossman seems to need to say is that Plato's view of equality is different from that of the liberal-democrats. The saving grace of *Plato Today* is, thus, that it does not purport to be philosophical.

There are nonetheless certain claims made by Crossman that it will be necessary to challenge below, particularly the view that Plato hated 'the mob', thought that 'the working classes must be put in their places' and was 'ignorant of human nature'.[12] The last charge in particular interests me, and I shall argue that it more properly fits the liberal-democrats, with their assumption that, because they are equipped to benefit from, and enjoy, a large degree of personal responsibility, so must everyone else be.

But Crossman also has some very interesting and pertinent things to say. His review of the three evils that Plato was out to combat (class-warfare, irresponsible government, and bad education) is straightforward and, in my view, accurate.[13]

The weakness of *Plato Today*, as I hope to make clear, is that its basic method of approach to Plato is illegitimate. The *Republic* is a complete structure, many of the parts of which there is no reason to suppose that Plato would approve in different circumstances; the importance of Plato, today, lies in his principles and not in his detailed proposals. To take an obvious example: Plato must be understood to believe that censorship can be justified; but we are not justified in concluding either that Plato would accept any censorship under any conditions, or that today in our world he would censor Homer.

Thus the suggestion that Plato today would approve of fascism, and admire Hitler's success in propagating National Socialism as an example of the ruler's use of a noble lie, is nothing short of facile.[14] Whether Plato would approve of National Socialism, and the use of censorship and propaganda to perpetuate it, must depend upon the doctrine of National Socialism: the suggestion that he would believe that the Aryan race was superior and that the Jewish race deserved extermination, is entirely without foundation, and, in so far as it seems to involve discrimination between peoples on no recognisably relevant criteria, it would in fact be anathema to Plato, whose Republic is formally founded on the principle of discrimination in accord with relevant criteria only.[15]

We come now to the third and greatest wave that has to be faced if any clear understanding of Plato is to be arrived at: the work of K. R. Popper: *The Open Society and its Enemies*.

One of the most extraordinary features of Popper's criticism of Plato is that he more or less admits that he is not a philosopher and does not want to be one; he is rather a social technician. And yet he has considerable admiration for Plato as a sociologist;[16] it is Plato's philosophy which he dislikes.[17]

The social engineer believes that the scientific basis of politics
would consist of the factual information necessary for the
construction or alteration of social institutions, in accordance
with our wishes or aims . . . speaking more generally we may
say that the technologist approaches institutions rationally as
means that serve certain ends . . . and that he judges them
wholly according to their appropriateness, efficiency, simplicity,
etc.

This is reasonable enough from the point of view of the social
engineer; but Plato is a philosopher and one who is concerned with
ends. What are our aims and ends to be? By contrast Popper seems
to regard this sort of question as impossible to answer. He pours
scorn on what he calls 'methodological essentialism, i.e. the theory
that it is the aim of science to reveal essences and to describe them
by means of definition',[18] and contrasts it with 'methodological
nominalism' which[19]

aims at describing how a thing behaves in certain
circumstances . . . in other words it sees the aim of science in
the description of things and events in our experience . . . the
methodological nominalist will never think that a question
like . . . 'what is an atom' is an important question but he will
attach importance to a question like 'under what conditions
does an atom radiate light?'

This is reasonable enough as an account of what the business
of science may be, and one may agree with Popper when he goes
further[20] and argues that social scientists ought to be asking the
same kind of question about 'government' or 'civilisation'; but
whether philosophers ought to be social scientists would seem to be
an altogether different question.

The importance of Popper's apparent hostility to the philosopher
who is concerned with the analysis of and the attempt to justify
ends becomes apparent in his chapter on totalitarian justice.[21]

What do we really mean when we speak of 'Justice'? I do not
think that verbal questions of this kind are particularly
important . . . since such terms are always used in various
senses. However, I think that most of us, especially those whose
general outlook is humanitarian, mean something like this

and Popper goes on to delineate justice in terms of 'equality'. But
the question 'What is equality?' then becomes extremely important,
and we are not really any nearer knowing what Popper regards as
just, let alone why he does so.

5

Later he argues that the proper approach is not to ask essentialist questions such as 'What is the state?', but rather 'What do we demand from the state?'; but these are simply different questions, asked for different purposes. 'What do we demand from the state?'[22] is a question about what we as a matter of fact do; different people might demand all sorts of things; the question that Plato is interested in is not what people *are* doing, but what they ought to be doing. 'What is the state?' is a way of questioning what one thinks the role of the state ought to be. Popper's question can only become equivalent, if it is already agreed that all moral injunctions or values are simply arbitrary expressions of approval which Popper specifically denies at one point,[23] and indeed the whole tenor of his book implies that certain things, such as freedom, are good in an absolute sense.

In view of Popper's reluctance to analyse or defend the values which he sees as ends that ought to be aimed at, particularly humaneness, reasonableness, freedom, equality, and individualism, and in view of his respect for Plato as a sociologist, the real purpose of his attack is hard to discern and we need to look more closely at what he is doing.

Fundamentally he is inspired by an optimistic enthusiasm for 'a movement which began three centuries ago . . . the longing of uncounted, unknown men to free themselves and their minds from the tutelage of authority'.[24] And he dislikes closed or tribal societies in which people are the victims of various taboos. So far this merely amounts to the expression of an opinion; one may not share Popper's conviction that the progress of America gives good reason for optimism; one may disagree with his assumption that the members of a tribal society are to be numbered amongst those '*longing* . . . to free themselves . . . from the tutelage of authority'. However, since it is merely an opinion, there is no need to do more than note it. He records approval of the attempt 'to reject the absolute authority of the merely established', which I share, if we understand this to mean that the mere fact that something is the case, does not establish that it ought to be the case.

He then gives an analysis of 'historicism', a doctrine that would seem to involve the view that society follows a certain law of development which can be predicted and hence anticipated, but not, of course, altered (since, by definition, the law is 'inexorable and irresistible').[25] Popper objects to historicism on the grounds that 'the future depends on ourselves and we do not depend on any historical necessity'.[26] And the impetus to his hostility to Plato seems to come from his assumption that Plato is a historicist.

Popper makes an inadequate attempt to justify this assumption, by arguing that Plato promulgated the historicist law that 'all

social change is corruption or decay'.[27] Even if this extraordinary
assertion could be itself justified, it still would not be true that Plato
is a historicist since, as Popper admits, he seems to believe that
'it is possible for us to break the iron law of destiny'[28] and that is
tantamount to saying that 'the future depends on ourselves'.

However it is not the historicism, or 'the definite limitations'[29]
on his historicism, but 'the totalitarian tendency of Plato's philosophy' that Popper now wants to criticise. He assumes that Plato
assumes that the conditions of the Republic 'were realised in ancient
times',[30] and that that is why Plato regards them as admirable.
Apparently the admitted fact that the notion of philosopher-kings
was not 'realised in ancient times', and yet is regarded by Plato as
the necessary condition for his ideal state, does not upset the thesis
that for Plato what is good is what is ancient.[31]

Popper then claims, entirely without foundation as we shall see,
that the Republic is divided on racialist grounds into a superior
class and an altogether inferior race who are 'human cattle' and
'do not interest Plato at all'.[32] Plato is, therefore, now in the un-
enviable position of being apparently firmly convinced of an
inexorable iron law of destiny leading towards disintegration,
which can nonetheless be easily broken by advocating racialist
supremacy. The resulting society is not good, firstly because it is
not just (this, I would agree, would be a valid criticism at this
point, if it could be established that the society is racialist in Popper's
sense of the term); secondly because it is not free; and thirdly
because it is a closed society. And there, rather surprisingly, the
matter is left. A concluding chapter merely acknowledges that
Plato was a good psycho-sociologist, who rightly diagnosed unhappiness in his fellow men and prescribed a removal of the strain
of personal responsibility. However 'we must bear the strain'.[33]

We are thus back at square one, faced with Popper's enthusiasm
for the open society. There has been considerable and detailed
interpretation of the *Republic* almost all of which is quite inaccurate.[34]
But what there has not been, at any point, is analysis of and argument in favour of the freedom, the happiness, the equality of the
open society, which we are asked to enthuse over. Presumably on
the grounds that we ought not to ask 'What is freedom?' or 'What
is the open society?', but ought rather to assume the desirability
of these 'demands' and ask 'How can we realise the open society?'[35]
It goes without saying that if we demand the open society, which is
defined by Popper in contrast to the Republic, we shall not also
demand the Republic. His book therefore is in a real sense wholly
unnecessary, except for those, surely a minute number of people,
who were unaware that the Republic was a closed or tribal society.

2 Liberal-democratic philosophy

It is not only the quality of liberal-democratic criticism of Plato, however, that causes one a certain amount of dismay. There is also the fact that liberal-democratic philosophy itself—the alternative viewpoint that we are asked to admire in preference to Platonism— is at best obscure and at worst incoherent.

Prima facie at least it seems that the lynch-pin of liberal-democratic theory is a belief in a plurality of ultimate moral principles, amongst which are a principle of equality, a principle of freedom and a principle of happiness.[36] These ultimate principles are articles of faith. It cannot be shown that they ought to be adopted. One cannot demonstrate, for example, the truth of the claim that all men ought to be free or that all men are equally entitled to happiness. Furthermore, implicit in the belief that these various principles are ultimate is the claim that they are of equal weight. I draw this implication out because of its importance. It appears that the liberal-democrats would endorse this statement from Warnock: 'It is clear that moral principles *may* point in opposite directions; and I can discern no ground on which one could pronounce *in general* which, in such a case, is to predominate over another'.[37] In other words, in the case of a clash between two or more principles one cannot say that one *necessarily* ought to take precedence over the other.

Given this lynch-pin to their thought, it is readily understandable that the liberal-democrats should feel hostile to Plato and his approach to education. It is scarcely surprising that they should tend to favour such notions as individual autonomy, and hence an educational pattern that promotes autonomy, partly because autonomy involves freedom which they value, and partly because autonomy is incompatible with the business of causing people to believe things that they have not worked out for themselves. In view of the presumed status of moral principles as no more than articles of faith, it is repugnant to them in this important area to cause people to share their particular beliefs—as Plato prima facie advocates in the *Republic*. For the same reason they have a great abhorrence of indoctrination. They also tend to interpret the claims of equality, in the educational or any other sphere, as a demand for equality of opportunity, since they would otherwise be continually faced with a clash between the claims of equality and the claims of freedom. Putting the matter negatively we may say that one would naturally expect the liberal-democrats to be hostile to any educational programme that ignores any of their principles, particularly the principle of freedom, or that, in the large and important sphere of values, ignores their contention that ultimate values are essentially unknowable.

The problem for the liberal-democrats is surely this: if we accept their assumption about a plurality of ultimate principles of equal weight, as many contemporary philosophers, who do not necessarily see eye to eye on all matters with the liberal-democrats or with each other, do, it follows that we cannot make a reasoned choice between a wide variety of educational (or social or any other) proposals; for, of the widely different, but seriously intended, educational programmes that have been put forward, there are few which could not be defended by appeal to one or other of the plurality of ultimate principles. If one cannot in general decide on the relative importance to be attached to principles, how can one ever decide in particular cases between the claims of two ultimate principles? And if one cannot decide, how can one criticise others who do in general attach more importance to one principle than another?

Let me illustrate this important point by further reference to Warnock (not forgetting that I am not intending to associate Warnock with the liberal-democrats, but merely citing him as an example of one who shares their belief in a plurality of principles). On page 115 of *The Object of Morality* he writes:

> We saw, however, that there are other moral principles than
> this one [the principle of non-deception], and therefore other
> sorts of 'moral reasons' why one ought or ought not to do
> things; we also saw that reasons may conflict, point in opposite
> directions, and that one cannot in general say that, where
> conflict arises, any one principle is necessarily to predominate
> over others.

Now, given a belief in 'the plurality and independence of moral principles', this is clear and presumably true. What is not at all clear is whether it is consistent with this view or coherent on these terms to talk, as some would do, of attempting to make 'judicious' or 'wise' assessments of the relative claims of principles in particular circumstances. What is involved in 'carefully weighing' the claims of, say, non-deception against those of benificence? When Warnock continues by saying that, if principles can clash, 'it is quite clear that where I have an obligation—that is, *a* reason for acting in a definite way determined by the requirements of the principle of truth—there may be *other* reasons why I should *not* act in that way', he is obviously correct. When he concludes that 'those other reasons may sometimes be found preponderant',[38] one is simply at a loss as to *how* they can be *found* preponderant (except by a reversion to naked intuitionism). How does one establish that there is good 'moral reason' for regarding one type of 'moral reason' as preponderant over another type of 'moral reason' in one situation and not in another? The point that I wish to bring out here is that, notwithstanding the fact that the liberal-democrats tend sometimes to talk of making choices between the claims of conflicting principles, (or, more often, implicitly make such choices, as if they were the correct choice in the circumstances), their commitment to a plurality of principles involves not simply recognising that these principles may clash, but also recognising that there is no rationale for deciding between them when they do.

The lack of precision and the plain inadequacy of liberal-democratic philosophy is well evidenced in Bertrand Russell's writings on education. For essentially we are presented with proposals that are more compatible with the communism, authoritarianism and Platonism that Russell elsewhere castigates than with the demands of liberal-democratism as expounded by him. There is still formal stress on the principle of freedom and its claims. We are reminded that 'it is important not to forget individualism's just claims', that 'the case for the greatest possible freedom in education is a very strong one' and that 'there is something better than a slothful contentment, and if a free education promotes this, parents ought not to shrink from the incidental pains which it may involve for children.'[39] But it is not clear how we are supposed to begin assessing the 'just claims' of individualism, or what the 'case' for freedom is. Russell merely makes some vague psychological claims about the undesirability of intimidating children, and comes to the conclusion that without liberty we may destroy 'originality and intellectual interest': 'the killing of spontaneity is especially disastrous in artistic directions'.[40] Clearly this kind of a 'case', whether persuasive or not, is dependent on further assumptions, some of which are empirical and some evaluative, which Russell certainly holds but does not attempt to explain or justify, such as that Goethe 'as an individual must be reckoned superior to' James Watt.[41] However, the coherence of the case for freedom is, surprisingly, ultimately of little importance, for when it comes to the point Russell announces that 'considered *sub specie aeternitatis* the education of the individual is . . . a *finer* thing . . . but the education of the citizen must . . . take first place'. 'The argument in favour of some education designed to produce social cohesion is overwhelming', though we are not told what it is.[42] 'Individualism . . . needs to be more controlled . . . than in former times. . . . A sense of citizenship, of social co-operation, is therefore more necessary than it used to be'.[43] He therefore turns a cold eye on 'progressive educators in the West' (which has not stopped educators in the West turning a warm eye on Russell as a 'progressive'), and in a chapter that is remarkable for its apparent inconsistency with Russell's views expressed elsewhere, concludes that communism[44] offers a solution of the difficult problem of the family and sex equality—a solution which we may dislike, but which does, at any rate, provide a possible issue. It gives children an education from which the anti-social idea of competition has been almost entirely eliminated. It creates an economic system which appears to be the only practicable alternative to one of masters and slaves. It destroys that separation of the school from life which the school owes to its monkish origin, and owing to which the intellectual, in the West, is becoming an increasingly useless member of society. It offers to young men and women a hope which is not chimerical and an activity in the usefulness of which they feel no doubt. And if it conquers the world, as it may do, it will solve most of the major evils of our time.

One of the problems that particularly exercises the liberal-democrats, naturally enough since it arises from the conflict between freedom and various other principles, is the conflict between the individual and society. Russell recognises this problem and in his second book on education, *Education and the Social Order*, takes it as his starting point. But one cannot be satisfied with his solution, even if his actual proposals appeal to one's taste, for we must be aware that they do not appeal to everyone's taste. With a world as full of diverse tastes, ideas, proposals and so on as ours, what is needed is convincing argument in support of some set of ideas or proposals—not more unsubstantiated ideas or proposals. But Russell nowhere substantiates. Naturally not, for he takes the view that 'as to ultimate values, men may agree or disagree, they may fight with guns or with ballot papers, but they cannot reason logically'.[45] As we should expect, throughout his writing on education it is assumed that there is something—freedom—that is inherently desirable, and that the claims of freedom can be raised against the claims of other principles. Consequently, while the claims of justice, equality and happiness are advanced to justify various restrictive measures, we are treated to other odd, unsubstantiated remarks about how bad a thing it is to restrict—although, of course, it is hastily added, a little restriction is sometimes necessary. This bland assumption of an Aristotelian mean which we are all supposed to recognise without difficulty ('too much difference is a barrier . . . but some difference is essential')[46] I call the Manfred syndrome, in memory of Gilbert's line from *Patience*: 'A little of Manfred, but not very much of him'. The Manfred syndrome does not contribute towards a solution of any conflict there may be between individual and society. It merely restates the problem in a polite manner that need cause no offence.

Introduction

I realise that the problem inherent in liberal-democratism that I have outlined—that it allows of a variety of sometimes incompatible proposals to be judged 'right' and denies any way of deciding between the claims of rival principles—does not show that liberal-democratism is wrong. It may, for all I have said so far, be the case that we are faced with a plurality of principles of equal weight and that therefore this consequence simply has to be accepted. But there is something else to be noted about the liberal-democratic struggle to impose pattern in the light of basic assumptions that necessitate that there should be no pattern, besides the fact that their specific injunctions are arbitrary—that is that they apparently do not realise it. For we are repeatedly told that we *ought* to do such and such. It would be quite consistent with liberal-democratism to opt arbitrarily for giving more weight to the claims of one principle in the case of a clash in a specific instance, and to opt to giving more weight to another principle in another instance. But what is not consistent with the view that various principles are ultimate and of equal weight is the claim in specific instances that the claims of one principle *ought* to outweigh those of another. This the liberal-democrats continually do, as we shall see, and it is scarcely surprising that they do, for not to do so would be to refrain from judgment on any issue that could be related to more than one of the principles of happiness, equality or freedom. But in so far as they do this, in so far as they are prepared to assert in even one specific instance that the claims of one principle ought to override those of another, they are being inconsistent, for it transpires that they are not committed to the view that there are various ultimate principles of equal weight. One principle, it appears, is more important than another, or else appeal is being made to some further principle, in which case the principles in question are not ultimate.

The first weakness of the liberal-democrats, then, is their commitment, in common with many contemporary philosophers, to a plurality of principles of equal weight. In the body of this book I shall argue that there is good reason to reject this idea of a plurality. For the moment I merely suggest that much of the practice of the liberal-democrats (i.e. many of their specific pronouncements) seems to be inconsistent with what is actually involved in taking up a pluralist position. And if that is so, the request for some account of how they arrive at those judgments that they do make, can hardly be ignored.

This brings me to the second weakness of the theory of the liberal-democrats. Although snappy sentences about the unknowability of moral principles are not in short supply, it is very unclear precisely what the liberal-democrats mean by saying that ultimate values cannot be reasoned about, cannot be settled by philosophy, are not subject to publicly acceptable evidence, and so on. What is clear is that there is an inconsistency between saying that value judgments cannot be known to be true or false, and that other people's value judgments are known to be wrong. The liberal-democrats, perhaps, do not explicitly do this. But implicitly they do it all the time. They do it by offering prescriptive definitions of normative concepts that they regard as self-evidently satisfactory, because the value content involves appeal to one of their principles, and by rejecting other proposed definitions that involve appeal to other values. (A stark example of this procedure is to be found in Popper's treatment of the somewhat crucial concept of justice. 'But was Plato perhaps right?' he asks. 'Does "justice" perhaps mean what he says? I do not intend to discuss such a question.')[47] They do it by treating it as self-evident that certain proposals are object-tionable by pointing out that the proposals offend one of their principles. Since they have many principles to call on, there are few proposals that they happen to dislike that they cannot seemingly repudiate by announcing that they offend man's right to freedom, right to equal treatment, or right to happiness. They ignore the fact that, on their own admission, the principles to which they adhere, and by appeal to which they condemn specific proposals of others, are merely articles of their faith, and they ignore the fact that on their own assumption of a plurality of principles of equal weight it is not necessarily an objection, even for liberal-democrats, that a proposal infringes people's freedom, equality or happiness, provided that it also promotes one of them.

A glance at the work of Popper, Crossman and Russell will show that they take their own fundamental assumptions for granted and that a large part of their objection to other philosophers, such as Plato, is that they are not liberal-democrats. This seems a curious charge, since no reason is given, nor apparently can it be given, as to why they should be liberal-democrats (even assuming that liberal-democratism was more helpful and less inviting to contra-dictory proposals than it in fact is). But this point reaches its acme of importance, when a philosophy, in the vulgar sense, is offered that does not involve values that are quite distinct from the liberal-democratic values, but that takes over one of the liberal-democratic principles and gives it pride of place as the supreme principle. Here, in essence, is the liberal-democratic dilemma: not only cannot they show that such a philosophy is unacceptable (a small point, given the view that ultimate values are matters of faith), but accord-ing to the logic of their own theory it would be quite inconsistent of them to object to it. For if it is true that the principles they adhere to are of equal weight, and that there is no way of making a 'right' decision between their claims, then there is no way of making a 'wrong' decision. It cannot be 'wrong', for instance, to lay stress consistently on the claims of freedom and to be prepared to sacrifice equality and happiness to that end, or to advocate a sacrifice of freedom to the claims of equality.

Liberal-democratic theory is a tolerant, attractive, and, in a sense, untouchable sort of affair. If one asks a liberal-democrat how he knows that people ought to be free, he replies with disarming honesty that he does not know. He believes. If one asks him how, in a specific instance, he comes to the conclusion that freedom should be restricted, he puts his hand into his bag of principles and comes up with the claims of some other principle. If one suggests that it is inconsistent to pull out one principle on one occasion and another on another, and that this procedure turns the making of value decisions into a kind of Bingo, he will reply that since the principles are of equal weight one cannot give priority consistently to one of them. And so we merely try to give due attention to each of them. Hence the Manfred syndrome. But the price of tolerance is impotence. It does not follow from the assumption that the claims of happiness, freedom and equality are of equal weight, that one ought to juggle with them in an arbitrary manner giving happiness priority on one occasion, equality on another, and freedom on another. It follows that it cannot be wrong to opt at any time for one rather than another.

So far my criticisms amount only to the conclusion that if we accept liberal-democratism we are rather more at a loss as to what ought to be done than the liberal-democrats sometimes seem willing to admit. The only way to discredit liberal-democratism is to offer a convincing argument for an alternative value scheme.

I shall try to argue in the following pages that a strict utilitarianism is the alternative to be accepted, that this was recognised and its consequences worked out in social and educational terms by Plato, and that the liberal-democrats' criticism of Plato neither shows understanding of what he is saying nor succeeds in discrediting him. I shall not simply be repeating the point that, since happiness is one of their ultimate principles, the liberal-democrats cannot meaningfully object to utilitarianism, although that point is obviously extremely important. I shall argue the strong thesis that happiness ought to be the supreme consideration, that equality should be interpreted as a distributive principle, a formal principle that takes its substance from the principle of happiness, and that the principle of freedom is merely another formal procedural principle that has to be interpreted in the light of happiness.

It hardly needs to be said that, although acceptance of utilitarianism will not necessarily make practical decisions as to what ought to be done in the sphere of education any easier, it will provide a blueprint of principle in the light of which we may know how to set about evaluating educational proposals and practice. But I do not appeal for utilitarianism on the grounds that it would be very convenient to get off the hook of liberal-democratism that offers us no specific guidance at all. I appeal for utilitarianism because I think (and shall argue) that it makes sense to say that it is true that happiness ought to be the supreme principle. Educational debate must therefore take account of this and recognise the consequences.

Notes

1 Popper, K. R., *The Open Society and its Enemies*, Routledge & Kegan Paul, London, 1966, 5th edn (revised), vol. 1, p. 1.
2 Crossman, R. H. S., *Plato Today*, Allen & Unwin, London, 1963 edn, p. 84.
3 Ibid., p. 84.
4 Popper, op. cit., p. 88.
5 Russell, B., 'Philosophy and politics' in Bambrough, R., ed., *Plato, Popper and Politics*, Heffer, Cambridge, 1967.
6 Russell, B., *History of Western Philosophy*, Allen & Unwin, London, 1946. 'Philosophy and politics' in Russell's *Unpopular Essays*, Allen & Unwin, London, 1950. Reprinted in Bambrough, op. cit.
7 Russell, *History of Western Philosophy*, p. 129.
8 Crossman, op. cit., p. 66.
9 Russell, *History of Western Philosophy*, p. 125.
10 Ibid., p. 36.
11 'Philosophy and politics', in Bambrough, op. cit., p. 116.
12 Crossman, op. cit., p. 64.
13 Ibid., chapter 4.
14 Ibid., p. 144.
15 See chapter 7.
16 E.g. Popper, op. cit., p. 171 and chapter 10 *passim*.
17 Ibid., pp. 22–4.
18 Ibid., p. 32.
19 Ibid.
20 Ibid., p. 33.
21 Ibid., p. 89.
22 Ibid., p. 109.
23 Ibid., p. 65. 'Our view . . . does not imply that they [moral decisions] are entirely arbitrary.' However, it is by no means clear what Popper's view of moral norms *does* imply for their status. See chapter 3.
24 Ibid., p. ix.
25 Ibid., p. 14.
26 Ibid., p. 3.
27 Ibid., p. 19.
28 Ibid., p. 21.
29 Ibid.

30 Ibid., p. 45.
31 'Our society can never grow into a reality . . . until philosophers
   become kings' 473 D. For Popper's apparent awareness of this point,
   see *The Open Society*, p. 45.
32 Popper, op. cit., p. 47ff.
33 Ibid., p. 176.
34 In the words of a moderate review of *The Open Society*, that book
   contains 'much that is careless, confused, badly argued or unjust'
   J. Plamenatz, *British Journal of Sociology*, 3. Reprinted in Bambrough,
   op. cit., p. 145. It is not entirely clear to which of the two volumes
   of *The Open Society* Plamenatz here refers. He certainly regards the
   first as 'much the better of the two' but nonetheless feels that it
   contains 'many weak arguments'.
35 Popper, op. cit., p. 112, where Popper argues that the justification
   for his view of freedom 'is not historicism or essentialism . . . it says
   nothing about natural rights . . . it is just a demand'.
36 Ibid., p. 1 refers to equality and freedom, as does Crossman, op. cit.,
   p. 84. But it is clear from their writing that they also acknowledge a
   third principle of happiness. The same principles are implicitly
   recognised by Russell. The fact that they regard the principles as of
   equal weight has to be deduced largely from their use of the
   principles.
37 Warnock, G., *The Object of Morality*, Methuen, 1971, p. 88.
38 Ibid., p. 115.
39 Russell, B., *Education and the Social Order*, Allen & Unwin, London,
   1932. Quotations in this paragraph from pp. 143, 19 and 58
   respectively.
40 Ibid., p. 20.
41 Ibid., p. 7.
42 Ibid., pp. 16, 17.
43 Ibid., p. 143.
44 Ibid., p. 115.
45 Ibid., pp. 128, 129.
46 Ibid., p. 42.
47 Popper, op. cit., p. 90.

What the *Republic* actually says   2

The first book of the *Republic* shows us Socrates at the house of Cephalus, whose natural unreflective assumption is that *dikaiosune* (the necessary practice of a just man) is 'telling the truth and paying one's debts' (331 B). When Socrates suggests to him that sometimes it may surely be the wrong thing to return what one has borrowed (e.g. the return of a knife to a delinquent bent on murder), Cephalus gives formal agreement, but immediately bows out of the argument, handing over to his son, Polemarchus.

It is evident that Cephalus's moral precepts are (a) merely conventional dicta, the validity of which Cephalus has no ability to establish, (b) inadequate as a total account of *dikaiosune*, and (c), though perhaps good working rules, positively immoral, if the letter rather than the spirit is adhered to. In Plato's view, 'actions vary according to the manner of their performance'. No act such as telling the truth, returning what has been entrusted to one, 'drinking, singing and talking', is in itself good. 'These actions are not in themselves either good or bad, but they turn out in this way or that, according as they are well or ill done'.[1]

Polemarchus also represents a conventional viewpoint; in arguing that 'it is just to give to each man what is due to him' (331 D), he appeals to the poet Simonides and echoes the gnomic utterances of Theognis. Socrates's argument with him (331–6) is not a model of rationalism, involving as it does a play upon the two possible meanings of *blaptein* (335): either 'to hurt' or 'to make worse'. We know very well, from Plato's dictum that it is better for a man who has done wrong to be punished (i.e. 'hurt' in some sense) rather than not, that he was capable of distinguishing the two meanings of the words, and yet here he chooses to allow Socrates to equivocate. The explanation is to be found in the purpose of the argument with Polemarchus, which is not to solve the problem of what *dikaiosune* is. For Polemarchus is in no position to help with this enquiry, being, like his father, incapable of offering a rational justification of the precepts he holds. The dictum that 'it is just to give each man what is due to him' is quite inadequate as it stands, because all depends on what we mean by 'what is due to someone'. If we try to specify the content, by saying, as Polemarchus does, 'it is just to help your friends and harm your enemies' (334 B), the second half of the claim at least becomes dubious (and the first half also, if 'help' is understood to cover the example, already considered, of offering the knife to a friend to help him kill; if, on the other hand, it is understood more generally as doing 'good' for one's friends, it is clear that we have made no progress until we can give some account of what this 'good' may be).

At this point (336 B) Thrasymachus enters the debate. He is of fundamental importance to the *Republic*, because he represents the enemy that Plato is riding to meet: the ethical relativist. 'Justice', he says, 'is nothing but the interest of the stronger party' (338 C). Despite arguments as to the possible interpretations of this statement, there is no doubt that, whereas Polemarchus and Cephalus had retained the evaluative force of *dikaiosune*, and tried to describe the sort of activity that is commendable, Thrasymachus does the reverse. Having in mind the sort of activities that people call just, he scornfully denies their worthiness, and says that this sort of behaviour is simple-minded folly, and that in any instance you will see that what is 'just' (i.e. called just) is in the interests of the stronger party, or the ruling faction as it shortly becomes (338-9).

It follows that Thrasymachus denies any absolute validity to moral injunctions: they are essentially man-made, imposed and encouraged by those who have the power to do so. If an individual says 'it is right to obey the laws', he is simply expressing his own approval of an injunction devised and promoted by the ruling factions, whose interest it is that the laws should be obeyed. A man of sense will therefore have no fear of breaking the law, if he can do so with legal impunity.

The argument that completes Book 1 between Thrasymachus and Socrates is generally agreed to be most unsatisfactory on a purely logical level. For instance at 340 D, in reply to Thrasymachus's claim that a ruler governs in what he believes to be his own interests, Socrates denies the claim and argues that a doctor treats patients in their interest; a captain looks to the interests of his passengers; and, therefore, a ruler rules in the interests of his people. Clearly the argument is absurd. In so far as the doctor receives payment and may well be negligent, he does not treat patients in their interests, but in his own. And no justification of the analogy is given, besides which counter examples can easily be produced, as Thrasymachus does: a shepherd fattens his sheep for his own good.

Since Plato is writing both parts of this script, we cannot assume that he is unaware of the weakness of Socrates's argument. It is surely clear that he is intent on illustrating the gulf between Thrasymachus and Socrates. The former thinks that a ruler *is* like a shepherd watching over his flock for his own ultimate self-interest; the latter thinks that he *ought* to be like the idealised doctor caring for the interests of his patients. Socrates can try to argue that in fact a shepherd does watch over the interests of his flock, and Thrasymachus can attempt to counter by saying that the doctor does consider only himself. None of this is much to the point so long as there is an unbridgeable gulf between them; namely the fact that Thrasymachus recognises no morality, except as an alternative name for convention, whereas Socrates does.

By contrast with the wrangling of Book 1, the second book opens with a lucid and powerful account of Thrasymachus's case. It is not in dispute that, in society as it is, a man who is known to do those acts which are generally termed 'just' will in fact acquire honour, and that there is therefore quite a reasonable motivation towards being 'just'. But, it is argued, this 'honour' is gained because society has conditioned people into fearing to praise certain types of action, which are conventionally grouped in a category marked 'unjust'. Besides which, this 'honour' is a mere consequence of being seen to do certain so-called 'just' things, whereas Socrates has firmly declared that 'justice' is good in itself. The crucial question, therefore, is what reason can be given to persuade the individual to do 'just things' rather than 'unjust things', even if he could acquire the honour normally reserved for the 'just', while being in fact 'unjust'. Appeals to rewards in heaven are ruled out as being, however valid, unconvincing.

Glaucon outlines a contract theory (359 ff). His purpose is merely to show that the conventional moral injunctions can well enough be explained as deriving their value from the fact that they represent a compromise in everyone's favour. He does not prove that man in a state of nature would act as a self-interested beast, and he does not prove that the 'just' man in a society acts under the compulsion of legal and social pressure. He merely puts it forward, as a prima facie reasonable view, that anybody, if he had absolute power, and was thus free from all legal and social restraints (including the social process of making him believe that some things just ought to be done), would in point of fact simply look after his own aggrandisement. The advantages this 'unjust man' is pictured as heaping unto himself are, not surprisingly, all of them material-istic (money, women, murder: 360 B).

Adeimantus adds that, if one cares to look at the way society actually tries to inculcate adherence to moral injunctions, it will be seen that it is always on the level of promising the rewards involved in earning a respectable reputation (363). 'What argu-ment, then, remains for preferring [what is thought to constitute] justice to the worst injustice, when injustice, provided it has a veneer of respectability, will enable us . . . to do as we like with Gods[2] and men' (366 B ff). What, in short, is inherently desirable about being just? Socrates proposes to look for justice in a community (by considering its origin and growth), to throw light on justice in the individual.

The first stab at creating a city (369 ff) involves no more than adopting a principle of specialisation: 'Quantity and quality are more easily produced when a man specialises appropriately on a single job for which he is naturally fitted'.[3] Those who are physically weak will be suitable for the relatively static task of being retailers stationed in the market; those of great physical strength but little intellect will do well as manual labourers.[4] No justification is offered for this arrangement; but, on the amoral assumption that communal life is to be valued in terms of advantage to the individual, it is necessary to organise the state in such a way as to maximise advantage; the principle of specialisation is introduced as a rational means of achieving efficiency. No slur attaches to occupation, because no difference of material reward or social status is accorded to any group. Plato clearly does not distinguish, in respect of worthiness, between the trader, the farmer or the labourer, and he is content that all men should occupy some such role. For this austere city is for Plato the 'real city'—'the healthy city, so to speak' (372 E). And the reason for this judgment is clear: there is no luxury and so there is no corruption—no tendency to aggrandisement; there is no competition, only co-operation, and therefore there is no envy. Essentially it is at peace and not torn by any kind of conflict: 'They will sit down to feast with their children on couches of myrtle . . . they will enjoy each other's company . . . they will lead a peaceful and healthy life' (372 B). There is no argument, and Plato knows well enough that his picture is little more than a wish-fulfilment dream. But this first city gives us a fair indication of one of Plato's central ideals: a co-operative peaceful community.

'A community of swine', comments the prosaic Glaucon. And so luxuries (i.e. non-necessities) are introduced. But if we are to approach more nearly society as it is (which is what treating non-essentials as necessities involves), we shall need 'artists, sculptors, painters and musicians'.[5] And we shall need more land to suit an expanding population, which involves us in a war with our neighbours. 'For the moment we are not concerned with the effects of war, good or bad; let us merely note that it arises out of the same causes as most evil, private or social'.[6] These causes are clearly a desire for luxuries, acquisitiveness or aggrandisement.

The state therefore needs a defence, which in terms of Plato's historical position will have to be an army. The army will also be responsible for internal defence and protection of citizens, hence their title of Guardians. If the Guardians are going to offer a satisfactory defence of the country's boundaries and effectively keep law and order within the state, then, on the principle of specialisation, they need to be professionals. This argument does not show either that Plato wants soldiers (he did not have them in 'the real city'), nor that he wants a military caste such as Sparta enjoyed in his time. In referring to the job (*ergon*) of the Guardians as the 'greatest' (*megiston*: 374 E) of those available for citizens, he is making no value judgment about the inherent superior worthiness of those who are Guardians, *qua* human beings; it is greater than the job of, say, the cobbler, both in that it requires longer training and in that the effects of its being done relatively well or ill are a great deal more far reaching: without external and internal defence the state is bound to fall flat. Because the job is therefore important, and because the Guardians 'must be gentle to their fellow citizens and dangerous only to their enemies' (375 C), their training will be particularly important and take considerable time.

Stage one of the educational programme is now outlined. It is explicitly introduced only in reference to the Guardians,[7] and we may infer that Plato is not thinking of applying it in its entirety to the traders, retailers and manual workers. Fite is therefore correct to observe that 'the only education that is treated, is an education designed explicitly for Guardians or the children of Guardians'.[8] But Popper goes altogether too far in dismissing the caution of Shorey that 'we cannot infer, as hasty critics have done, from 421 A', where Plato says that cobblers who are badly brought up are less dangerous to the state than Guardians who are badly brought up, 'that he would not educate the masses at all',[9] and in claiming that 'As in Sparta the ruling class alone received education'.[10] That would only be true on the assumption that *paideia*, or education, is properly defined only in terms of the full educational programme laid down for the Guardians. Plato's refusal to 'clothe the farmers in robes of state',[11] which is a metaphorical way of saying 'give the farmers the upbringing and way of life designed for the Guardians', does indeed indicate that the farmers will not receive precisely the same *paideia*, but equally it implies that they will receive their own distinctive *paideia*. It is quite clear, from Plato's introduction to the 'noble lie', that all citizens are presumed to be educated: 'I hardly know how to find words to persuade the rulers, the Guardians and the rest of the city, that all our training and education of them were things they imagined'.[12] Certainly some aspects of the education specifically introduced now in relation to the Guardians, such as the censorship and the promotion of certain *exempla bona* would be pointless, if a similar control of influences were not extended to cover the non-Guardians; and certainly the Republic is unlikely to survive if the farmers, for instance, are not taught to farm. All we can safely say is that Plato chooses to concentrate on outlining the education of the Guardians, some aspects of which must also be presumed to have application for all citizens, and that some other aspects of the specific education of the non-Guardians are not explicitly talked about.

This first stage of education makes use of the traditional content of the *paideia* of the upper-class Athenian: music and athletics. It also resembles that *paideia* in being primarily concerned with moral training and character-building rather than with the development of intellect or the acquisition of a wide range of knowledge. As Protagoras is made to say:[13]

> From the moment that the Athenian child can understand
> what he is told, all the adults with whom he comes into contact
> are primarily concerned to make him as good as possible. At
> a later stage the schoolmaster too is expected to give more
> attention to good behaviour than to letters or lyre playing.

Protagoras goes on to point out that even reading, music and gymnastics are subordinated to the aim of producing the good man: the reading matter is selected for its inspiring ideals, the musical rhythms for their appropriateness in terms of developing a sense of order, and physical fitness is advocated, at least partially so that the individual shall be literally able to carry out his duties in life and not be incapacitated by weakness, fear or sluggishness.

In principle Plato retains all this. Children are taught the rudiments of literacy and the fundamentals of arithmetic;[14] they learn to sing, to dance and to play the lyre. They undergo athletic training. Such instruction, in a sense, provides them with the basic skills or the means necessary both to playing the part of the educated man as conventionally understood in Plato's time and also to advancing to the second stage of education that Plato advocates for some. The training in literacy and music gives them access to the poetic heritage that enshrines, in Matthew Arnold's words, 'the best that has been thought and said in the past'—a point of view that Plato does not formally dispute, although, of course, he is about to do a little carpentry on the said poetic heritage, just to ensure that the 'best' is good enough for the ideal state. The emphasis on dance, coupled with Plato's concern to distinguish between various musical modes as more or less acceptable, and the intense consideration that he gives both to the kind of characters that children are called upon to represent (in their recitations) and the way in which they should do so, are, in my view, beyond our grasp; there is very little we can say on this matter, except that (a) Plato evidently sees a connection between graceful movement, liking for harmonious rhythms and the enactment of calm and ordered characterisations on the one hand, and the development of a calm and ordered personality on the other, and (b) that he thinks that he can distinguish the graceful from the graceless and the harmonious from the cacophonic. Popper regards this view that music can cause people to be heroic, cowardly, disciplined, anarchic and so on as 'superstitious . . . backward and silly'.[15] I would hesitate to be quite so dismissive, bearing in mind such examples as the effect that Tyrtaeus's martial elegies were alleged to have on the Spartans marching into battle, the play made with music at the Nuremberg rallies, the claims made for psychedelic pop music, the potency, for some, of Elgar's *Pomp and Circumstance March* No. 1, and the similar faith held by some today in the value of dance and movement as being of educative value. On the other hand I am not all that convinced by Bosanquet's suggestion that a degree of truth in Plato's view is perhaps evidenced by the thought that many of us would not feel entirely happy if our children 'had surpassed [themselves] mainly in acting Sir John Falstaff, or in singing opera bouffe'.[16] The fact is that we know next to nothing of Greek music and next to nothing about the wider implications of a feeling for 'harmonious music' or 'graceful movement'. I therefore intend simply to duck this question (merely noting, in passing, that it is no bad thing that we should from time to time confess that we do not really know what we are talking about).

The emphasis on gymnastics is a quite different matter. Here the reasons for Plato's concern are entirely clear. In the first place he wants physical fitness for the straightforward reason that fitness and health are a necessary condition of the performance of most activities (and he would seem to include in this the performance of intellectual activities). Secondly, the Guardians, being soldiers, require physical strength. Thirdly, physical health was regarded as an end in itself by the Greeks. And finally, the athletics exercises whereby the young developed their healthy bodies were also seen as enjoyable activities in themselves: as a result of being fit the citizens of the Republic can continue to take part in the javelin throwing, wrestling, racing and discus throwing that they delight in.

To some extent, in the early years of this first stage of the education programme, the teacher is to avoid laying down a rigid programme, and should rather follow or build upon the interests of the child.[17] But Lodge's statement that 'the Administrator tries to build civic virtues on spontaneous activity'[18] must be qualified. It must be stressed that the 'spontaneous' activity is only uncorrected within limits. In the first place, as we shall shortly see, there is very little if any spontaneity allowed in the moral sphere itself; secondly, such spontaneity as there is, is clearly advocated as a means to an end:[19]

> Athletics, geometry and all branches of the preliminary
> education . . . should be introduced in childhood, but not in
> the guise of compulsory instruction. Enforced exercise does no
> harm to the body, but enforced learning will not stay in the
> mind. So avoid compulsion, and let your children's lessons
> take the form of play. This will help you to see what they are
> naturally fitted for.

In other words there is nothing here of the peculiar view that
education is only education, if what goes on in its name is decided
entirely by reference to what the child at the time wants to do or
happens to value. A degree of freedom is advocated for motivational
and practical reasons; above all, so that the division later to be made
between children on the basis of their different 'natures' shall
indeed be, as far as possible, a division based on their innate
proclivities and not on enforced or deliberately cultivated
proclivities.

The crucial point about this first stage of education is that it is
the 'stage in which feelings and habits undergo a discipline necessary
for social life'.[20] It is a stage concerned with dispositions and basic
skills; it is fundamentally non-intellectual. There is no emphasis
on encouraging the mind to expand, to question or to activate
itself. The approach to poetry, which forms the main content,
is not one of enquiry or probing for response, so much as of simple
imbibement. Consequently Plato desires that the poetry read should
embody standards that are socially desirable.

We have already seen that Polemarchus quoted Simonides as if
he had biblical authority and Adeimantus expressly said (364 E)
that the poets advise us that the Gods' favour can be bought. Plato
objects to the tales that tell of the wayward behaviour of the Gods
on two counts: first that they are not true, and secondly that 'even
if they were true I should not have thought that we ought to tell
them lightly to the thoughtless young' (378 A). The second argument
is clearly the more crucial of the two, since it can have application
regardless of one's view of whether Plato is entitled to assert that
certain characteristics are not true of Gods. For the moment we
merely note that the social utility of Plato's move is obvious. The
kind of God-figure (i.e. ultimate authority figure) that we want
people to grow up with in mind, must not be one who can be
bribed, etc., for, if that is the case, they will not think it amiss to
bribe and be bribed in life.

Thus there is nothing aesthetic in this censorship; its justification
must depend to some extent on the validity of the factual premiss
that people are affected by the stories they hear. But Plato is not
in doubt on this premiss, as is clear from the beginning of Book 3,

where, considering moral objections, he says, 'it is not that they are bad poetry or unpopular', on the contrary, 'the better they are as poetry the more unsuitable they are', being more efficacious in direct proportion to their subtlety.

Plato sees environmental pressures (including the books and music one likes, and the characters one watches on the stage), as influencing the individual; they are teachers, to be sifted as carefully as any other prospective teachers. Art for art's sake is not, for Plato, a sufficient justification. 'We shall thus prevent our Guardians being brought up among examples of what is evil and so gradually doing themselves grave psychological damage' (401 B).

An excess of doctors and lawyers is the mark of a state in trouble (405 A), for the need for doctors indicates a lack of health, which in part will be due to sybaritic living, and the need for lawyers indicates friction and faction between citizens, which cannot indicate harmony and happiness. The conclusion of this section argues forthrightly for an educational programme that will aim to harmonise energy and intellect (412 A).

In section 412 Plato divides the Guardians into rulers and auxiliaries. It is not explicitly said why it is necessary to do this, but the principle of specialisation obviously demands it (as might practical considerations, such as the wisdom of dividing the authority of a state from the power). The rulers are selected from the Guardians because some of the qualities that were demanded in a Guardian ('a philosophic disposition, energy, acuity and courage', 376 C) are needed equally, if not more, by a ruler. It is claimed that obviously 'the elder must have authority over the younger'; since this is not perhaps obvious to us, we must assume that Plato, besides following Greek sentiment, is identifying age with experience, as he did in the case of appointing judges (409 B); besides, if we assume that he already has in mind an education that will extend to the fiftieth year, his assumption of age is fully explained.

Sections 412 and 413 are arguably the most important in the *Republic*. 'Those who govern must be the best', that is to say, 'the most regardful of the state', and that, in turn, means 'the most intelligent and capable in respect of watching over and caring for the interests of the whole state'. The *polis*, here translated 'state', means the community or body of citizens. Consequently it is the common interest of their fellow citizens that the rulers are to watch over, and this will be best done by those who love their fellow citizens (412 B). And the rulers must not be amenable to irrational persuasion or influence, nor must they be careless or fearful.

The passage is important because, although it is purely formal (nothing has been said, for instance, about what the interests of the community are, beyond the fact that one aspect of the perfect state will be harmony and stability), it makes it absolutely clear that Plato's ultimate criterion of good government is the interest of the community. This formal criterion is to be contrasted, as it is in Book 9, with the specific criteria of wealth, success, popularity or *de facto* power.

Plato now proposes 'an innocent fiction'. There are now three groups, which may be separately classified: those who, by dint of superior intellectual ability and moral integrity, are most fit to rule in the interests of the whole community; those who just fall short of this ideal; and those whose aptitude and interest place them in the largest group, comprising all who are neither rulers nor auxiliaries.

The myth, which tells how Mother Earth gave birth to all, but gave to different people different qualities, making some suitable for this way of life and some for that, is designed: (a) to foster unity (via the notion of common motherhood, which may be seen as a primitive embodiment of the concept of the brotherhood of man); and (b) to convince all of the correctness of their function in society. The myth will have 'the good effect of making each of them more inclined to care for the community as a whole and each other' (415 D).

Book 3 ends with an account of the austere conditions under which the rulers and auxiliaries will live (415 ff). They will live in communal dwellings, without private property and without money, their food being provided for them by the other citizens. The object of these strictures is clear: on the rulers hang the harmony and health of the state; if they are at variance with each other, or tempted by goods desired by the majority of citizens, should they succumb to temptation, the harmony of the state is ended. What Plato fears is that, if the rulers 'acquire private property in land, houses or money, they will become farmers and businessmen instead of Guardians, and harsh tyrants instead of partners in their dealings with their fellow citizens, with whom they will live on terms of mutual hatred and suspicion' (417 B). His rulers and ruled can be real partners because their needs are different; Plato has preserved harmony by divorcing what all might regard as an advantage (wealth) from authority; consequently, provided that the ruling is equitable, nobody need resent being excluded from it.

That is all very well, says Adeimantus, but what about the rulers? *They* are not getting any of this wealth which, it is admitted, all might regard as an advantage. Socrates's direct reply is that we are concerned with the happiness of the whole community, not that of a select group (420 B).

There follow some comments on the relatively greater harm that is done to the community as a whole by irresponsible rulers than by irresponsible anything else (421), on the danger of a city too wealthy or too poor (422), on the size of the ideal community (423), on the fact that education is the key to a healthy society (424),[21] and on the absurdity of trying to approach the problem of creating a harmonious and healthy society by piecemeal methods (426), prior to an examination of this state (which was created in accordance with rational considerations and Plato's opinion of what was desirable) in the search for justice.

The search for the virtues (wisdom, courage, moderation and justice) does not seek to form any kind of a proof. Plato simply says (428 ff) that we should regard a city as wise in respect of it showing good judgment. A community's judgment is exhibited in its social organisation and the principles that organisation embodies. This community is wise in as much as it wisely adopts wise rulers who rule wisely. It is steadfast (courageous/*andreia*) in as much as those responsible for external and internal defence, the auxiliaries, 'being convinced and receiving the laws like a dye as it were' (430 A), can be relied on, and will ensure courage against the enemy and stability within the community. It is moderate essentially in as much as it is reasonable and involves the leadership or guidance of the irrational impulses in society (emanating naturally enough from the relatively irrational citizens) by the rational. Thus Plato is advancing the proposition that a community organised on the principles and in the manner so far advanced would be wise, steadfast and moderate.

What then is just about the community? Or where do we see justice? The answer is (433) that this community is just because it is built on rationally defensible principles; it is just because its measure of social arrangement is appropriateness. In other words Plato claims (*not* proves) that a community constituted on the principle of relating a man's activity to his needs is a just one, but it is important to remember, since he does not explicitly state it here, that all along, in constructing what he is now calling a just state, Plato has taken for granted the aim of the happiness of the whole community. In short, in saying that '*Dikaiosune* is in some sense the doing of what is peculiarly one's own' (*to ta hautou prattein*), Plato is saying: the just principle of distribution of social roles is distribution according to aptitude and ability. But he says this in the light of his commitment to a principle of happiness.

He now puts forward his view of the three-part soul (435 ff). The state acquired its wisdom from wise men; its courage from courageous men (435 E). We see then that broadly speaking there are three types of men: the irrational, the energetic and the rational. A man becomes one of these types as the result of the supremacy in his soul of the rational part, the energetic part or the irrational part.

Sections 435–445, on the three-part soul, amount to the formal statement that a just man will be one who acts on rational principle and not on whim; he is characterised, not as the sort of man who does X and Y, but as the sort of man who uses his rationality by way of justification and not his immediate inclinations. The inclinations or desires are not supposed to be quashed or obliterated, merely controlled by the demands of rationality. Plato's ultimate claim that the just man is the happy man thus becomes explicable. Happiness, for Plato, necessarily involves the absence of unfulfilled and conflicting desires, as well as the control of certain desires at certain times which will lead to trouble.

All, including Thrasymachus, who is surprisingly still with us, want to know what happens to the women and children of the rulers and auxiliaries, if they are supposed to have all things in common. With logic that is a good deal more appealing than that of his critics, Plato argues thus (451–7). Although women are by nature less physically strong than men, and although they are biologically different in certain respects, these are not, prima facie, valid criteria for discrimination in respect of social roles. Though the strongest men are stronger than the strongest women, some women are stronger than some men, besides which strength is not a valid criterion for all jobs.

In Plato's view there are no valid reasons why a woman *per se* should be discriminated against in respect of a social role; if men are chosen to rule on the criteria of intelligence and moral integrity, then it is quite illogical to say that a woman ought not to be chosen if she has the same qualities. Therefore the state will aim to classify women by the same criteria, aptitude and ability, and to educate them alongside men. The need to foster unity amongst the auxiliaries and rulers, and the need to prevent them from acquiring acquisitive possessive instincts, led to a decree that they should lead a communal life (416); it follows as a matter of course that the same regulation will apply to women who, on grounds of aptitude and ability, are being trained for either of these two groups. To preserve the institution of marriage amongst these groups would be to foster private interests and would lead on occasion to disharmony (via jealousy, for instance). Therefore 'wives and children will be held in common' (457 C). But random mating would be contrary to the spirit of the perfect state, and might lead blood father to blood daughter, etc. (458 E).

A rational approach would seem to lead to the conclusion that, so far as the birth of children is concerned, the community would benefit (a) from keeping numbers more or less constant, and (b), if control is to be exercised, from encouraging the mating of those 'in the prime of life' and generally superior in respect of bearing healthy children. Any children born who are obviously not auxiliary material we intend to *katakruptein*;[22] the rest will be brought up in crèches. The rulers alone will understand the true system of alloting partners for sexual intercourse, and the reasons behind the system; the auxiliaries will think that the act of intercourse is a reward or part of some festival.

Section 462 begins another important passage. Plato restates his creed: 'Nothing is worse for a state than disunity, nothing better than cohesion or unity'. Cohesion is the result of an identity of interest; a unified society prevents the occurrence of conflicting interests. In the Republic, therefore, the rulers will not be masters (because 'master' implies a distinctive interest from that of the 'mastered'), but fellow-citizens, defenders and protectors. I.e., though the function of the individual may vary, the ultimate interest is the same. The familiar loyalties and solidarity of the family, and the happiness they inspire, are transferred to the larger community.

In the wake of the wave abolishing private family life, Glaucon asks whether this state is a practicable one (472 B). Socrates's answer is that he has provided a *paradeigma poleos agathēs*: 'a formal presentation of a good society'. We must be content to get as close as we can in practice to this *paradeigma*, to the ideal demands of rationality; but we see that basically one change is necessary from the actual practice of existing societies: 'those we now call rulers must really and truly become philosophers' (473 D). This is to say that principle and reason should alone inform government practice, as becomes clear in what follows (474) where Plato defines what he means by a philosopher. He is one who loves (*philei*) wisdom (*sophia*), without qualification or reservation; therefore a technical expert in the field of, say, astronomy is not a philosopher, no more need a professional logician be, for neither stars nor formal logic represent *sophia*. *Sophia* (wisdom) is the truth of what is, in any respect.

The Theory of Ideas is now introduced (476). Whereas a deed or a man may be just, they are not justice. Justice is the essence of which just men and deeds partake; it is *to on* (the reality/the existence) by virtue of which particular things become just. The same applies to beauty. The *philomousike* (the lover of music) is not a philosopher; he recognises beauty in music, no doubt, and loves it, but he sees only an example of beauty, not beauty itself. To see beauty itself (*to kalon*) would involve recognising all examples of beauty and knowing them to be but examples. To be able to do this, to know and distinguish the essence itself and the particulars which partake of it (*auto kai ta ekeinou metechonta*) is to be awake to reality, and not a dreamer gazing on the image or example of the essence or Idea.

Knowledge and opinion are to be distinguished (477); the former has as its object what is, what has absolute existence. Opinion, on the other hand, is appropriate neither to something that is, nor yet to that which is not, but to something in between. Now beautiful things sometimes seem ugly from a different point of view (479); we cannot say this symphony *is* beautiful, because to another man, or at another time, it may not be beautiful. This symphony neither is, nor is not, beautiful; its beauty is therefore a fitting object for opinion or belief (*doxa*); you opine that it is beautiful, I opine that it is not. We neither of us 'know'. Thus the man who comprehends the beauty of a beautiful statue is possessed of a belief or an opinion. If he desires to be a man of knowledge he must go beyond the particulars, for only the Idea can be known. What Plato means by a philosopher is thus very simple: a man who is capable of a high degree of conceptual thought and who is not wedded exclusively to empirical information about the actual world.

In short the non-philosopher is one, who, by definition, looks at a particular (for example, returning what one has borrowed) and decrees that it is good, because he is of the opinion that it is; he therefore assumes that he knows that it is absolutely good, and is not aware that it might not always be a good habit; for 'it' was not good; nothing is *per se* good; it merely partook of goodness in a certain situation. The philosopher must rise above the level of acquired taste and prejudice. He must love the idea of goodness, and by conceptual leaps advance beyond the particular which strikes him here and now as good. Besides being capable of this high degree of conceptual activity, it is argued (485 C), the philosopher will necessarily love truthfulness;[23] he will not be 'grasping after money—other men, not he, will be eager for what money can buy';[24] he will have developed an acute intelligence, a breadth of vision and a sense of proportion.

Not unreasonably, Adeimantus objects that philosophers in practice seem to be, if not pernicious, utterly useless as members of society, (487 D). This, replies Socrates, is for two reasons: (a) most of the alleged philosophers are in point of fact corrupt, and hence not philosophers at all in the Platonic sense; they have some of the qualities necessary (acuity, cleverness) but they have not been educated properly. The sophistic philosopher is indeed gifted, so far as the skill of handling the people goes, but he makes no attempt to evaluate their various appetites and moods. A great skill, without moral backing, is the most dangerous leader a state can have. (b) What good philosophers there are, are thus disillusioned or else are flatly rejected by the state. 'There is not a society in existence fit for the true philosopher yet' (497 B). Returning, therefore, to the *paradeigma* of the ideal state, Socrates now argues that philosophy (i.e. the intensive pursuit of conceptual analysis and enquiry into moral values) should be reserved until late in life, and he holds out a hope that in time the ideal may be realised.

The next question is the precise nature of the education to be given to potential philosopher-kings; the real problem is that a rare combination of facets is required: a sharp volatile mind is needed alongside a steady reliable one, and therefore the ruler must go beyond the auxiliary in his education; he must come face to face with the Idea of Good, which is to say the fundamental principle of morality; he must understand what goodness or morality is. He will quickly see that it is neither 'as most people think Pleasure'[25] nor knowledge (505 B).

In point of fact Plato is very loath to tell us what the idea of goodness is, but it is clear that he identifies it with rationality; and he tries to explain it by analogy (507). Goodness is to the realm of the intelligible what the sun is to the realm of the visible. The sun causes the visible world to be seen, and it can be seen itself; in the same way, goodness is what causes the intelligible to be understood by the intellect; it both gives meaning to and is the meaning of the universe, and the intellect can also grasp the notion of goodness. That is to say, without the light of comprehension spread by recognition of the ultimate reality, our understanding of justice, beauty, etc. is nebulous (508/9). In prosaic terms: moral discussion is worthless with those who do not understand the problems inherent in the peculiar status of moral principles, and yet an understanding of moral truth is necessary to give meaning to life.

The divided line, now introduced, is not bewildering. The Theory of Ideas and the sun analogy have already introduced us to the idea that there are various stages, or degrees, of reality and different responses opposite to each other. Here these stages are formally arranged in hierarchical order as a preliminary to the superb, but wholly emotive, saga of the cave. In the physical world we may gaze on reflections or shadows; our attitude to them must be one of illusory opinion. We may also gaze upon material things, which are concrete embodiments of an Idea, in which case we believe. We believe that this is good, but we do not, merely by observing an instance, know anything.

The intellectual sphere may take us to a higher level of reality: reasoning about the abstraction triangularity, based upon examples of triangles, or any other reasoning about logical abstractions related to physical objects approaches reality, but it is reasoning about the forms or Ideas of abstract concepts that represents the activity peculiar to the philosopher-kings.

Plato summarises his despondent view of man's actual condition, his idea of the intellectual climb needed to escape it, and the problems facing the fully fledged philosopher on his return to a merely mortal level, in the simile of the Cave. The human predicament has most of us as prisoners to illusions: like men locked into a position where they can only see the shadows of puppets thrown on to a wall (514), we accept what we see as all that can be; we have no criteria to judge the shadows against. All that we believe, we assume that we know. And if we release one of the prisoners in the cave, and show him the puppet that is casting the shadow, he would at first disbelieve in the reality of the puppet, and if we then drag him out of the cave into the sunlight, he would be dazzled at first and see nothing, for he is not familiar with seeing things in the light of the sun; and yet finally he could adapt himself to look even on the sun itself. Thus, as is explained in 517 B, a man may be turned away from his prejudices to learn to gaze upon the truth, but the change will be very difficult, as has been graphically illustrated.

But the more important point, perhaps, is that if, having gazed on the sun, the cave-dweller returns to the cave, the fact that he has seen the real physical world will not help him at all in his attempts to convince his fellow-men. For a man can only judge by what he feels he knows. Furthermore, the returning man will appear to be more ignorant than those who idly ruminate on shadows and imagine them to be the ultimate reality, for he will be judged by them on his ability to discriminate between shadows, an ability that will be impaired by lack of practice and the blinding of the sun.

Education is a process of turning the mind in the right direction. Since, in fact, we see in our cities that many clever men have no moral integrity, and many true philosophers turn their back on the problem of adapting to a world of shadows, it is necessary to persuade those who understand the rational moral nature of the universe to go back to the cave. 'Surely', says Glaucon, 'to compel them to be concerned in a shadow world would be unfair'. 'The object of our legislation', Socrates replies, 'is not the welfare of any particular class, but that of the whole community. It uses persuasion or force to unite all citizens and make them share together the benefits . . . we shall be justified in compelling the philosophers to have care and responsibility for others' (520 A). They have a moral obligation to repay, by service, the state to which they owe so much; and finally it will actually be a great benefit to the community that those who rule do so reluctantly. Quite explicit is the charge that since those who love 'the happiness of a right and rational life' do not want to rule, those who, in practice, do want to, are 'hoping to snatch some compensation for their own inadequacy from a political career' (521 A).

What we have to understand about the programme of higher education, with which the remainder of Book 7 is taken up, is the principle that underlies it rather than the actual content. That principle is that the philosopher-kings should transcend the world of the here and now, the familiar and the conventional, and seek knowledge of what is eternally true. In Nettleship's words[26]

> to know the truth of the world would be to know the Good of the world, or the 'reason why' of its existence and to understand human life thoroughly would be to see the end or purpose which governs it in the light of that larger end or purpose which makes the whole universe luminous and intelligible.

Plato is concerned to replace the notion of an educated man as one who has information, who knows that the conventions of his society are such and such, that the moral rules are this and that, that Sparta led the Peloponnesian League, who knows how to play the lyre or wield the sword, with the notion of a man who, to use Hirst's terminology, understands the various forms of knowledge.[27] What matters is not particular historical claims or specific aesthetic judgments, but what is involved in historical claims or aesthetic judgments. He is not advocating a complete dismissal of the material world, for throughout the years of higher education the potential philosopher-kings are simultaneously taking an active part in the everyday life of the community and gaining experience of and information about the here and now. But Plato's concern is to put his students in a position to make something of their acquired experience and information.

Mathematics, arithmetic, geometry, astronomy and harmonics, are introduced by Plato as graded exercises in the handling of abstract concepts. By working through these exercises the student will prepare himself for handling the supremely important abstractions of ethics. I know of no better summary of the culmination of this programme than Shorey's:[28]

> The consummation of it all is described poetically as 'the vision of the Good' (540 A)—which, however . . . turns out to mean—for all practical purposes the apprehension of some rational unified conception of the social aim and human well-being, and the consistent relating of all particular beliefs and measures to that ideal—a thing which can be achieved only by the most disciplined intelligence.

Before leaving Book 7 we should note that at the very end (541) Plato's claim that any attempt to actually found this state would necessitate starting from scratch, with a community consisting only of children under the age of ten, and hence not yet set in their ways and opinions, indicates his profound conviction that conventional prejudice in any society is more or less ineradicable.

Plato returns to the study of the four forms of constitution that are to be found in practice and all of which are imperfect; that is to say they bear no relation, or little relation, to the principles embodied in the *paradeigma* of the true state. Fundamentally it would seem that they fall short in two respects: their arrangements are haphazard and irrational, and they do not promote the harmony and happiness of all the members of the community. There is the Spartan type of society, a timocracy in which reputation is earnestly sought. Such a society may arise out of a perfect society should unworthy rulers ever take control, 'neglecting us—and underrating education' (546 B); if the group of rulers and the group of auxiliaries are not well chosen, if they ignore their rigorous education, then 'Stasis' will break out between them:

> they pull in different directions; those with iron and bronze
> in their make up [i.e. those whose character makes them unfit
> for the position they are in] towards private property and land,
> profit, houses and gold and silver . . . while those whom they
> once ruled as freemen and friends are reduced to the status of
> slaves and menials. . . . Such a state will have a fear of
> admitting intelligent people to office . . . it will prefer simpler
> and more hearty types who prefer war to peace . . . it has one
> salient feature due to its emphasis on the 'energetic' element
> in us . . . covetous contention (547 B).

What becomes very clear from Plato's disapproving account of timocracy are some of his values: he does not want rulers who neglect the welfare of the community as a result of personal motivation towards private property and profit; he does not want rulers who have had no training and who show no concern for the citizens over whom they have power. He does not approve of individualism, if that means a pride in personal acquisition or success; he does not want education to be a 'matter of force rather than persuasion', by which he would seem to mean he prefers persuasion towards the rational to dictation from circumstances (548 B). He does not like a competitive society: he does not think that the population ought to be in subjection.

The individual, who likewise allows his *thumos*, his energy, which is here clearly allied by Plato with acquisitiveness, to direct his behaviour, the timocratic man, will also display 'arrogance and ambition' (550 B). But nonetheless such a man, and such a society, are not completely given over to the irrational. The timocratic man has reasoning ability, but he uses it to promote his ambition and is not ultimately ruled by it.

An oligarchy to a Greek meant the rule of the minority of rich people, not simply rule by a few. Thus, whereas in the timocracy it was prestige and honour, rather than the rational view of what was good for the community, that motivated people, in the oligarchy it is, more simply, money. Love of wealth leads to 'disrespect for and disobedience to the laws' (550 D). We cannot underestimate Plato's hostility to wealth, which he sees within society as a more or less reliable pointer, in inverse ratio, to the degree of goodness to be found. (551). In section 551 he makes it very clear that he understands all that is formally involved in the principle of impartiality. 'Wealth is an invalid criterion for discriminating in respect of positions of responsibility' and much else besides, as we shall see. It is also important to note another example of Plato's horror of 'a society split into factions; in this case the rich and the poor, who live in the same state and are always plotting against each other'. The oligarchy is also prone to throw up examples of those who, as a result of their wealth, contribute nothing by way of activity to the community, and reduce the poorest to a state of total subjection; poverty, in turn, and need, are potent causes of criminal behaviour (552). Plato's criticism of these features also makes clear his attitudes and values.

All this is mirrored on a small scale in the oligarchic man whose high evaluation of money is his ultimate motivation, to which rational processes are subordinated (553 ff).

Democracy, according to Plato, arises when the poorer section of the community rise up against the wealthy and overthrow them. 'The people plot against those who have deprived them of their property' and win by superiority of numbers and physical strength; it is to be stressed that there is no reason to suppose that Plato would blame the people for 'longing for revolution' (555 D); praise or blame is neither here nor there, for we have long since left the principle of a justly organised society. But certainly Plato sees no inherent value in 'treating all men as equal in all respects, whether they are or are not' (558 C), nor in the fact that all citizens are 'free to do as they like' so that there is no 'compulsion on those who could contribute in some way to the welfare of society to do so, nothing to make people submit themselves to a rule, and no qualifications beyond currying popular favour, necessary for being a prominent politician'. The fact that Plato thus criticises 'democracy', as it is known to him, is obviously unimportant compared with his implicit condemnation of the belief that it is rational or good (a) to avoid pressurising people into considering the community; (b) to promote autonomous behaviour as good in itself; and (c) to reduce the art of government to carrying out the wishes, according to the lowest common denominator, of the people.

This last point leads Plato on to distinguish between necessary and unnecessary desires (559); the former may be subdivided into those that are necessary in the literal sense of unavoidable, such as desire for food on a minimal level, and those that are beneficial if satisfied. Unnecessary desires are those which do not do any good, beyond the fact that when satisfied they remove an irksome craving, and 'which can be got rid of by practice'. Plato points out that many desires, such as the desire for food, may be judged either necessary or unnecessary, depending upon their strength and the precise nature of the food desired.

The democratic man and the democratic state, because reason, or the rule of what ought to be, is not in control, are motivated, led and enslaved by any desires they happen to have, regardless of whether they be necessary in the sense of ultimately beneficial or not. Plato's real attack, then, is directed against the notion that a man's desire *per se* has any relevance to deciding what ought to be done. Only reason can decide whether a specific desire is worth championing.[29]

Though one would hardly realise it from the attacks of Toynbee, Popper, Russell and Crossman, Plato reserves his most strenuous scorn for the 'tyrant', thus making it clear beyond all doubt that he is no worshipper of absolute authority *per se* (or anything else *per se*, as I have tried to stress). Russell remarks scathingly that 'only the veneer of virtue on the Republic prevents one from detecting its abhorrent totalitarianism', as if this were some vital discovery. It is, of course, the fundamental tenet of Plato's position; authoritarianism is only justified and is the only sane form of social organisation, provided that its aim is the welfare of the citizens. In other circumstances it becomes the most abhorrent of methods of government and is to be known as tyranny. If we ask in what respect the 'tyrant' differs from the philosopher-king, the answer will tell us in what circumstances the government may be absolute or, in other words, what principles Plato thinks ought to be implemented, even against the vote of the people; and the answer is that the tyrant rules in his own interest, not in that of the community; he is cruel and, above all, he does not rule on any rational principle beyond that of securing his own supremacy, which Plato feels cannot be justified. It is worth noting, finally, that in these circumstances Plato is willing to champion freedom; for although the doctrine that freedom is *per se* good is ridiculous, it is, nonetheless, obnoxious that the tyrant should 'find ways of suppressing anyone who has ideas of freedom and of not submitting to his rule' (567 A).

Plato fears that the natural soil of the embryonic tyrant is a democracy that is excessive in its liberty (562 C). Once 'freedom' is exalted to the status of an ideal and a good in itself, the people 'will abuse their leaders as oligarchs and reject them, unless they are very lax and promote a policy of non-interference', 'the least vestige of restraint is resented as intolerable, and respect for discipline and law crumbles into nothing'. Ultimately, via intermediary stages, 'from an extreme of liberty' there will be 'a reaction to an extreme subjection'. The tryant arises as the champion of some faction who claims that he will restore the state to its pristine order.

But a state under a 'tyrant' is really enslaved in an evil sense, for it is enslaved to an evil man and his evil principles, just as the tyrannical individual is enslaved to some consuming passion; this is liable in the long run to be unpleasant in fact, and is evil in principle, because it is irrational. No man is really free of every kind of restriction, but the rational man may be emotively described as the most free, because he is ruled only by reason.

For the last part of Book 9 Plato returns to the question of whether a just man or an unjust man will lead the happier life, it being presumed that the happier life is the preferable life, assuming that we do not consider the possibility of an after life or a theosophy which makes different demands. The detailed argument is perhaps not overwhelming, but it is not of overwhelming importance. Plato's position is clear: a man may be motivated predominantly by love of honour, love of material wealth, or love of the immediate gratification of immediate desires whatever they happen to be; or he can be motivated by reason over and above these separate impulses; this last motivation, when embodied in an individual, Plato calls justice and this, he argues, is the surest guarantee of happiness.

Rationality is the divine element in man (590), and rationality should be the arbiter of what be done; if the individual is relatively irrational, then his conduct should be guided, as that of a child is, by those who are more rational, but the guidance should be given 'in a friendly spirit'. The crucial problem is obviously: who decides who is rational?

Book 10 will not detain us now, because its first half involves another discussion on censorship, which will be discussed below, and it culminates in an argument for the immortality of the soul, and the Myth of Er. Plato's evident belief in an after life makes him want to add, now that he has argued that the just man, being the rational man, is the happy man, that he will also meet his reward in heaven and in the life to come. The significance of the Myth, in the structure of the whole *Republic*, lies in the emphasis on the fact that those who are choosing what they will be in their next life on earth have but to study carefully before making their choice and they can assure themselves of happiness.

Notes

1 *Symposium,* 181 A.
2 Because, as people say, the Gods can be bought off, 365 B, E.
3 370 C.
4 371 E.
5 373 B.
6 373 E.
7 376 E.
8 Fite, W., *The Platonic Legend*, Scribner, New York, 1934, p. 18.
9 Shorey, P., Introduction to *Plato's Republic*, Heinemann, London, 1935, vol. 1, p. xxxiii.
10 Popper, op. cit., p. 46. Cf pp. 52, 227.
11 420 D.
12 414 D.
13 *Protagoras,* 325 C.
14 536 D.
15 Popper, op. cit., p. 229.
16 Bosanquet, B., *The Education of the Young in the Republic of Plato*, Cambridge University Press, 1932, p. 7.
17 536 D. The extent to which the teacher should 'follow' is ultimately decided by reference to the claims of a just and happy community.
18 Lodge, R., *The Philosophy of Plato*, Routledge & Kegan Paul, London, p. 244.
19 536 E.
20 Bosanquet, op. cit., p. 14.
21 Education is the key to a healthy society for two reasons: (a) only by taking trouble to educate people can one ensure that some people will develop the intellectual capacity necessary for superintending the affairs of state successfully, and (b) only by education can one ensure that all citizens acquire a pro-attitude towards the values of the state. This, of course, is purely formal, and one might point to examples of states, such as Hitler's Reich, in which government is efficient and most citizens have a pro-attitude towards the values of the state, but which nonetheless one would condemn as unhealthy, because one objects to the values in question.
22 Literally 'hide-from-under'. Nobody *knows* what Plato means here. It seems most unlikely that he means 'kill'. He does not use euphemisms and he is not afraid of killing (cf. 410 A). Since he talks of transference between groups later, it is to be presumed that here he means 'surreptitiously transferred to another group'. But there are problems. See chapter 7.
23 Which does not mean that he could never see the need for telling a lie. In Plato's metaphysic, as we shall see, the idea of Good is supreme. The philosopher loves to be truthful, but the true Good may demand a lie.
24 485 E. Now we see clearly why Plato did not need to provide material wealth for his rulers; they are not interested in it.

25 Plato does not think that the Good is the pleasant; but he does, as we shall see, think that it is good that people should be happy.

26 Nettleship, R. L., *Lectures on Plato's Republic*, Macmillan, London, 1964, chapter 10.

27 See, however, chapter 8.

28 Shorey, op. cit., vol. 2, p. xl.

29 Nor is the formal position upset by the suggestion that we do not and cannot 'know' ultimate moral truths; we may still have ultimate moral values, and the democratic man is one who cannot abide by the principles he believes in.

3   **Preliminary problems**

The attempt to argue that Plato was a utilitarian may be challenged at the outset on the grounds that Plato himself effectively denies that he is one and that, in any case, the only reason for even supposing that he might be one is his reference to *eudaimonia* as an objective, which, although it is conventionally translated as 'happiness', does not in fact mean 'happiness'. Neither of these points, however, are sufficient to discredit the notion that he was in some sense a utilitarian (although, of course, they may have some bearing on the precise nature of his utilitarianism). The view that Plato explicitly denies that he is a utilitarian seems to rest on his assertion that 'the Good is not, as most people think, Pleasure' (505 B). This assertion cannot be ignored: 'good' and 'pleasurable' therefore cannot be identified as far as Plato is concerned. But nor in fact can they be regarded as synonymous even for a relatively uncompromising utilitarian such as Bentham. For even if it is taken as true that 'quantity of pleasure being equal, pushpin is as good as poetry', once one has introduced some distributive principle, which all utilitarians do, and indeed once one is prepared to differentiate between pleasures, even if only by reference to quantity, it ceases to be true that anything that gives pleasure is *ipso facto* good in the sense of morally desirable. What we may say at this stage is that it is quite coherent for someone to argue that pleasure and good are not synonymous, but that nonetheless what is morally good has to be decided essentially by reference to considerations of pleasure and pain. The Good is therefore not identical with that which gives pleasure, but nonetheless the Good may have to be determined by reference to what maximises pleasure, or, if pleasure and happiness are seen to be intimately related, to what maximises happiness. With regard to the second point, it is probably most convenient at this point to concede that the Greek term *eudaimonia* is complex and should not casually be identified with a loose ordinary usage conception of happiness. But, of course, one cannot reasonably divorce the two terms except as a result of analysis of both of them. Whether Plato did or did not mean 'happiness' when he wrote of *eudaimonia* depends partially on what we mean by 'happiness'. It therefore does not seem to me, at this stage of the argument, to be necessarily destructive of the thesis that Plato was a utilitarian to insist that

40

eudaimonia does not simply mean 'happiness'. What I shall attempt to do in the next two chapters is explicate a conception of happiness to which Plato is clearly committed and which he picks out by use of the term *eudaimonia*.

Neither of these two points, then, automatically rules out the possibility that Plato was a utilitarian in the general sense that he regarded the ultimate criterion for assessing right and wrong and/or good and bad, as people's happiness. (Any precise interpretation of this general formula being, of course, something that is yet to come.) But in outlining the *Republic*, I have drawn attention to Plato's concern for order, system and symmetry, his theory of Forms and his clearly displayed passion for truth and knowledge. It is not only that he cares that truth rather than ignorance should inform the way in which we live our lives; there are passages in the *Republic* where he goes further than this and almost exults in the idea of the individual bent on the pursuit of truth and knowledge. This, he seems to say, is the highest activity for man. Now, in view of all this, in view of this conviction that truth and the pursuit of truth matter, in view of this positing of a noumenal world which is somehow more real in its existence than the reality of the natural or material world that we perceive, is it even prima facie reasonable to attribute to Plato the relative earthiness of a utilitarian ethic?

It will be appreciated that the question of whether Plato may legitimately be classified as a utilitarian is distinct from the question of whether the features of the *Republic* listed in the previous paragraph are *necessarily* incompatible with a utilitarian position. In this chapter I am concerned with the latter question only and I shall therefore proceed on the hypothesis that he is committed to what can only reasonably be described as a utilitarian ethic.

It is certainly the case that Plato talks of the form of the Good as being supreme, and that his language in respect of the theory of Forms does not read like a stark representation of utilitarianism. But, of course, the manner in which Plato, writing at the dawn of philosophy, chose to present his argument is neither here nor there. We must distinguish between this manner and the substance of what he has to say on specific questions. What matters is what lies behind the language, particularly when we are dealing with the language of a mystic, a metaphysician and a poet, which, without any doubt whatever, we are when we are dealing with Plato.

Besides insisting on the supremacy of the Good, Plato consistently refuses to offer elucidation as to what exactly it is. What Plato is trying to say can only be communicated by analogy, myth and poetry. But what *is* he trying to say? We do not know, but we do know that in talking about the form of the Good, he is not talking about what moral principles have validity, but about the status

41

of whatever principles there may be. The theory of Forms is essentially no more than a poet's way of asserting his commitment to an absolutist view of ethics rather than a relativist one. What is fundamentally being conveyed, and what is important, is the view that, for example, justice is not a chameleon concept that derives its content from the habits or attitudes of a specific society at a specific time, but that it is a concept with a determinate content and absolute validity. Some things simply are just and others not, and their justness or lack of it is determined by fixed criteria, regardless of what anybody may happen to think at any particular time. The idea or form of Justice is more real than specific instances of justice, because specific instances are variable in the light of circumstances.

But none of this metaphysical speculation has anything to do with what Plato actually thought were the criteria of justice, good, or moral right. To find that out we have to look elsewhere, and leave the form of the Good to stand as a way of expressing the conviction that whatever Plato does regard as morally desirable or right can be seen to be so by those who travel along the right path. In other words there is certainly no necessary contradiction between the proposition that there is a form of the Good that exists, whatever Plato meant by that, and commitment to a principle of happiness as supreme. All we would need to say is that in Plato's view the form of the Good demands or involves the supremacy of happiness.

Similarly, although Plato clearly believes that the cosmos is governed by a rational spirit and that all things are therefore capable of rational explanation and have their proper function and their one proper place, so that, it may be said, the *Republic* embodies Plato's view of the proper place and proper function of different kinds of people, this consideration does not discredit the attribution of a utilitarian position to Plato. The belief that the cosmos represents a systematic rational whole does not obviate the need to produce some principle or principles of substance in the light of which to explain it. There has to be some criterion (or criteria) by which to assess what is the proper function or place of various people. The order that Plato is committed to is not just any order; it is what he regards as the true order. And the fact that it is the true order may well be evidenced by the fact that it is the order that leads to the happiness of the whole.

More interesting is the suggestion that Plato cares about the pursuit of truth and knowledge and that this is something that he values at least as highly as happiness. This, as far as one can judge, is true. He is evidently quite prepared to subordinate telling the truth to the claims of happiness, but that is not the same thing as saying that he would be prepared to subordinate the value of pursuing truth and knowledge to the claims of happiness. Would he be prepared to advocate a community that was happy, but in which nobody was pursuing truth and knowledge in the manner of the philosopher-kings?

The trouble with this question is that one cannot meaningfully address it to Plato, so long as he maintains his view that the cosmos is a rational structure and that everything can be known. For him pursuing truth and knowledge is one with pursuing understanding. Certainly he values this pursuit but then it happens to be, for him, a necessary part of maintaining the happy state, partly because the philosopher-kings who have this understanding—understanding, amongst other things, of the overriding need to maintain a harmonious and happy state—base their rule upon it, and partly because this pursuit of knowledge is necessary for the happiness of a particular kind of individual. (These points will be elaborated on in the following chapters.)

The only way to attempt to break this circle is to ask what Plato would say if the philosopher-kings were to discover that happiness was not supremely important. Would he argue that happiness was more important than truth and that the ideal state should continue to be maintained as before, or that truth was more important? But, of course, hand in hand with the realisation that the truth is otherwise than as originally imagined, is the demonstration that it is not the case that happiness has supremacy. An error has been made. Now there can be no doubt that Plato would not countenance an error, but this will not show that he should not be classified as a utilitarian, so long as he believes that it is not an error to maintain the supremacy of the principle of happiness. If it is a necessary condition of being properly described as a utilitarian that one should persist in advocating the supremacy of happiness even when one has come to see that it is not supreme, then Plato is no utilitarian. No more is Bentham, Mill or anyone else. But if the assumption is that utilitarians are those who believe it to be true that happiness is the supreme end, then Plato may be one, despite the undoubted fact that he values the pursuit of knowledge and truth, which includes, for him, the pursuit of understanding the supremacy of happiness.

It is clear that a great deal of weight is being thrown upon this assumption that moral knowledge is possible and that the philosopher-kings have such knowledge. So far I have merely indicated that given Plato's belief in the possibility of moral knowledge there is nothing necessarily inconsistent between the suggestion that he is to be classified as a utilitarian and the admission that he values truth, order and knowledge. But we now have to face one final preliminary problem and that is the suggestion that whether Plato can technically be described as a utilitarian or not is ultimately neither here nor there, since his whole argument is grounded on the false assumption that moral knowledge is possible.

If ultimate moral principles could be incontestably proven true, and if Plato's claim was that happiness was the supreme principle and if that were known to be true—well, that might be one thing. For instance, Bambrough argued that 'the claim that there is moral knowledge' in the sense that it is actually possessed 'would be necessary, even if it would not be sufficient, to justify the claim that an authoritarian state is the best state'.[1] But is such moral knowledge possible? Surely we are familiar with the view that moral propositions belong to a class of propositions that are not known to be true or false. Bambrough himself had gone some way towards suggesting, in a previous article, that Plato's evident assumption that his philosopher-kings would have moral knowledge, just as a doctor has medical knowledge, was his fundamental mistake.[2] Even if it can be shown that Plato did regard happiness as the supreme principle and that the argument of the *Republic* is internally consistent, does that whole argument not founder on its false premiss that what Plato regarded as true could be known to be true? Do we not have to accept that, even if propositions such as 'it is good to promote happiness' are not, as the logical positivists one day announced, literally meaningless, nonetheless they are not demonstrably true or false? And do we not therefore have to accept that it simply is not true that the pursuit of moral knowledge will go hand in hand with understanding that the claims of happiness are supreme, that there may be a clash between the value placed on truth and knowledge and the value placed on happiness, and that the philosopher-kings do not know the Good and do not have the authoritative expertise that was supposed to justify their position? Does all this not lead to the conclusion that even if the *Republic* could be shown to be grounded on a coherent utilitarian ethic, it would still be open to question whether the provisions of the *Republic* were or were not morally acceptable?

The situation is complicated by the fact that it is by no means clear where the liberal-democrats stand on the issue of the possibility of moral knowledge. Crossman regards Plato's 'dogmatism' as his fundamental error. 'Philosophy, by itself, can never discover what is right and just'; one cannot assert 'the existence of an absolute truth'.[3] And Russell states that 'Ultimate values are not matters as to which argument is possible'. 'As to ultimate values, men may agree or disagree, they may fight with guns or with ballot papers, but they cannot reason logically'.[4]

One could hold the view embodied in these quotations, without necessarily being a relativist of Thrasymachus's type. In other words one could believe, as I imagine that Crossman and Russell may, whereas Thrasymachus does not, that there is an absolute truth, that there are absolute moral demands, but that man can never be sure that he knows them. However, whichever of these positions the liberal-democrats take up, it is clear that their criticism of Plato is wholly impertinent. For if one *cannot* know the validity of one's ultimate values, one cannot *know* the invalidity of somebody else's. And if one cannot know the validity of ultimate values, whether through the limitations of man or the fact that no ultimate values have validity, Thrasymachus's position is a great deal more coherent than that of the liberal-democrats. If there is no knowing the truth then there is little point in trying to know, and no known moral reason to refrain from doing what suits one. This in itself and the dire consequences that might result from the adoption of such a view, does not unfortunately, as Wild seems to think, constitute an argument for establishing that the view is mistaken.[5] But it does mean that Russell and Crossman are quite inconsistent, both in arguing that the open society is to be commended for 'searching for truth'[6] and in insisting, as they emphatically do, that we ought to do and refrain from doing certain things. Once one involves oneself in arguing that certain ideals are preferable to others one is being no more and no less dogmatic than anybody else who does the same thing. Once the liberal-democrats have asserted that the state ought to ensure the observance of even one moral norm, as they certainly do, they are as guilty as Plato of dogmatism.

Popper, in a chapter that begins quite acceptably by rejecting various versions of the naturalistic fallacy (although he wrongly attributes most versions to Plato), attempts to explain his thesis of critical dualism.[7] This thesis certainly does not amount to the view expressed by Russell and Crossman; rather it appears to be a theory that would suit their practice, as opposed to their proclaimed principle. Critical dualism involves seeing the difference between true natural laws (i.e. laws of nature that govern the universe) and man-enforced normative laws.[8]

> Taboos are different in various tribes . . . they are imposed
> and enforced by man . . . laws are altered and made by human
> law givers. These experiences [sc. the realisation of these facts]
> may lead to a conscious differentiation between the
> man-enforced normative laws, based on decisions or
> conventions, and the natural regularities which are beyond
> his power.

In view of such statements as this it is not surprising perhaps that Wild assumed that Popper was a moral relativist. But that is not the whole story, for Popper goes on to say that this 'has nothing to do with the assertion that norms originate with man, and not with

God. . . . Least of all has it anything to do with the assertion that norms, since they are conventional, i.e. man-made, are therefore "merely arbitrary".'⁹ Presumably what Popper means is simply that, although moral laws may have absolute validity and may therefore be true, nonetheless we have to rely on man's intuition and reasoning to discover what they are. He would clearly seem to feel that we can be sure that some suggestions do not constitute bona fide moral laws (for the choice is not 'merely arbitrary'), but that nonetheless we cannot ever claim to be absolutely certain that a particular moral law does have validity.

On the assumption that critical dualism is a fair summary of the liberal-democratic position (since it clearly suits their practice), the charge that Plato does not know what ought to be done, as a doctor knows what ought to be done in the sphere of medicine, loses its significance. It may be conceded that ultimate values have a peculiar status that divorces them from the possibility of some conclusive empirical proof and that relies for substantiation on man's reasoning, which may in fact be faulty though man does not realise it. But in so far as society is going to insist on the observance of any moral norms, as the liberal-democrats no less than Plato demand, all that is required to justify the adoption of a norm is all that *can* be required, since it is all that can be done—namely that man's reasoning should assent. And the question of which man's reasoning is to settle the issue applies no more to Plato's society than any other.

This obvious point was well enough known to Aristotle, who referred to the wisdom of expecting only the degree and kind of certainty appropriate to a given field in that field,¹⁰ and to Mill, who explained that there was a wider sense of proof than what he called 'direct proof' or 'proof in the ordinary and popular meaning of the term'.¹¹ What both authors may be taken to have meant is that ultimate ends cannot be proven, as empirical claims are taken to be, by corroboration directly by one of the senses. They can only be reasoned about. What one may be forgiven for wondering is why the liberal-democrats bother to reason about them. For there is quite literally no point in distinguishing between coherent and incoherent reasoning, if there is not a presupposition that coherent reasoning is the way of establishing what ends to adopt.

The liberal-democrats cannot have it both ways. Unless they are prepared to eschew all interest in making any moral demands on anybody in society, they cannot shelter behind the shield of the unknowability of moral norms. By raising the question of whether the *Republic* is morally acceptable or not they involve themselves in an attempt to answer it; the only way to answer it is by reasoning. The truth is that men convince themselves of the truth of moral norms. And we require conviction as to the relative truth of the liberal-democratic norms and Plato's utilitarian norms.

It is undoubtedly true that Plato believed in the absolute validity of *his* moral principles, and he therefore assumed that the philosopher-kings, who gaze upon the form of the Good, who come through study to understand the nature of morality, would adopt the same principles. But since the liberal-democrats would have us incorporate certain principles and injunctions that follow from their theory in the organisation of our society, it is incumbent upon them to do more than point out that Plato cannot prove the validity of his principles with the same convincing crunch as, by dropping stones, he can prove the law of gravity. They must show by the kind of argument the case allows, why they do not accept Plato's principles and why they advocate their own in preference. They must convince us.

Popper's extraordinary digression to prove that Plato fashioned the philosopher-kings in his own image, is, therefore, a trifle absurd.[12] Of course he did. If one believes that certain things ought to obtain in society, one tends to approve of the sort of government that thinks likewise. Popper is presumably as anxious that the government of the liberal-democracy shall share his 'demands' and reject Plato's moral principles, as Plato is anxious that the philosopher-kings shall share his and reject Popper's. Besides, as I have tried to bring out in the previous chapter, the philosopher-kings are not simply those who, as Plato would put it, recognise those moral principles that do command our assent. They must be seen on a lower level as well, which could have application even if one believed, as the liberal-democrats do not, that choice of ultimate values was entirely arbitrary. They are not only defined in terms of recognising that happiness is the supreme principle, but also as people who are adept at seeing means to ends and resisting temptations to deviate from ends, whatever those ends may be; who do not reason fallaciously (for instance, who do not indulge in the naturalistic fallacy or hold mutually exclusive beliefs); and who are of a certain disposition (essentially concerned for the well-being of others and courageous in abiding by this concern). Even if we ignore the question of ultimate ends, it seems odd to call such a person 'a monument of human smallness'.[13]

If the liberal-democrats lay stress on the unknowability of ultimate ends, they cannot consistently claim to know that happiness is not the end. If they concede that only some kinds of proposed ends make sense as moral ends, and that happiness is one of them, they cannot consistently object to exclusive preoccupation with happiness. But whatever position they adopt, in the face of a specific claim such as that happiness is supreme, there is only one acceptable way of countering it, and that is to show where the argument has gone wrong.

It is surely clear that in the face of specific proposals for a particular kind of society and a particular attitude to the nature and distribution of education, it is quite inadequate to argue that the proposals in question can be ignored because they are based on the questionable assumption that they are *known* to be desirable. Our procedure must be to elucidate precisely what argument lies behind the proposals in question and then to attempt to assess that argument. In this instance it is therefore necessary first to consider what argument there is in favour of a utilitarian position and whether there is good reason to interpret the *Republic* as the embodiment of utilitarianism, and secondly to examine those principles, such as freedom and equality, to which Plato's liberal-democratic critics are committed, in order to see whether Plato offends the claims of these principles, and, if he does, whether a convincing argument can be produced for concluding that he ought not to. None of the points raised in this chapter can serve to remove the need for that procedure.

In short it is one thing to say that Plato cannot prove that rulers ought to be as he depicts them, and ought to recognise his moral ends, with the finality that we feel is possible in certain empirical proofs. It is another to say that we cannot assess this proposal and distinguish and judge between it and others. Indeed, in condemning it, the liberal-democrats would seem to be doing precisely that. Our distinguishing may be faulty, but in the nature of things we either have to attempt it or hold our peace.

Notes

1 Bambrough, R., 'Plato's modern friends and enemies', *Philosophy*, 37, 1962, p. 110.
2 Bambrough, R., 'Plato's political analogies' in Laslett, P., ed., *Philosophy, Politics and Society*, Blackwell, Oxford, 1956.
3 Crossman, op. cit., p. 174.
4 Russell, *Education and the Social Order*, pp. 128, 129.
5 Wild, J. D., *Plato's Modern Enemies and the Theory of Natural Law*, University of Chicago Press, 1953, pp. 70, 71.
6 Crossman, op. cit., p. 185.
7 Popper, op. cit., chapter 5.
8 Ibid., p. 60.
9 Ibid., p. 61.
10 Aristotle, *Nicomachean Ethics*, I. 3.
11 Mill, J. S., *Utilitarianism*, chapter 1.
12 Popper, op. cit., pp. 153ff, p. 155.
13 Ibid., p. 156.

What is happiness?   4

1   Introduction

Plato is quite explicit that the aim of the arrangements of the Republic is to ensure 'the greatest happiness of the city as a whole'.[1] Russell contemptuously dismisses the idea that the citizen of the Republic will be happy, with the remark that 'Man needs for his happiness not only the enjoyment of this or that, but hope and enterprise and change', none of which he sees in the *Republic*.[2] It is not immediately obvious what he means by hope, enterprise and change, nor that they are absent from the *Republic*. But Russell does not think that Plato cares about the happiness of his citizens anyway: 'Whether people are happy in this community does not matter, we are told'.[3] Now in point of fact we are told the exact opposite of this, but Russell draws this conclusion from the Platonic dictum that 'excellence resides in the whole, not in the parts'.

Popper likewise argues that[4]

> Plato says frequently that what he is aiming at is neither the happiness of individuals nor that of any particular class in the state, but only the happiness of the whole, and this, he argues, is nothing but the outcome of that rule of justice which I have shown to be totalitarian in character.

This passage is a fairly good example of Popper's technique: it is true that he has argued that the Republic is totalitarian, but what he has not done is shown that totalitarianism, or rather Platonism, is evil, still less that it precludes happiness. In point of fact Popper goes a long way towards admitting the sincere, though in his opinion misconceived, benevolence of Plato's intentions. He admits that, 'with deep sociological insight', Plato saw signs of severe strain amongst people, which he sought to alleviate, and that totalitarianism might answer 'a real need' for many people,[5] but at no stage does he consider that this might be a justification for Platonism. Platonism, according to Popper, being totalitarian, is indefensible. The result is that, since the happiness of the Republic is dependent upon totalitarian justice, Popper does not see the need to enquire further into the nature and the claims of happiness.

There are three distinct points here. (a) Is there a real distinction between aiming at the happiness of the whole and aiming at the happiness of individuals? (b) Does the Republic provide happiness?

49

and (c) how important is happiness? Is it, for instance, worth the price of Platonism? The last question can only be answered after we have considered what exactly the price of Platonism is; it is with the first two questions that I am immediately concerned.

Holism is the term used by Popper to castigate Plato's preoccupation with the whole. And the suggestion (it is never made very explicit) is that Plato, because he is concerned about the whole state, therefore has no feeling for the individuals within it. But this seems a most perverse interpretation of the *Republic*. What is the state, i.e. the whole, except the sum total of the individuals in it? To say this is not to endorse some mystic doctrine of the destiny of a nation without regard to its actual members, it is simply to say that, when one talks about what is good for England, one means what is good for the English people. Naturally in doing that, in talking about what is good for the English people, one is guilty of generalising. A proposal that is regarded as in the interests of the English people will not necessarily be in the interests of every single individual. But to suggest that, when advancing proposals of a political nature, one should not so generalise, would immediately bring an end to all political proposals. In proposing any legislation we are likely to distress certain people, but we persevere nonetheless, if we believe that on balance it will alleviate distress for the country as a whole. And that is all Plato means: the welfare of the community as a whole is to be put before the welfare of any individual or group, should the two conflict.

It is quite true that Plato uses the language of whole and parts, and that he explicitly states that the interests of the whole are superior to the interests of the part.[6] What he does not do is assume that the whole, be it the physical body or a community, is something separate and distinct from its parts, the legs or the individuals. In using the phraseology of whole and parts, Plato is thus doing no more than stating a principle of utility. This is absolutely clear from a passage in the *Laws* which Popper does quote, but not in its entirety. His version is the stark statement: 'The part exists for the sake of the whole, but the whole does not exist for the sake of the part . . . you are created for the sake of the whole and not the whole for the sake of you'. Plato's version adds some important details:[7]

> the purpose is . . . to win happiness for the life of the whole
> [i.e. the whole world]. The whole is not made for your
> advantage, so much as you for its advantage . . . just as a
> doctor works on a part [i.e. the leg] for the sake of the whole,
> to contribute to the general good, and he does not work on
> the whole [the body] for the sake of the part [the leg].

Since the 'whole', in political terms, the state, can only be understood as an abstraction referring to the members of the community, the distinction is between the benefit of the individual and the benefit of the citizen body as a whole should they conflict. On two of the occasions on which he refers to the happiness of the community as an aim, Plato uses the expression 'the whole city',[8] the second time he talks of producing happiness '*in* the whole city'; on the third occasion he talks simply of making 'the city most happy, rather than fixing our eye on making one group happy'.[9] This terminology surely makes it clear that 'city' is being used as a collective noun exactly akin to 'flock' or 'herd'; could one seriously suggest that a man intent on feeding his flock is not concerned with feeding the sheep in it? The implication that Plato regarded the 'state' as some entity divorced from its members is equally false and meaningless; the language of whole and parts itself logically implies a connection: the concept of 'body' (in other than the restricted sense of 'trunk of the body') involves the notion of arms and legs. Undoubtedly Plato intends this analogy to suggest that the individual outside community life is but a helpless limb, and it may be objected that this is not the case. But he is concerned with political matters, which is to say that he is presupposing a *polis* or community; it is therefore surely legitimate to raise the question whether, given that a number of individuals are trying to make something of a corporate existence, the claims of the individual or the claims of the corporate existence take priority. To opt for the former suggestion is to deny the purpose of community life; whereas, once it is realised that the claims of the corporate existence, community, whole or state, are no more than the synthesis of individual claims, it seems impossible to deny that these should be the concern of the political philosopher.

We thus cannot accept that Plato lays himself open to the charge 'that there is a difference between the happiness of the State, which is important, and the happiness of the citizens, which is not'.[10] Rather, I should say, that Plato would endorse Aristotle's claim that 'happiness is not a conception like that of evenness in number which may be predicated of the whole number without being predicated of its component parts'. The state may only properly be described as happy if its citizens are happy; that is precisely why Plato is not interested in making some minority group happy at the expense of others, for he is trying to construct a just city, and a just city, like a just man, will in Plato's view be happy; if it can be shown that citizens are not happy in the Republic, then it has been shown that the state is not organised on just principles, according to Platonic doctrine.

But whether the Republic is in fact likely to provide happiness clearly cannot be answered until we have given an analysis of that concept, which we shall now proceed to do without reference to Plato.

2   The concept of happiness

It is doubtful whether we can ever hope adequately to describe the state of 'happiness', if by 'describe' we mean put into words the feelings that we experience when we feel happy; and ultimately it is unlikely that we shall ever know whether the experiences of two people who are happy are similar or identical in any respect.

The problem of describing, of course, applies to all words of 'feeling', such as pain, cold or warm. There is no way of proving that your feeling is in any way akin to mine when we sit in a room and the heat is increased. We can point out that similar biological reactions take place, such as sweating, or perhaps that similar behavioural responses take place, such as an effort to open the window; we can even say that neither of us like the experience after a certain point. But we cannot with absolute certainty describe the nature of that feeling in the same way that we can describe the room in which the scene takes place.

No more can we describe 'yellow' in this sense. But this inability, the impossibility we find in describing 'happiness', does not mean that the word has no rules governing its use and it does not make the concept unusable, any more than the concept of 'yellow' is unusable. The question then is what can we say to give content to the concept of happiness.

A frequent gambit is to attempt to provide content for the concept by listing certain external conditions as either sufficient or necessary. I suggest that this procedure is unacceptable. Such conditions might be health, wealth, companionship or a job of work to do. But none of these is obviously necessary to happiness, still less sufficient. It is not logically odd to say: 'I am poor and happy' nor, conversely, 'I am rich and unhappy'. Furthermore to claim that, although it is not logically odd, nonetheless, in fact, nobody could be poor (unhealthy, alone, etc.) but happy, would surely go against evidence with which we are all familiar: people claim to be happy and are said to be happy in a bewildering variety of circumstances. Clearly to rule out certain claims to happiness as being false, because they do not convince us, at this stage would be an arbitrary procedure. If Diogenes says that he is happy in his barrel, and the martyr on the cross, our analysis of 'happy' must take account of these examples before we rule them out.

Some people, we said, might be happy in most unlikely situations. Is it perhaps that certain specific mental attitudes are necessary or sufficient conditions of happiness? Could we say that provided you are clever, long-suffering, imaginative, dull, intellectually curious or endowed with some such character trait, you will be happy (sufficient) or that at least without it you will not be (necessary)? Once again to make such a claim runs against our experience, and makes a criticism of our use of the word 'happiness', without producing grounds for so doing. 'He is dull but happy' is no more logically contradictory than 'he is intellectually curious but happy'. One has heard of boring people who claimed to be happy, and fascinating people who claimed to be happy; bored and excited people, listless and energetic people. It may be that we shall establish criteria for ruling out some of these claims as illegitimate; but we cannot start by saying that they are self-evidently illegitimate, when to many people the self-evidence is not apparent.

If we accept that theoretically X may be happy in any circumstances; or that anyone may be happy in circumstance A; that Y is nonetheless not happy in circumstance A; that Z may be happy where X is not, and so on, it becomes apparent that concentrating on either the circumstances or the character of the individual to the exclusion of the other is a mistaken approach. Happiness involves a relation between two variables, the person and his circumstances. (By person I mean nothing philosophically remarkable: the person, here, is the individual inclusive of his physical and mental make-up, the latter including his prejudices, opinions, beliefs, knowledge and taste. Thus the 'person' includes character traits, even if they have been developed by a certain social context.) The circumstances necessary for happiness cannot be pinned down in the form of a specific list, because what is intolerable to the character that is X, is not necessarily intolerable to the character that is Y. But nor can a specific type of character be delineated as a necessary condition of happiness, since circumstances are not static.

'X is happy', in so far as it is true, tells us something about X. It does not automatically tell us anything about the circumstances in which he is placed. If X is known to us, we may on empirical evidence rule out certain circumstances, e.g. if X is my brother, and very well known to me, I may presume that, if he is now happy, he is not now eating my mother. But if X is some wild native of a newly discovered prehistoric tribe deep in the jungle it would be foolish to assume that, if he is happy, he cannot possibly be eating my mother.

Nor does the information that X is happy tell me anything about X's character, unless I know something about the circumstances. I certainly do not know whether he is clever or stupid, nor do I know whether he is easy or difficult to please, alert or insensitive. What I do know, as a result of the information that 'X is happy', is that X's relationship with the circumstances in which he finds himself is of such a sort that he is satisfied. But we can do better than this. In the first place we can recognise happiness, and in the second place there are some very definite logical rules governing the use of the word. When we describe a man as happy we attribute to him satisfaction with the relations existing between him and his situation (i.e. his situation might be 'surrounded by other people', his relation 'friendliness' and the resultant feeling in him 'satisfaction'). It is therefore logically impossible that the man should be at the same time described in any way that attributes to him dissatisfaction with those same relations. Thus X cannot be happy and frustrated, because to describe him as happy is to attribute satisfaction to him in respect of his situation, while to describe him as frustrated is also to say something about him in respect of his situation but it is to say precisely the opposite: namely, that whatever his circumstances may be he is dissatisfied by them.

This point is best brought out by considering the two predicates 'alone' and 'lonely' in conjunction with 'happy'.[11] To predicate 'alone' of X is simply to describe a specific aspect of his situation: so far as the question of other people goes, he is without contact with them. In other words 'alone' simply describes an aspect of X's situation, just as 'wealthy' or 'poor' do. As such it tells us nothing, logically, about X's happiness, because we know nothing about X's attitude to this aspect of his situation. (A man may be happy and alone.)

But to describe X as 'lonely' is to do two things: it is (a) to assert that he is alone, and (b) to assert that he is not satisfied with this state of affairs. It is therefore contradictory to predicate both 'happiness' and 'loneliness' of the same man at the same time, unless one specifically means that he is happy except for the fact that he is lonely, (i.e. that the only feature of his situation which does not satisfy him is that he is alone,) since to be 'happy' is to be satisfied.

It would therefore seem at this stage that whereas we have no grounds for accepting that there are certain necessary factors in a man's situation for happiness, there are nonetheless some necessary conditions for attributing happiness and they are the absence of certain conflicting attitudes to one's situation such as frustration, loneliness, agitation, depression, annoyance, irritation, guilt, remorse, regret and resentment, or, more generally, misery.

On this list of conditions which guarantee the absence of happiness one or two points should be made:

(a)   It is not an exhaustive list. It will be seen that some of these words, such as guilt and remorse, are closely related and just as I have included both of these so I might have worked through the

Thesaurus and added disappointment, dejection, etc. as close relations of frustration. To make the list exhaustive would be a lengthy
business and not obviously helpful.

(b) There is no principle of unity linking these words beyond
the fact that if correctly predicated of a man they all indicate a
wish on his part that something about the situation he is in, or about
himself, were otherwise, which would seem to me to be equivalent
to restating the premiss: that each of them is incompatible with
happiness conceived of as something complete.

(c) Agitation, depression, annoyance, irritation, resentment and
regret are all words which draw attention primarily to the nature
of the dissatisfaction felt; in practice they draw attention generally
to behavioural patterns: 'the depressed man' is dissatisfied and may
show it by a glum countenance, the annoyed man by anger, the
irritated man by temper. The distinction between some of the
words is obviously minute. In theory anything may cause any of
them.

Loneliness, guilt and remorse, on the other hand, are tied more
securely to specific situations: loneliness indicates a feeling of dissatisfaction, but it specifies the source of the feeling rather than the
nature of the feeling: it does not tell us whether the man's dissatisfaction is expressed by anger, depression, etc. but it does tell us
what is causing the dissatisfaction: namely being alone. Frustration
does not primarily describe a sphere of the situation, as loneliness
does, nor does it tell us anything about the manner in which the
man is expressing his dissatisfaction; rather it tells us that in respect
of some part of his situation the man recognises a barrier between
himself and his object. Finally misery seems to be one of the generic
words, synonymous for our purposes with unhappy, covering all the
more specific words and obviously, by definition, incompatible
with happiness.

Clearly, if one is trying to judge whether a man is happy or not,
only the first group of words will help, since the only way one could
judge whether a man may be correctly described by a word from
one of the other groups, is to see whether he exhibits annoyance,
depression, irritation, etc. A man does not betray his loneliness
except through one of the first-group words.

(d) Such being the varied nature of the words any hope that we
can use their opposites to provide a positive list of necessary conditions for happiness is surely doomed. When the words are specific
about the source of dissatisfaction, as e.g. lonely, it is not true that
the opposite, which would involve both being with other people and
welcoming this state of affairs, is either a necessary or sufficient
condition of happiness. When the word is taken from the first group,

E

e.g. annoyance, irritation, one is not sure what the opposite is. Is the opposite merely an absence of these feelings? If this is the case then clearly, by definition, they (the opposites) are necessary conditions of happiness: if annoyance is incompatible with happiness, then naturally non-annoyance is necessary for happiness. If on the other hand one tries to creat opposites of more substance such as 'bliss' for 'annoyance', or 'elation' for 'frustration', one is either committed to the view that elation is merely another word for happiness, in which case again it is necessarily a necessary and sufficient condition, or else, more plausibly, to the view that, though all elated people are happy, not all happy people are elated, in which case we have a sufficient condition, but only by understanding elation to be a particularly intense sensation of happiness.

In conclusion we can say that no man who is any one of these things, lonely, depressed, anxious, etc. is completely happy, but we cannot confidently argue either that any man who is not one or some of these things is happy, since if he is not lonely but is frustrated, he will not be happy, nor can we assert that the opposite of any one of these predicates is obviously necessary or sufficient as a condition of happiness unless we define the opposite in such a way as to make it more or less synonymous with 'happy'.

This brings us back to the question of recognition. Obviously the conditions of happiness outlined here are very formal. We are no nearer being able to describe a feeling of frustration than we were a feeling of happiness, and perhaps more important we do not know what causes a man to feel frustrated or anxious. But surely this is precisely because theoretically anything may make a man feel frustrated or anxious, just as a man can theoretically be happy in any circumstances. We cannot predict what will frustrate until we know something about the other variable: the man.

But although it is true that no absolute conditions can be laid down for happiness in specific terms, it does not follow from this that there is nothing we can do or say in practical terms about happiness. We recognise very easily whether we ourselves or other people are or are not happy, or, as we should say, since presumably few if any are ever completely happy, whether we or they are *relatively* happy or unhappy. In absolute terms we cannot state, for instance, that crying is an indication of unhappiness, since we sometimes cry for joy and some societies have actually used crying as the normal expression of joy. But even here, within our society we can, and do, assume that in default of special circumstances when a man cries he is not happy. More generally we may state that if a man is making a positive attempt to extricate himself from or alter his situation he is not happy;[12] the fact that we might judge him as ill-advised to alter what we regard as a favourable situation is, of course, neither here nor there, even if he later implicitly endorses our judgment. Thus if a man throws up his job and emigrates and then ten years later says: 'I didn't realise how happy I was then', we surely cannot accept an analysis of 'happy', which says that he *was* happy before his emigration, but only realises it now. To realise that you are happy involves feeling happy; how could this man have felt happy then and not realised it, and yet now realise that he felt happy then? This would be like saying, ten years after the event, 'I was in pain when I caught my hand in the door'; if at the time the speaker did not notice that his hand was caught, can we fairly describe him as being 'in pain'? Surely all we can say is that he experienced something which we are surprised did not cause him pain. (Unless all we mean is that he has only recently learnt the sort of situations in which we use the word 'pain'). Likewise we must interpret the immigrant as meaning not so much 'I didn't realise how full of satisfaction I was at that time, but I do now', as 'I didn't realise how *lucky* I was' or, 'I wish I had accepted conditions then' or, 'I am even more miserable now', none of which, though they may be true, can lead us to the conclusion that he was happy then, in the sense of satisfied with his situation, but didn't realise it. The mere fact that he emigrated, unless he was forced to do so, indicates that he was not entirely happy and thought that he could be happier.

We thus entirely reject the claim that there is any distinction to be made between being happy and feeling happy, except when we predicate happiness of another in its original sense of 'lucky'. We will accept that there is a use of the phrase 'he is happy', meaning 'he is lucky or fortunate', such that the predicate 'happy' is used to refer to the situation in which a man finds himself, without reference to his response to that situation. It might be argued that it is odd to call another 'lucky' if he does not appreciate his luck, but at any rate we will allow that as a matter of fact people sometimes do say such things as 'X is lucky and he doesn't realise how lucky he is', and, in saying such things, they take for granted, with the person they are talking to, that there are certain circumstances which may be objectively described as more rather than less acceptable. Thus if A and B are talking about X, and X is known to have won the pools, to have landed the job that he had said he hoped to get, and to be getting married tomorrow, and yet X claims to be miserable, A is quite likely to say to B: 'X doesn't know how lucky he is' which amounts to saying, 'X will not find himself in circumstances more favourable than these'. A and B are taking it for granted that these circumstances are productive of happiness, or at least necessary for it, and they may be right, certainly as far as they themselves are concerned, and possibly as far as X is concerned. But if they are right it is because of the particular character of themselves and X; and if they are right about X, i.e. if as a matter of fact X will never find himself in circumstances which he might regard as more favourable, it follows that he will never be luckier or happier in this sense. But if X does not feel happy, if, however foolishly, he insists or desires to alter his circumstances, he cannot be described as happy in the sense of satisfied with his circumstances. All that we could conclude is that, assuming A and B are right in their factual claims, X is never going to be happy.

Nor can we argue that a person might feel happy and not be happy, except in the sense that the person has misunderstood the word 'happy'.

Mrs Austin has suggested in 'Pleasure and Happiness' that a man experiencing euphoria, induced by drugs, feels happy but is not happy; it is the only example she gives, but she feels that it clinches the argument that there is a distinction between being and feeling happy. There are, however, two points about our actual use of the word 'happiness' that might account for the plausibility of this suggestion, without establishing its truth. In the first place, when we indulge in theoretic discussion we quite naturally deal with 'happiness' as a complete state describing a man's total condition; in theory the happy man is not beset by fears of the morrow and, more particularly, is not only happy because he is hiding from himself certain important facts. Our imaginary and ideally happy man is not a man who simply refuses to acknowledge that his wife is dead, that his job is in jeopardy, etc; such a man as this takes us into the world of the abnormal and we simply do not have him in mind when we try to imagine the 'happy man'. But, although such a man is a rarity, there seems no logical reason why he should not be 'happy'. We accept that a man may be happy today, because he is in ignorance of certain facts, which, if he knew them, would certainly make him miserable. If then it is psychologically possible for a man to put himself in ignorance of certain unpleasant facts, then it is surely possible for him to be happy even in circumstances which he would normally admit he regarded as most upsetting. Thus, though the drug addict is almost certainly only feeling happy because he has artificially closed his mind to everyday experiences, it is difficult to accept that he is not happy, so long as he is successful in keeping the everyday world at bay. The impossibility of establishing necessary conditions of circumstance for happiness has led us to see that happiness is dependent on a relation between two variables: the individual and his circumstances. The drug addict has achieved his happiness by taking extreme measures with one of the variables.

This brings us to the second point about our use of the word 'happiness' in philosophic circles. We seem very often to want to distinguish between various qualities of happiness, and because we envisage such a scale of quality we are inclined to dismiss 'happiness' on the lower end of the scale as in some sense unreal. It may be possible to argue that the Aristotelian *nous* provides a better happiness than de Sade's lechery, if we mean, either that it has more chance in practice of being permanently fulfilled, or that the circumstances in which happiness is found in the former case are in themselves more worthy; but it is very difficult to see what grounds could be produced for saying that the feeling experienced by the man happy in intellectual contemplation is of a different order to the feeling experienced by the man happy in lechery; and in default of grounds being offered, it is impossible to accept the contention. Thus, although we accept that to Mrs Austin, and indeed ourselves, a man who claims to be happy while under the influence of drugs may be pursuing a poor way of life and may ultimately be lessening his chances of permanent and frequent happiness, we deny that it can be established that a man who feels happy when taking drugs is not happy.

We accept that the feeling of happiness in this case is achieved by artificially controlling the individual, that it is perhaps an unwise way to seek happiness, and that we prefer the picture of Socrates satisfied to Jimi Hendrix high and happy, but we have no grounds for claiming that Hendrix when drugged could not feel in respect of his situation the same kind of feeling as Socrates in respect of his.

Words which involve 'feeling', such as 'happy' and 'pain', are, at the same time, both absolute in one sense and relative in another. There are degrees of intensity of pain, with the result that, when I am pinched, I may feel less pain than when a nail is driven through my flesh. But I am in pain on both occasions and it is perfectly legitimate for me to describe my experience as 'painful' without qualification on both occasions. It is therefore possible for me to say 'I thought I was happy but I wasn't', if I mean by that 'judging from my experience since, it is clear that I am capable of more intense feelings of happiness than I realised when I described myself as happy in the past'; thus it may be true that I was not, 'in the past', as intensely happy, as I am capable of being, but naturally at that time I had no way of judging that. What is not possible is to claim that I therefore was not happy in the past, although I felt happy, unless we defy our use of the word 'happy' and insist that it only has application when an individual is experiencing the most intense feeling of happiness which he, given his individual character, could ever feel. Provided that he was not frustrated, anxious, miserable etc., in the past, he was happy; and if he *was* frustrated, anxious, miserable, etc., then he must have been aware of it at the time and could never have thought of himself as happy except either by misunderstanding the word, or in a qualified sense (i.e. 'I am happy in general, but one thing frustrates me').

It follows that if a person feels happy he is happy, however insensitive, blind, lacking in forethought, etc. he may be. It may be possible for us to scorn him for feeling happy in a given situation, but we cannot deny that he is happy.

Because Mrs Austin believes in a distinction between being and feeling happy she is enabled to say that a man cannot be 'unkind and happy', a remark which strikes me as preposterous and therefore cannot be claimed as self-evidently true. To say that a man cannot be unkind and happy is once again to lay down necessary conditions for happiness, but this time conditions about the person rather than his circumstances; and once again an argument to support the contention is needed and is not forthcoming. It may very well be generally true that unkind people are unhappy, but if it is, it is empirically true. There is no logical reason why an unkind man should not be happy and there is therefore no reason why there should not prove to be exceptions to Mrs Austin's rule. The point is that 'unkind' is similar to 'alone' in its logic. It describes a relation, in this case from the point of view of the agent; he is related to others by a behaviour pattern we describe as 'unkind'; but nothing has been said about the agent's reaction to this situation: we have not moved, so to speak, from 'alone' to 'lonely'.

We are left with the following contentions:

(a) If a man feels happy, he is happy, although he may later discover that he is capable of more intense feelings.

(b) Conversely, if he does not feel happy, he is not happy.

(c) There are no necessary conditions of happiness, although if we know a man we may predict accurately conditions necessary for his happiness.

(d) To make a man happy we must remove sources of frustration, anxiety, depression, etc.

(e) We can in practice recognise symptoms of frustration, anxiety, etc. They may be broadly categorised as indications that the individual would alter his circumstances if he thought that he could.

These points tell us something about happiness, just as we might say that yellow is a colour and cannot be predicated of abstracts like justice. We turn now to the question of trying to depict 'happiness', and here more than ever we feel that philosophers are, in Berkeley's words, guilty of kicking up 'a cloud of dust and then complaining that they cannot see'. It is true that what makes you happy does not necessarily make me happy, that what makes me happy today does not necessarily make me happy tomorrow, that there are no necessarily universal indications of happiness (if we mean by that certain specific activities such as smiling or laughing), and that logically incompatible predicates such as frustrated are equally obscure. But it is not true that we cannot recognise happiness, when we see it, though we should stress once again that in our experience when we refer to a man as 'happy' we are usually making a relative assessment: few people, if any, are absolutely and completely happy, because few people are entirely without fear, anxiety, frustration, worry, etc. in any respect.

We can tell when we ourselves are happy. We cannot assess how happy we are in relation to others, nor in relation to our own potential, but we can recognise when we are happy rather than unhappy. The happier we are the easier it is to recognise it, no doubt, but we can always recognise 'happiness' by an absence of its opposites: 'happiness', being a general word and one applied to man's total condition, is much harder to deal with than the various specific incompatible concepts opposed to it. In short although I may not know *why*, I always know *that* I am frustrated, anxious, afraid, miserable, lonely, repressed, etc. and when I am any one of these I am not happy. My fight for 'happiness' is therefore a fight against these enemies.

We can also tell when another is 'unhappy'. In practice we can make use of certain external symptoms particularly within a society. Thus, despite what has been said above, if I see somebody I know crying, it is prima facie likely that he is 'unhappy' (although it *may* turn out that he is crying for joy). More to the point, since 'being happy' cannot be divorced from 'feeling happy' and since the same applies to those predicates that are incompatible with 'happy', we can always find out whether X is happy or not by asking him whether he feels happy or not. In practice, given that there is a mystique about the word 'happiness', we should be better advised to ask X whether he feels 'frustrated, miserable, depressed' etc. It may well be that he will not be able to tell us *why* he feels any of these things but it is inconceivable that he should feel them and not be aware that he feels them. If he is not aware that he feels 'unhappy', assuming he understands the word, then, however stupid we may think he is, whatever reason we have for thinking that he ought to be unhappy, the fact remains that he is not unhappy.

It might be asked whether we could really allow that a man whose life was by any objective standards a complete and total failure could be called 'happy' just because he said he was. We reply that short of proving that he is in fact frustrated, etc. (which amounts to proving that he is misusing the word 'happy') he is 'happy' if he says he is, and that all we can point out is that his psychological make-up is odd; to insist on divorcing his feelings from his actual state, is to insist on objective criteria for happiness, which involves making positive claims about human nature in the face of evidence to the contrary, and which would require substantiation which has never yet been, and is never likely to be, forthcoming.

I am arguing, then, that the reason that we cannot lay down substantive conditions that are either necessary or sufficient conditions of happiness, is not that the task is difficult, but because there are none. Insofar as it is true that this that or the other is necessary for people to be happy, it is only contingently true, and it is true because of the psychological make-up of those people which might have been different. When we pause to consider whether a man who retires to bed for life and passes the time 'transferring dried peas, one at a time, from one saucepan to another'[13] could truly be said to be happy, we cease philosophising and begin a psychological enquiry. There is nothing in the concept of happiness that necessarily rules out this or any other activity or behaviour as incompatible with happiness.

All that we are entitled to say is that people are happy in so far as they feel happy, and that people feel happy in so far as they feel that things are as they should be. This, it should be stressed, is not a psychological but a definitional point. I am *not* saying 'Take your conception of happiness and agree with me that people do not experience it when they do not like the look of the world'. I am saying 'Drop your conception of happiness, unless it is such that you agree that people are to be called happy in so far as, and only in so far as, they feel that things are as they should be; for that is all that can finally be said about it'. When people feel that things are as they should be, they do not feel any impulse to alter their situation, and the most general symptom of unhappiness (implicit in all those concepts that are logically incompatible with happiness) is an impulse to alter one's situation in some way if one could. Conversely, a positive formulation might be that the individual is happy when he feels that he *enmeshes* with his surroundings or situation. This is not to say that happiness is identical with enmeshment, but rather that happiness is the feeling that arises out of and is dependent upon enmeshment.

It may be allowed that there are different degrees of intensity of happiness that may be felt as a result of enmeshment. One man may experience ecstatic feelings of happiness, which I shall characterise as whoopee feelings, while others may experience more moderate feelings. When we come to consider the question of attempting to provide happiness for members of a community, I shall not be concerned to talk in terms of promoting specifically whoopee feelings rather than moderate feelings, because of the practical difficulties involved. One can, as will be argued, ensure enmeshment and hence happiness; it would seem to be an altogether different question whether one can ensure whoopee feelings. And indeed, as I shall also argue, some of the arguments advanced to support the claim that people do not necessarily pursue their happiness are in fact based upon the assumption that some people do not always pursue whoopee feelings.

What is meant by saying that a person is enmeshed with his surroundings is that he is in such a relation to his situation that the demands of that situation are willingly met, and the restrictions of that situation are not irksome. It is the positive formulation of the claim that the individual is not subject to frustration, envy, boredom, etc. A man is enmeshed with his job, for instance, if all aspects of his persona that relate to the job (his ability, interest, enthusiasm) are suited to the job, and given the opportunity to find fulfilment. To say that a man is 'wholly enmeshed', or simply 'enmeshed', without qualification, is to say that all aspects of his life are as he would have them be.

It may be objected that total enmeshment, if it were feasible, would lead to boredom. Surely there are some people who like a challenge and who find their happiness in striving and struggle? This may well be so. Certainly, if a man is bored he is not enmeshed, for boredom involves an impulse, however listless, to alter one's situation, and this is a symptom of unhappiness. But to say as much is to say something about the persona of the man in question. The man who likes challenges, in order that he may compete, has a specific persona which depends for its enmeshment on a situation that will provide this challenge. In the same way the notion of 'divine discontent' can be accommodated by this view of enmeshment as the cause of happiness. For 'divine discontent' is the feeling of happiness that accompanies the attempt to ameliorate a situation that is dissatisfying. Now, of course, not all people who attempt to ameliorate a dissatisfying situation do experience divine discontent, or happiness, in the process of improving the situation. Some merely look forward to the improved situation that they are aiming at, and regard the process as a tiresome means to an end: others may derive relative comfort from the thought that the process is under way. But in so far as a man really experiences happiness in the process of amelioration, then it may be said that his character is such as to enmesh with the situation involved in the process. In other words, if he is really experiencing happiness in the process, he will not be finding it frustrating, irritating or depressing. It is also quite possible that a man should enmesh both with the process and with the static end result, provided that as a result of the process he has worked out those aspects of his persona that seek for a challenging situation for their enmeshment.

So that there shall be no doubt on this important issue, let me stress that the point I am making at this juncture is purely formal. Happiness, I am suggesting, means an absence of such things as anxiety, depression or frustration. To be happy is to be devoid of such feelings as those that indicate a desire that the world as it impinges on oneself should be in some respect otherwise. The individual who is devoid of such feelings I characterise as enmeshed with his surroundings. I have said nothing at all so far about what sort of things do as a matter of fact cause frustration, anxiety or whatever, and hence diminish enmeshment, thereby diminishing happiness.

The reader may feel that I am to be forgiven for this omission, on the grounds that the question of what does cause frustration is an empirical rather than a philosophical question. This, of course, is true. But if the reader leaves it at that he may be missing an important point. For although it is true that in specific circum-stances the desire to promote happiness would lead us to locate sources of frustration and anxiety, etc. and attempt to remove them, this is not the only way of achieving the object of a happy society, and indeed it might in practice be impossible to achieve the object by approaching it in this way, since sources of frustration, anxiety, etc. might differ from individual to individual. If we were to take a particular state we might pick out specific sources of dissatisfaction such as, if you will, censorship or great wealth differentials. But as soon as we do this we realise that, whatever our views on the subject, it seems clear that by no means everybody is caused a degree of unhappiness by censorship or wealth differentials: even poor people may sometimes be quite satisfied in respect of their poverty. It is not necessarily going to be possible, then, to increase happiness by altering circumstances.

It follows logically from the fact that happiness is a feeling dependent on enmeshment that, in order to promote happiness, we have to correlate the aspirations, attitudes, beliefs, desires and so on of the individual with the demands and the ethos of the circumstances in which he finds himself. One way to do this is to alter the circumstances to suit him, but another way is to alter him to suit the circumstances. More to the point, the obvious way to aim at the creation of a happy state, is to bring children up so that there is this correlation between individual and situation (and, of course, coincidentally, so that there is not conflict between different individuals requiring mutually incompatible situations for their enmeshment). Fairly obviously there are certain broad areas on which any society that was concerned to promote happiness would need to concentrate. In particular, given that there are different kinds of functions to be performed in society it would be important that the individual's character should be adapted to meet the specific role or situation which, for whatever reason, he is in fact going to face; that is to say that, so far as happiness is the aim, the development of the individual should follow a course that relates the man to the way of life he will lead. Technical expertise obviously plays a necessary part in this, but by no means the only important part. Of much more significance is that the individual should have attitudes, tastes and characteristics that suit the overall manner of the life he is expected to lead. For example, if the individual is destined to live a life in which there will be very little formal guidance or structuring from external pressures, he will need to have the kind of character that welcomes making decisions, taking responsibility and acting on its own initiative. If he is destined to live for the most part circumscribed by various pressures, then he needs, if he is to be happy, to find such direction acceptable.

That impracticable dream, the totally happy society, would be a society in which no individual had any impulse to alter any aspect of it. It would, of course, be open to anyone to condemn the society in which people have found happiness as immoral or shortsighted in some respects, but it is not legitimate to claim that a society in which everybody feels happy, on whatever conditions, is not in fact happy. To do that is once again to argue (a) that people have no right to feel happy except on certain conditions and (b) that anyway they don't feel happy, although they think that they do.

3 Plato, the liberal-democrats and happiness

Plato's view of happiness is the same as that which I have outlined above. Adeimantus takes the view that certain external conditions are necessary for happiness, consequently he immediately assumes that the Guardians will not be very happy, since they do not gain the sort of benefits from the city that can be acquired by 'owning lands and building fine big houses . . . and enjoying the possession of gold and silver and all that is customary for those who expect to be happy'.[14] But these things are not necessary for happiness, they are only necessary for a certain kind of character, namely the character in which desires for such things are rampant; but the desires of the Guardians have been deliberately channelled in a different direction:[15]

And surely we are aware that when a man's desires incline strongly to any one thing, they are weakened for other things. So when a man's desires have been taught to flow in the channel of learning and all that sort of thing they will presumably be concerned with pleasures of the soul and will be indifferent to those concerned with the body . . . such a man will have little lust for wealth and the things for the sake of which money is sought.

Plato admits[16] that we could bring up our prospective rulers in a different way so that the sort of conditions that made them happy would be different; and he is aware that each of the three groups in his state will find their happiness in different circumstances, as their nature or character dictates.[17] Cephalus, although he does not use the word 'happiness', talks of other elderly men whom he knows and who are clearly depicted as being unhappy, as being so because they are maladjusted to their situations.[18] And Sophocles is 'most glad' to have outgrown his sexual desires, because, without the desire, sexual release is not necessary for his happiness.

The cave dweller who climbs out into the light and at first finds it painful, comes eventually to count himself happy; but if he returns to the cave, those who dwell there, habituated to their way of life, would laugh at him: they too feel happy.[19]

However, Plato still feels that the just man is most happy[20] and that the Guardians in particular are perhaps especially happy because they are 'rich in the wealth that makes happiness—a good and wise life'[21] and it may be felt that he is here making a certain kind of character a necessary condition of happiness. But this is not so. Undoubtedly Plato himself felt that the manner in which the Guardians find happiness, through intellectual contemplation and the pursuit of truth, was more admirable than various other manners; that is to say that he prefers the man who is happy doing philosophy to the man who is happy eating large quantities of food; he also feels that happiness that is not dependent on material wealth is more permanent, a practical observation which is obviously true: the Guardian is able to be happy regardless of the ups and downs of the material world; others are dependent on a certain degree of possession which none can guarantee. This is an important truth that lies behind Plato's metaphysical language: the pursuit of, say, fine houses is less 'real', less secure, than the pursuit of intellectual satisfaction. But Plato does not mean that the Guardians will be able to say 'we feel happy to a degree of 100 per cent', while members of the largest group will only be able to experience happiness to a degree of 50 per cent. Both groups will feel equally happy and hence be equally happy, but the outsider is entitled to approve the manner in which either group find their happiness to a greater or lesser extent.

Happiness is thus seen as a form of harmony or enmeshment by Plato, and correctly so in our view. The just man is one in whom the three parts of the soul are harmonised rather than in conflict; the just state involves the willing interplay of the various groups of citizens; it is happy because rational men can see that it is just and therefore do not feel that it ought to be otherwise, while those of less rational ability feel that it is right as a result of conviction. The stability of the state denies the possibility of anxiety, the correlation between aptitude and function denies the possibility of frustration, the careful provision of different types of desiderata to different types of people denies the possibility of envy and, more generally, the faith generated amongst the people ensures that there shall be no dissatisfaction with the *status quo*.

The nature of happiness being as outlined above, a mental state concomitant on the individual being 'enmeshed' with his situation, it becomes at once apparent both why Plato has insisted that his citizens should not be allowed to foster feelings that they are miscast in their various roles, and also that he is indeed, as he claims, organising affairs in such a way that the happiness of all the citizens may be secured. The citizen in the Republic will as a matter of course be 'enmeshed' with his social role, for his social role is decided by his nature. The farmer will be happy farming simply because Plato has made it a feature of the Republic that those who farm have been brought up in such a way that their interest and ability both find their fulfilment in the farmer's way of life: he is not resentful, frustrated, envious nor anything else that is incompatible with happiness because he is doing what he wants to do, has no motivation to do anything else, and does not feel that he has any reason or right to do anything else that is being denied to him.

It is clear then both that Plato claims to be concerned to provide happiness for all individuals in the community and that, if the view of happiness outlined in the previous section is substantially correct, he is indeed trying to do what he claims to be doing. What is the next move of the liberal-democrats going to be? Their next move is to make grossly inadequate noises about the concept of happiness, such as Russell's bald declaration that 'man needs for his happiness, hope, enterprise and change'. But, if what I have already said about happiness is anywhere near the truth, this claim is simply not necessarily true.

'Hope' in fact would appear logically to involve an actual state of unhappiness; if the individual is in the position of entertaining 'expectation of something desired', then, at the time of hoping, he is deprived of that desideratum, and in as much as his hoping indicates an awareness of his deprivation he is, to a certain extent, frustrated. Of course for most of us in practice 'hope' is a valuable compensation for an actual deprivation: if I neither have what I desire nor any expectation of it, I am likely to be more miserable than if I can console myself with hope. But there is a great difference between the man who has neither what he regards as necessary to his happiness nor hope for those necessities, and the man who has no need of hope, because he is happy now. What Russell has exposed here is that 'hope' is a necessary compensation for full happiness in a certain kind of society: any society that, by whatever means, leads its members to regard a certain amount of success in competition as leading to happiness, must promote 'hope' as fuel for the system. A competitive economy, for instance, can only work if a sufficient number of people see the making of money, or the rewards obtainable with money, as important to their happiness, and it can only keep the game going by giving everybody hope that they may be successful. There is no point in my competing if I have no chance of success; it is therefore important that I should have some hope, however delusive, of success. The precise 'hopes' that Russell intends to deny to citizens of the Republic are not clear, but it should be remembered that the hopes they lack are hopes that they have no need of; to hope is to confess a present need; the less need a society has of hope, the less need it has of anything to increase its happiness.

Something similar may be said of 'change'; it is not clear whether Russell intends to say that 'change' is a necessary logical requirement for happiness, or empirically tied up with it. It is not logically necessary, or at least Russell has done nothing to show that it is, and if it is, one would presumably have to deny that certain stabilised communities such as those of monks or nuns can be happy. As an empirical observation it would certainly seem to be true that many of us need 'change', in the sense of variety, in order to combat frustration and the various other feelings incompatible with happiness, but that is because our characters are of a certain sort; we are examples of the democratic man who 'lives out his life in this fashion, day by day indulging the appetite of the day, now drinking wine and luxuriating in music, then drinking only water and going on a diet; at one moment having a fad for exercise, at another a fad for philosophy and at another a fad for lounging about'.[22] One might suggest again that the individual who needs change for happiness, the neophiliac, in fact betrays a deep-seated unhappiness, an anxiety, but for the moment we need only stress that change is not necessary for happiness in any logical sense.

The claim that 'enterprise' is necessary for happiness, i.e. the claim that men cannot be happy unless they have opportunities of engaging in 'undertakings of difficulty, risk or danger' would seem to be demonstrably false. Here, as with 'change' and 'hope', Russell seems in fact to give further substantiation to our analysis of happiness given above. Some people in our community certainly do seem to have need of enterprise in order to be happy, but some equally clearly do not. It depends entirely on the character of the man in question: the adventurous spirit will be unhappy if curbed; the placid man will resent being dragged up a mountain.

Popper does not believe any more than Russell that Plato is seriously concerned about the happiness of the largest group, and he criticises Crossman's acceptance of Plato's aim as fundamentally 'the building of a perfect state in which every citizen is really happy'. As far as he is concerned Plato's view of happiness can be scornfully dismissed:[23]

> True happiness, Plato insists, is achieved only by justice, i.e.
> by keeping one's place. The ruler must find happiness in
> ruling, the warrior in warring; and, we may infer, the slave
> in slaving . . . in view of all this, it seems to be a consistent
> and hardly refutable interpretation of the material [sc: related
> to happiness] to present Plato as a totalitarian.

As pointed out above, showing that Plato is a totalitarian has got nothing to do with showing that Plato is either wrong or insincere in his view of happiness, if one refuses, as Popper does, to consider 'happiness' itself. On the other hand, stripped of its emotive overtones, Popper has given a more or less accurate account of Plato's view of happiness, and that view, we have argued, is correct. 'Keeping one's place' can be made to carry implications that discredit it, for one is inclined to think of social situations which one dislikes for other reasons such as their inherent unfairness. One thinks of the servant in the last century who was expected to 'keep her place', which place one may feel was unduly exploited by others better placed. But even so one may feel, with George Bernard Shaw, that, *if* one *is* a servant, the secret of success and happiness in that role is 'to have the soul of a servant': 'the way to get on as a lady is the same as the way to get on as a servant: you've got to know your place: that's the secret of it'.[24] The question of whether the place one is expected to keep involves a morally acceptable social arrangement is quite distinct from the question of what is necessary for the happiness of the individual placed in a certain situation.

Plato believed that a just social arrangement would concentrate on allocating social roles in society according to aptitude rather than any other criterion, and since this is the basis of his society's arrangements and he claims to be promoting happiness, it follows that he thinks that the happiness of individuals is promoted by suiting the individual to his role in society, and with this view, which Popper has done nothing to discredit, we see reason to agree. True happiness is not achieved simply by keeping one's place, but happiness will necessarily be diminished in proportion to the extent that the individual is not suited to or enmeshed with the way of life he is expected to lead.

But it is with the rest of the chapter from which Popper's remark on happiness is drawn that I am primarily concerned,[25] for Popper more or less admits that Plato has correctly diagnosed the causes of unhappiness in the world that he knew *and* that he offers the solution. Formally Popper denies the latter point, for he says that Plato 'knew what was amiss... he understood the strain, the unhappiness, under which people were labouring, even though he erred in his fundamental claim that by leading them back to tribalism he could lessen the strain and restore their happiness.'[26] But, in point of fact, all that Popper then goes on to say supports the thesis that a closed or tribal society is at least more likely to promote happiness than an open society. Popper's objections, which obviously will have to be met later, are of an altogether different order: fundamentally they boil down to the claim that there are moral principles, particularly that of freedom, which ought to stop Plato doing what he intends to do; but such an argument, however valid, clearly does not show that Plato 'erred in his fundamental claim' that he could restore happiness.

Stasis, civil war, was a prevalent feature of the Greek world in which Plato grew up. The nature of Greek politics was such that even 'democracy' did not mean a constitution in which all citizens were formally united. Democracy signified not the 'reconciliation of class conflict but the pre-eminence of a single class'[27] namely the majority class of what we may legitimately call 'workers', whether farmers, manual workers or labourers, as opposed to the minority party of wealthy oligarchs. Athens herself twice experienced the overthrow of the democratic party and the supremacy of the oligarchs. Thucydides devotes a memorable part of his history to the *stasis* on the island of Corcyra.[28]

> So savage was the progress of the revolution, and it seemed all the more so because it was one of the first which had broken out. Later, of course, practically the whole Hellenic world was convulsed, with rival parties in every state.

In view of the facts, it is scarcely surprising that Plato aimed at a stable state and physical security. A stable political situation cannot be regarded as necessary for the happiness of all men, since some individuals may be so constituted as to enmesh with a fluctuating and exciting scene of turmoil, but it is surely legitimate to claim that such individuals as a matter of empirical fact are relatively rare, and for the rest the conditions of an unstable state necessarily militate against their happiness, since, if the situation is permanently changing, the character of the individual must also continually adapt to enmesh with new situations; anxiety and insecurity are likely to afflict most people.

Nor is it surprising that the term *stasis* is taken over by Plato and given a wider metaphorical significance. The conflict in the soul of the man in whom the absence of rational control indicates a state of affairs contrary to the requirements of the principle of justice is described as 'some kind of *stasis*'. *Stasis*, which for Plato has come to mean any conflict, arises out of an unjust state of affairs, for an unjust state of affairs gives rise to resentment and hatred; justice on the other hand, being rational, removes due cause for resentment and promotes unity. To remove *stasis* it is necessary to remove the causes of conflicting interests between people, notably acquisitiveness for limited goods; envy and hatred do not arise amongst a unified group.

If the aim of happiness is to be achieved therefore, two kinds of *stasis* need to be guarded against. Literal *stasis* in the state, because it is an empirical truth that most people cannot adapt to a revolutionary situation. And metaphorical *stasis* in the soul of the individual, because it is a necessary truth that when the individual is pulled in different directions he cannot satisfactorily enmesh with any situation.

But Plato also saw something possibly even more important in the Greek world that he grew up in: anomy. This concept has been subjected to various interpretations of late, but I am taking it in essentially the same sense as Durkheim intended by the term. Anomy[29]

> arises when the influence of society on the individual tends to
> weaken and he finds himself in a psychological condition
> where deprived (or almost so) of enthusiasm, faith and virtue,
> he fails to adapt himself successfully to a new situation . . . the
> social directives of the belief-systems [sc. of the society] no
> longer satisfy the demands of the individual . . . at the same
> time no new belief-system has arisen to take the place of the
> foregone.

Anomy represents for the individual 'an intolerable void'. Anomy arises in the individual who suffers from 'the malady of infinite aspiration'; 'unregulated emotions are adjusted neither to one another nor to the conditions they are supposed to meet: they must therefore conflict with one another most painfully'; and Durkheim sees 'weariness, disillusionment, disturbance, agitation and discontent' as accompanying anomy.

The total breakdown of social mores and belief-systems in Athens during the Peloponnesian war is attested by Thucydides, and indirectly by Aristophanes. The plays of Euripides exhibit an intensely rational mind struggling to make order out of chaos, in comparison with the 'easy going' attitude of Sophocles, the child of a confident and bygone age. Nor do we need to look far for the cause of the new anomy: the war itself, of course, must have contributed to the change from heady assurance to baffled insecurity, but if that provided the immediate cause, the true explanation lies further back with the introduction of an age of rationalism, generally known as the growth of the sophist movement. The sophists, the new rationalising tendencies, killed the comfortable beliefs of the past. The gradual awareness that other people had different habits brought home to even the least enquiring mind the truth that what had been taken for granted in the past as *the* way to behave now stood in need of justification; tribal superstitions had lost their power.

One of the consequences was a tendency to moral relativism and it is this tendency, exhibited in fact in such aspects of Athenian history as the strictly amoral 'justification' of the massacre of the inhabitants of Melos,[30] and in principle in the characters of Thrasymachus and Callicles, that Plato is primarily determined to fight. Now most of the above is substantially admitted by Popper: 'I believe that Plato with deep sociological insight, found that his contemporaries were suffering under a severe strain, and that this strain was due to the social revolution which had begun with the rise of democracy and individualism.'[31] But we may go a great deal further than this.

A tribalistic or closed society, since we mean by this a society in which taboos, totally believed in by the members of the community, 'regulate and dominate all aspects of life' and in which 'there are few problems',[32] is a society in which enmeshment is relatively complete. There is no question of anomy, which is absolutely incompatible with happiness, no question of *stasis* either between groups or within the individual and no tendency to moral relativism which necessarily breaks down the tribal taboos. Thus whatever else we say of it the tribal society is a relatively happy society.

I do not wish to suggest that there is any necessary reason why a specific individual within an open society should not be happy; indeed, such is the adaptability of human nature, that it may well be that there is no society to which certain individuals could not adapt, with which they could not enmesh. There are, however, I think, certain features of an open society which as a matter of empirical experience seem to militate against the happiness of many people, and there are also features which make it necessary that some people should not be happy.

The exact meaning of the term 'open society' may be open to doubt; I am concerned with what the term seems to mean to Popper. Its most striking characteristic is its emphasis on freedom, and, in particular, its high evaluation of encouragement of personal responsibility, in the sense of personal decision-taking; that is to say it rejects the notion of 'taboos'; an open society seeks to minimise the influence of tradition and custom. As much as is possible the individual is encouraged to act on his own choice, after rationally examining any situation that confronts him. Popper and Crossman both talk of 'our' civilisation and 'our' ideals, from which one concludes that Western democracy is the epitome of the open society. One feature of Western democracy is competition, which in any case would seem to be demanded in a society that commends the freedom of the individual to make his own decisions to any great extent. We are therefore concerned with a society in which individuals will be encouraged to look only to themselves for guidance in decision-making, in which beliefs that are not susceptible to rational justification will be scorned, and in which the individual will freely compete with his neighbours.

Empirically one immediately has grave doubts about the likelihood of happiness in such a society. Voltaire's celebrated remark that 'if God did not exist, he would have to be invented' will be felt by many to represent a formidable truth: that in practice people need the comfort of a stable code of values for their happiness. Moral relativism destroys an anchor that people want to cling to. Increased freedom is not as welcome to most people as it may be to the successful and rational philosopher.[33] 'Man, in fact, is made for life in a determinate, limited environment'.[34] So might the argument run, and Popper himself seems to admit its validity, for he talks of the relative isolationism of a non-tribal society which results 'consequently in unhappiness', and admits that there is a 'strain created by the effort which life in an open society continually demands from us'.

The rather odd situation has hence arisen that Popper who a few pages previously claimed that Plato was not aiming at the happiness of individuals, despite Plato's straightforward statement that he was, is now in the position of admitting that in practice the tribal society does guarantee happiness and his own ideal state does not. This then is the first step: that whereas a tribal society such as the Republic guarantees happiness, the open society is unable to. However it is still possible to argue that the problems of the open society in respect of happiness are entirely due to the transition from the tribal past and that in time people will adapt to their new situation. Can it be shown that there is any necessary reason why all men should not be happy in an open society? The answer is, obviously, yes. Because although any specific individual may adapt to cope with the responsibility of freedom, the only way in which all may cope is if all achieve enmeshment with the phenomenon of change itself, which, quite apart from its inherent unlikeliness, would mean the end of the notion of society, for it involves the rejection of any stable mores, rules, patterns, customs and habits. The situation is this: the ideal of the open society is that every individual shall develop autonomously, that is to say without any external guidance or influence; it follows that ideally no attempt is made to suit the individual to his role in life, taking role to mean anything from the job he will perform to the status in terms of wealth, nature of employment, and power that he will acquire. Rather the intention is that he will find the role that fits the nature that has developed in him. Unfortunately since a competitive society needs to promulgate enthusiasm for certain ends, the individual's autonomy is in practice subject to considerable pressures; but since a competitive society also needs to maintain a hierarchy of success the net result is that many people inevitably do not find the role to which they aspire; they therefore find themselves in situations to which they do not aspire, to which therefore they are not fully suited and with which they do not enmesh. 'Someone can win only if someone else loses'.[35] Nor can one simply drop the competitive element in the open society, for the function of competition is to provide motivation where direction or compulsion is lacking; a free society without competition is either a society of angels or a stagnant pool. In addition, the open society intends that the individual will enmesh with a situation in which his conscience is his guide; he cannot at the same time be expected to enmesh with a rule-bound society such as even the liberal-democratic ideal state apparently is. 'Poverty', said Plato, 'is the increase of a man's desire and not the diminution of his property'.[36] Poverty is the inevitable result of a competitive society, and since wealth is generally the object on which all hearts are set, the result of poverty is misery.

Notes

1 420 B. The point is repeated at 446 A and 519 E.
2 Russell, 'Philosophy and politics'.
3 Ibid., p. 117.

4 Popper, op. cit., p. 169.
5 Ibid., p. 171.
6 Particularly in the *Laws*. E.g. 903 C, 739 C, 942.
7 *Laws* 903 C. For further comments on Popper's translation and argument, cf. Levinson, R. B., *In Defense of Plato*, Russell & Russell, New York, 1953, p. 519. For Popper's version, see *The Open Society*, p. 80.
8 420 B. 519 E.
9 466 A.
10 Wayper, C. L., *Political Thought*, Hodder, London, 1954, p. 39.
11 At this point I elaborate on, and attempt to explain, a point raised by Jean Austin in 'Pleasure and Happiness' in *Philosophy*, vol. XLIII, No. 163. Reprinted in Schneewind, J. B., ed., *Mill: Modern Studies in Philosophy*, Macmillan, London, 1968.
12 For a discussion of rejection and acceptance of situations as symptoms relevant to judging happiness, see Cowan, J. L., *Pleasure and Pain*, Macmillan, New York, 1968, chapter 4.
13 Dearden, R. F., 'Happiness and education' in Dearden, Hirst and Peters, eds, *Education and the Development of Reason*, Routledge & Kegan Paul, London, 1972, cites this example.
14 419 A.
15 485 D.
16 420 D.
17 421 C.
18 329 A-D.
19 516 A-B.
20 545 A.
21 521 A.
22 561 C.
23 Popper, op. cit., p. 169. Cf. Crossman, op. cit., p. 75.
24 Shaw, G. B., *Arms and the Man*, Act 3.
25 Popper, op. cit., chapter 10.
26 Ibid., p. 171.
27 Crossman, op. cit., p. 24.
28 Thucydides, 3. 70ff.
29 Joshi, N., *Political Ideals of Plato*, Manaktalas, Bombay, 1965, p. 21. For a summary of recent discussion of the concept of 'anomy', see Lukes, S. 'Alienation and Anomie' in Laslett and Runciman, eds, *Philosophy, Politics and Society*, 3rd series, Blackwell, Oxford, 1969.
30 See Thucydides, 5. 85ff.
31 Popper, op. cit., p. 171.
32 Ibid., p. 172.
33 Cf. most particularly, Fromm, E., *Fear of Freedom*, Routledge & Kegan Paul, London, 1960.
34 Durkheim, quoted in Lukes, op. cit.
35 Gouldner, A., *Enter Plato*, Routledge & Kegan Paul, London, 1967.
36 *Laws*, 736 C.

5   The pursuit of happiness

1   That happiness is necessarily pursued

Happiness is an emotion dependent upon a harmonious relationship between the individual and his situation, which we may summarise as 'enmeshment'; the characteristic form of appraisal associated with it is the belief that whatever aspect of one's situation one contemplates fits one's view of life. The Republic ensures happiness by ensuring enmeshment, but this is only achieved by means that a hostile critic summarises as 'the arts of indoctrination, inquisition, political lying and the censorship of opinions and tastes'.[1] The first question to be considered, therefore, is whether there is good reason to promote happiness in such a determined manner as Plato does.

Plato himself treated the matter as self-evident. 'Do not all men desire happiness? Surely this is one of those ridiculous questions which a sensible man ought not to ask: for what human being is there who does not desire happiness?'[2] 'Happiness is the most precious of human possessions'.[3] And in the *Republic* the actual argument in favour of men being just, comes down to an attempt to show that 'the just man is happy and the unjust miserable'.[4] It is taken for granted that it follows that all men must choose to be just, in Plato's sense of the term. But, of course, this assumption does not follow if there are other ultimate ends besides happiness that mankind may pursue. If Mill was wrong to suggest 'not only that people desire happiness, but that they never desire anything else',[5] then it would be quite possible for an individual to say in reply to Plato: 'I accept that a man who is just, in the specific sense that you intend, will be happy, but happiness is not my sole concern and I therefore see no overwhelming reason to be just in your sense of the word'.

It is therefore necessary to ask, not for the first time, can an individual ultimately desire anything other than his own happiness? But, as a preliminary, it is important to stress that it is not in dispute that the individual may choose not to pursue immediate short-term happiness, nor that he may not consciously calculate the advantage to himself in terms of happiness before acting. Mill himself did not dispute that because the individual internalises a great deal, he may come to regard certain things, such as virtue, as ends in themselves, with the result that he *feels* that he has adopted a certain course of action ultimately because he regards it as virtuous.

Mill's belief is simply that the desire to be virtuous is itself ultimately based on a desire for happiness. Utilitarians 'recognise as a psychological fact the possibility of virtue being, to the individual a good in itself, without looking to any end beyond it'.[6] The point at issue is whether it is meaningful to say that virtue is in fact an end in itself, such that an individual could pursue it rather than his own happiness, even when he is fully aware that the pursuit of virtue makes him ultimately miserable.

'Now it is palpable that [people] do desire things which, in common language, are decidedly distinguished from happiness'.[7] The question here is whether common language is making the same sort of distinctions as the philosopher is concerned with. To say that in common language we refer to a man as desiring virtue or desiring love, and that, as virtue and love 'are decidedly distinguished from happiness', it follows that all people do not always desire their own happiness, is clearly an inadequate argument as it stands. I may indeed desire these things; I may desire all manner of things, such as sweets, money, variety, work or leisure, and none of these things is happiness. But it is with the ultimate end or ends that we desire, that we are concerned, and not with specific things that we assume, rightly or wrongly, to contribute to that end or those ends. If I am a certain kind of person, then it may well be that I do as a matter of fact need a considerable amount of money for my happiness, and it may therefore come about that I regard money as an end in itself—something for which, in practice, I will entertain a fixed desire, without ever considering whether any specific activity I engage in in pursuit of money contributes to my happiness or not. But the outside observer may still feel that I could not pursue money as if it were an end in itself, were I to pause and reflect, and come to the conclusion that the pursuit of money made me more unhappy than not pursuing it would do.

I shall seek to establish that all men effectively pursue happiness as their ultimate end, by showing that all men necessarily pursue enmeshment, and hence happiness.

Desire of some sort is a necessary feature of freely chosen activity, provided that we do not restrict the meaning of desire to *strong* yearnings or *passionate* wishes. There have been arguments about the analysis of the word and some criticism of Mill has been based on an attempt to argue that his use of 'desire' is equivocal.[8] I intend no equivocation; it seems reasonable to argue that a 'desire' can indicate a relatively weak feeling of favour towards an object, and I mean to do more than use the word as a convenient shorthand way of referring to a feeling that draws the individual to an object or an activity, however strong or weak the feeling may be. To say that the individual desires X is therefore, on these terms, to say no more than that he has a pro-attitude to X in some degree. An emotional attitude of approval, in some degree, is necessary as motivation towards any action that is freely chosen. A man cannot deliberately choose to act in a way that he in no sense desires to act in. There must be some degree of pro-attitude towards the chosen course of activity in some respect.

In respect of a specific desire, for instance for sexual satisfaction, it seems legitimate to say: 'I have this desire, but I do not in fact desire to satisfy it'. The reasons for avoiding such satisfaction might be many: it could conflict with the satisfaction of some other specific physical desire; it could conflict with my desire to do my duty; it could conflict with my desire to preserve my health. But to make sense of the remark 'I have this desire, but I do not desire to satisfy it', it is necessary that the explanation of it should contain reference to some other 'desire' envisaged as conflicting. It is not a sufficient explanation to say: 'I have this desire, but I do not desire to satisfy it, because my mother is ill', since it may still be reasonably asked why the fact that my mother is ill has any bearing on the situation. If I reply that I regard it as my moral duty to see my mother, it is at once clear why I desire to rush off and avoid satisfying the sexual desire, because the nature or morality is such that we feel that anybody who sincerely claims to believe in a moral principle or moral duty, must have some desire to abide by it.

A sexual desire may certainly manifest itself in a different manner from a desire to abide by one's moral conscience; it may, for example, appear more suddenly, more violently and owe less to rationality, with the result that a man may do, on the impulse of a sexual desire, that which he would not on balance have desired to do had he had time to reflect upon the matter. But what he cannot do, if he understands the words he is using, is say: 'I have a desire for sexual satisfaction, and another conflicting desire; the conflicting desire is stronger, so I am going out to satisfy the sexual desire'. This would amount to saying, 'I am more in favour of doing that to which I have a less favourable attitude'. And, in so far as the man does go ahead and satisfy the sexual desire, we shall say that, at the time of decision, that desire was greatest; he desired, at the time, to gratify that desire more than conflicting desires, however much he may come to regret this later or to appreciate that from a long-term point of view he has miscalculated.

Thus whenever a person freely opts for one course of action out of more than one available to him, he is doing that which at the time seems to him to be most desirable or to which he has the strongest pro-attitude. The fact that, had he thought about it, he would have chosen a different course of action, or that he failed to foresee undesirable consequences and so on, makes no difference to the matter. It is true that we may talk of 'doing work which we have no desire to do', and such a remark is not meaningless. But here common language is using 'desire' to refer to inherently desirable objects: the work in itself I do not desire; I have no pro-attitude towards it. But it may still be desirable, even to me, for some further end; to put it another way, I may have no desire to do the *work*, but I do desire to *do* the work. In most choices laid before us there are many factors to be considered; that is why a course of action can be described as both desirable and not desirable. But if on balance, after working out so far as he is able all the consequences of various alternative courses of action and considering these consequences in the light of his values, hopes and tastes, the individual decides that he desires to do X rather than Y, then it is inconceivable that he should choose to do Y.

It will be said that this involves making it true by definition that all men must act according to their desires. But, as will become apparent in the remainder of this chapter, I am not trying to argue along the lines: all men must pursue happiness, because happiness involves the satisfaction of desires and whatever anyone pursues I will call the satisfaction of some desire. I am merely stressing an incontrovertible fact: that one cannot choose to do X without some pro-attitude that constitutes motivation towards X.

But happiness involves, ideally, total enmeshment with one's situation, which is to say total satisfaction of all one's desires, whatever they are, and however strong or weak they are. The completely happy man, if such a thing were possible, would be able to do or to realise all that he wanted to do or wanted to see realised; everything to which he had a pro-attitude (or for which he had a desire) would be fulfilled. This is not to say that, if I woke up tomorrow and found I had been given all that I say today that I want, and that the world had become such as I say today I would like it to be, I would be happy. It might turn out that I had wrongly predicted what would make me happy; it might turn out that my character is such that I was bored without things to complain and grieve about. But formally the completely happy man is one who does desire his situation to be as he finds it and who has no desire or motivation to change any aspect of it. The fact that many people seem to have a prejudice against this picture, and to resent what they might term, emotively, 'cabbage-like contentment', is, of course, wholly immaterial. One understands that these critics may have characters that either cannot envisage, or indeed in fact may not be able to endure, enmeshment with a situation that lacks challenge. But the fact remains that we may sensibly say that the completely happy man is one who is in all respects enmeshed with his situation and who therefore has no desire to alter any aspect of that situation.

In so far as a man has desires or pro-attitudes towards objects, notions or states of affairs that are not attainable, he is frustrated and hence not completely happy. Of course in practice we all have to put up with some thwarted desires, some unattained objects, and some unhappiness; a great deal of compromise is necessary at a low level between specific desires, between pro-attitudes towards conflicting or incompatible courses of action, between conflicting motivation. But we pursue, by definition, what at any given time we feel to be most desirable (i.e. that towards which we have, on balance, the strongest pro-attitude), and, in saying I desire X, I am also saying I desire that my desire for X be satisfied: I am in favour of the satisfaction of what I favour. The satisfaction of what I favour, the achievement of the object I desire, is 'enmeshment'. Inasmuch as it is true that motivation towards some freely chosen action is dependent on some pro-attitude or desire, and inasmuch as it is true that enmeshment involves the fulfilment or satisfaction of one's desires, it follows logically that one is always engaged in the pursuit of enmeshment, which is the necessary and sufficient condition of happiness.

Again, the meaning of those words judged to be incompatible with happiness, such as frustration and anxiety, seems to be such that nobody could deliberately desire them as ends, although, of course, one might in practice choose a course of action knowing that it will involve some anxiety or frustration. But one could not have a pro-attitude towards anxiety as an ultimate end; the term carries with it undesirable overtones. One must rather seek to avoid it and the other terms incompatible with happiness. One must ultimately seek to enmesh with one's situation, to achieve harmony between oneself and one's world, which in practice will mean to satisfy one's ultimate or most pressing desires, though in theory it could mean to alter one's desires to suit the situation in which one finds oneself.

Mill, as we know, claimed that the individual must ultimately desire his own happiness and that what is fundamentally going on when the individual freely chooses to act in one way rather than another is that he opts for that action which will give him more happiness in his view, allowing, of course, for such considerations as that ignoring a 'moral norm' that he has internalised is one factor that can diminish happiness. Mill however did not offer an analysis of the concept of happiness. The result of this omission was that his claim that people must pursue happiness was open to the objection that lots of people simply said that they did not always pursue happiness. And such denials seem entirely legitimate so long as the term happiness floats undefined.

This explains why I have argued that it is logically necessary that people should pursue enmeshment, and hence happiness, rather than that people must pursue happiness. It is very difficult for most of us to use the term 'happiness' without preconceived ideas of what causes it and what it involves; it is particularly difficult, I think, for many people to disassociate it from a whoopee feeling or from a sensation of considerable intensity. I am not, of course, arguing that all men must pursue whoopee feelings or vivid sensations of pleasure. But whereas it is convincing to point out that I cannot choose to do X, if I have a stronger pro-attitude towards not doing X, it is not so convincing, to those who have a more vivid notion of happiness than the sensation or feeling attendant on enmeshment, to point out that, in choosing to do X, I am pursuing my happiness as I see it. For those who accept my earlier arguments to the effect that we cannot reasonably do more than characterise happiness as a feeling dependent on enmeshment, it is of course *true* that in choosing to do X I am effectively aiming at what I believe will promote my happiness (but that does not mean that it will seem convincing). If however it be insisted that 'happiness' must be something more vivid than I allow, that will not materially affect my argument. For if happiness be identified, for instance, with some degree of whoopee feeling, then clearly I shall concede that men do not necessarily pursue happiness, and will revert to exclusive use of the term enmeshment. What matters is what is the case; the labels we use are of secondary importance provided that we understand one another.

But now, on the assumption that my use of the term 'happiness' is acceptable, I wish to examine closely a recent attempt to argue against the view that all men necessarily pursue their own happiness, that of Anthony Kenny'[9] He raises various examples of people who do not appear to be concerned about their own happiness. What I will try to do, broadly, is to show that the people in these examples clearly are seeking enmeshment, and hence happiness, unless, as I suggest Kenny is subconsciously doing, one assumes some view of happiness such as that it must involve whoopee feeling. In the process, it is hoped, the argument will be further clarified. We may say straight away that the fact that some people do not apparently plan their lives at all is quite irrelevant and does not show that all men do not desire their own happiness; it shows merely that some people are happier living without much conscious planning. Again 'a man may', indeed, 'map out his life in the service of someone else's happiness'.[10] But if he does this of his own choice he does so because, on balance, this is what he desires or has a pro-attitude towards doing. Putting into practice what he has a pro-attitude towards doing involves taking a step towards harmonising his character with his world; he does not do it despite the fact, or because of the fact, that this course of action will make him more miserable than any other, but because, given the alternatives open to him, and being the sort of man he is, which includes being a man with certain feelings and with a certain moral code, and calculating, perhaps mistakenly, that doing this will on balance make him less frustrated, less anxious and less depressed than any other course of action, he realises that in actual fact he has no real alternative. What, after all, does making a choice involve if not attempting to assess what alternative on balance fits best one's tastes, character, values, etc., which is to say what situation enmeshes best with oneself?

Likewise the man who 'devotes his efforts to the pursuit of some end which it may be possible to realise only after his death',[11] such as the martyr, does so because his belief in an after life and the demands of a God materially affect his character so that a state of 'enmeshment', for him, necessarily involves account being taken of these factors.

Kenny quotes the example of the man who, after some misfortune, says: 'I shall never be happy again', as evidence that some people do not aim at their own happiness. But, quite apart from the fact that what someone opines about his future has got little to do with the facts about his future, such a statement has nothing to do with what the man does, or will, desire. If it is true that he will never be happy again, he is restricted in his freedom of choice, but nothing can stop him trying to gain more rather than less happiness, and such at attempt involves aiming at happiness. I may well feel that I shall never be rich, and I may well be right, but that does not necessarily stop me trying to be rich. Naturally you cannot guide your actions by aiming at the impossible; consequently, if I sincerely believe that happiness is impossible for me in the future, I could not consistently claim to be guiding my actions in the light of my expected happiness. But here we are once again faced with confusion, caused by the fact that philosophers tend to talk as if aiming at happiness involves aiming at a complete blue-print of complete happiness that may easily be achieved, although, in fact, in aiming at happiness we are merely aiming at as much happiness as possible or as little frustration, misery, etc., as possible. It is difficult to see what 'it is impossible for me to be happy again' means; it is most unlikely that the individual has been completely happy all his life. He has found some happiness, some area of enmeshment, which he has now lost; it may be true that he will never be *as* happy again; if he really has been completely happy up to this point, it may be true that he will never be happy, in the sense of completely happy, again. But, so far as the choices he will have to make in the future are concerned, he will still be faced with alternatives that promise more or less happiness, even if all of them are on a low level.

What Kenny succeeds in doing, I feel, is restating the admitted truth that people often renounce their immediate desires, their more vivid desires and their most obvious desires in favour of more long-term, general or obscure desires. Furthermore some desires become internalised and acquire the reputation of habit or the status of ends in themselves, so that people do not always seem to be acting with a view to their own happiness. The claim that people always pursue happiness as an end is not intended to deny that sometimes people do not act purposively at all, nor to deny that the individual may come to regard truth-telling, for instance, as an end in itself (because he believes that the truth ought to be told and therefore has a desire to tell the truth quite apart from calculating the consequences to himself) so that in a specific situation he may feel that he desires to tell the truth, but that doing so militates against his happiness. Thus in applying for a job I may be asked to reveal some information about my past which will certainly prevent me from getting the job, which in turn will cause me a certain amount of frustration or anxiety, but I may nonetheless choose to tell the truth. And it may be asked whether this does not indicate that it is not the case that all men desire only happiness as an end.

One might argue against this suggestion by claiming that I am in fact calculating more happiness for myself as a result of telling the truth than I would gain if I told a lie and was given the job. Of the various facets of my character, all of which require 'enmeshment' for complete happiness, desire to tell the truth is but one, desire to get the job but another. And it is certainly possible that I should feel that my frustration, anxiety and depression would be greater as a result of telling a lie than they would be if I told the truth and lost the job. However the defence cannot be left at that, for it is undoubtedly the case that some people feel that they would choose to tell the truth, even though they are convinced they would have told a lie if happiness was their only consideration. To simply insist that they are really pursuing their happiness without explanation of how it comes about that they think otherwise, would be a dubious move.

Some desire or pro-attitude towards a course of action is necessary to provide motivation towards carrying it out; and enmeshment, and hence happiness, is dependent on the fulfilment of desires. But desires may be measured or weighed in respect of strength, duration or number. To say that the individual desired to do X more than Y does not necessarily tell us much about the nature of his desires. Now clearly, in the example we are considering, the gaining of the job is likely to produce a sense of elation, or a degree of what I call whoopee feeling, that telling the truth may not. Even those of us who feel deeply about the truth do not generally feel exuberant

83

every time we tell the truth, in the way that we might if we secured a job that seemed interesting in itself, well paid, secure, etc. It certainly makes sense, therefore, for the man who is troubled about a choice between a lie and a job, to claim that he told the truth but would have been happier if he had not, if he means by that that he would have been more full of whoopee feeling had he lied and been given the job. On the analysis that I am attempting to substantiate, we should say that, in telling the truth and losing the job, he has opted to 'enmesh' in respect of a rather dull, stubborn and persistent desire, rather than in respect of a vivid and elatory desire. But in so far as he did make this choice, he desired to satisfy the former desire more than the latter; that surely is irrefutable. He therefore sought to satisfy the desire that he felt most needed satisfying, which is to say that he opted for enmeshment in respect of his most pressing need: he did not opt for a maximum of whoopee feeling, but he did opt for a minimum of anxiety, guilt, frustration or whatever. To substantiate the contrary claim that he deliberately chose more rather than less misery for himself, it would be necessary to argue that it makes sense to say: 'Taking into account the intensity, duration, etc. of my various desires my motivation towards X is in every way stronger than towards Y, but I am going to do Y'. I cannot see that this does make sense. If the individual chooses to tell the truth his motivation towards telling the truth is stronger than his motivation not to. But the ultimate goal of the activity is still satisfaction of the stronger desire or motivation. Happiness, in the sense of enmeshment, relatively joyless though it may be, is still the ultimate end, even if the individual did not think of the matter in that way.

Since happiness is, ideally, the satisfaction of the whole man (that is to say, the ideally happy man is not only enmeshed with the demands of, for example, his job, while being dissatisfied in respect of his private life; ideally all his desires should be satisfied), and since in practice the pursuit of happiness is the pursuit of maximum possible satisfaction (which, of course, may be achieved by a stress on the satisfaction of those desires that are strongest in the individual rather than by the satisfaction of the largest number of desires) there is no reason to suppose, as Kenny does, that the daughter who forgoes the prospect of marriage, in order to nurse an invalid parent, is not pursuing her own happiness. To say that she cannot be, is surely to play the discredited game of laying down necessary conditions for happiness: namely 'marriage, congenial company and creative work'. Perhaps such factors in one's life contribute more to whoopee feeling than nursing an elderly parent does, but they do not necessarily contribute more to happiness.

In order to be absolutely clear, it is necessary to stress once again the admission that the word 'happiness' can be used in such a way as to suggest that men do not always pursue happiness. One cannot deny that people do say such things as 'He has chosen to do his duty rather than do what would make him happy'; 'He would be happy if only he would do such and such', or simply, 'He does not want to be happy'.

But all such comments on third parties either involve a view of necessary conditions for happiness on the part of the speaker, or else purport to be accounts of the third party in question's own view. Thus the speaker is either saying (in the first example), 'Clearly, *to my mind*, the course of action adopted by this man will lessen his happiness', or else 'he says that he will be more miserable if he pursues this course of action, but nonetheless he feels that he ought to do so'. If the former interpretation is the apposite one, then, clearly, the speaker needs to justify the necessary conditions for happiness that he implies, a task that we have already seen reason to regard as impossible, and even then it would be necessary to show that the man in question is aware that, in doing his duty, he is necessarily diminishing his happiness overall where he is not compelled to do so.

The word 'overall' is important since nobody denies that if the word 'happiness' may be used with reference to momentary or relatively short-lived sensations the individual may sacrifice the immediate happiness. The question is whether the individual, in so far as he is capable of seeing ahead and making assessments for the future, can choose to embark upon a course of action which he believes will minimise his happiness, i.e. his satisfaction, whether, in fact, he, the third party above referred to and not the original speaker, can sensibly say, 'I do not want to be happy', or 'I do not choose to be happy', or 'I will do this rather than that, although to do so will make me relatively unhappy'.

Since we have no reason to restrict the sensation of happiness to certain spheres of activity (i.e. it may accompany contemplation, eating, sexual activity or anything else the individual may do) when a man says 'I do not want to be happy' without qualification, he must be presumed to mean 'Given a choice I want to pursue that course of action in any sphere which will increase my dissatisfaction'. Yet one integral part of the notion of dissatisfaction is the tendency to reject; a dissatisfied man is one whose impulse is away from a dissatisfying situation. In so far as a man might conceivably choose to pursue his life in such a way as to place himself in situations he will wish to reject, we shall say, and surely it is legitimate to say, that his peculiar personality finds its satisfaction in continual rejection. What is inconceivable is that I, who know that I am happy whenever my mind is free of anxiety about X, should deliberately choose a course of action that will increase that anxiety, except in circumstances where not to choose the course of action would cause me a greater degree of anxiety (or frustration, etc.) for some other reason.

In claiming, then, that all men pursue their own happiness we are saying that, in any situation which offers a choice of activities to a man, he will select that course of activity which, it seems to him, will cause him least frustration, anxiety, guilt, envy or generically dissatisfaction. A man will not choose what he considers to be more rather than less unhappiness, but, of course, whether obeying the dictates of a sense of duty, or showing gratitude, will seem to him to be more or less necessary to feeling relatively happy than, say, pursuing immediate pleasures, will depend on the individual. We accept that some individuals are so constituted as to calculate their happiness by intensity and some by duration; some look further ahead than others; and all make mistakes at some time. But we say that 'in so far as a person really acts, rather than being acted upon, he acts on his own evaluation to try to make the world more nearly what he would like it to be'[12] and he will not want it to be what he would judge as frustrating, etc.

The fact that many situations do not admit of choice, that many situations offer choices incalculable or equally undesirable, the fact that in many situations we act by habit or without due care or consideration—all these facts are irrelevant to the point that, when we do act purposively, the nature of our purpose is a striving towards a satisfaction which, if it were ever entirely realised, could be described as a state of harmony between the individual and his situation in all respects.

Notwithstanding the possibility of miscalculation, in practice it is possible to recognise both that people are unhappy and the reasons which make them so in individual cases; within a community with a common culture that has to a considerable extent moulded the character, one can even make general observations: it is, for instance, generally true of individuals in our community that the loss of a child makes them unhappy for a time; it is true of most men at all times that physical pain contributes in itself to unhappiness.

And as final arbiter of happiness or lack of it in the individual, we have his word for it; the fact that we judge, in some cases, claims to happiness to be based on poor grounds, (i.e. find it hard to believe that anyone could be happy under certain conditions) is irrelevant, as our inability to understand how anyone could love the girl next door is irrelevant to the question of whether or not she is loved. It may well be true on occasion that, when X feels happy, he could in fact experience what he would then admit to be greater happiness in the sense of more intense happiness; but here, if ever, we may presume the truth of the adage 'what the eye doesn't see, the heart doesn't grieve over'. The pain of a drawing pin in my finger is less than the pain of a six-inch nail, but the aim of pain avoidance strategy is simply not to feel pained. In the same way the object of happiness-pursuit is simply to feel happy. No doubt when I have experienced a period of intense happiness, I shall not feel happy if my circumstances revert to such as I had experienced happily before my recent experience of intense happiness, but that is because this recent experience has increased my expectations, and a man's expectations are relevant to his character, which is one of the variables that affects the question of happiness.

2 That happiness constitutes the supreme moral principle

From the fact that people necessarily pursue enmeshment, and hence happiness, it does not follow simply that the principle of happiness should override any other proposed moral principle. If we assume, for instance, purely for the sake of example, that there is a God and that he is the ultimate source of moral demands, and, further, that he demands as an absolute injunction that we should not commit adultery, it would follow that, even if as a matter of empirical fact observance of this injunction caused more misery than happiness, the injunction should nonetheless override this consideration. And objection cannot be made to this example by an attempt to argue that ought implies can, and that therefore if people cannot pursue unhappiness (or rather the non-enmeshment that leads to unhappiness) it cannot be meaningful to say that they ought to do something which is known to cause them unhappiness. For, as we have repeatedly said, 'enmeshment' denotes a relation between two variables: individual and situation. It is entirely meaningful (if the assumption about God be accepted) to say that although men do not enmesh with a situation that prohibits adultery, they ought to. For, although they necessarily pursue enmeshment, they do not necessarily need to enmesh with a situation that allows of adultery.

It is, therefore, now necessary to establish both that the state can maximise the happiness of members of the community and that it ought to do so. There is no doubt that it can, provided that it has control over both variables—the individual and the situation. Happiness, being dependent on enmeshment between the two, can only be guaranteed where the pattern, values, rules and demands of the community are such as the individual is drawn to: acceptance of the norms of society that make demands on one is a necessary part of complete happiness. The tribal society, in so far as it is

G

relatively happy, is so, not because its members have less responsibility, but because there is very little discrepancy between the aspirations, hopes, values, etc., of the individual and the aspirations, hopes, values, etc., that the community promotes and encourages. There is no attempt here to make the argument rest upon dubious empirical generalisations about man: the Indian squaw, for instance, is not happy because women fundamentally desire to be down-trodden or relegated to the home, but because she does not entertain any assumption that her way of life could or should be different to what it is. The zealous missionaries who invade primitive tribes necessarily cause some unhappiness because, for a period of time at least, they upset the equilibrium between the social situation and the members of the community, by introducing new dimensions to the characters of the latter that are not provided for in the former.

The open society, or a society that encourages personal responsibility, must, if it is to ensure happiness, not only succeed in making people want this responsibility, but also in providing them with a social situation in which it can be exercised. Fundamentally the members of the community that will be happy must believe in the community.

The essential point is that, in so far as a happy community is one's aim, it is not enough to offer vague prescriptions such as 'give them freedom', 'give them bread and circuses' or 'give them access to culture'. It is not simply that it is an empirical question whether such 'handouts' will make people happy, and that people are different. It is rather that nothing will necessarily make anyone happy: freedom, bread and circuses, culture, *could* all contribute to people's happiness, but will only do so if there is a correlation between what is provided (or denied) and the nature of the individuals in question. To promote happiness, to remove frustration, anxiety, envy, etc., is to promote, by some means or other, an identity between the outlook of the individual and the claims and opportunities of the society. The state, in so far as it has control of education and educational influences and control of the way of life of the community, is in a position to maximise happiness, if it so chooses.

Finally it is necessary to establish that the principle of happiness is supreme and must override the claims of any other principle that may be put forward, should they happen to clash. I shall put forward three arguments to this end, although the third is merely the reverse side of the second and cannot be fully completed until the examination of the principles of freedom and equality in the next two chapters is completed. The arguments are: (a) that the notion of justice presupposes, and, apart from procedural principles, only presupposes, the principle of happiness; (b) that the principle of happiness is the only principle that commands universal assent and therefore does not need proof; and (c) that the other principles put forward by the liberal-democrats as being of equal significance to the principle of happiness, namely the principles of freedom and equality, cannot be substantiated except by reference to and as subordinate to the principle of happiness.

(a) Naturally in approaching this matter we must dispense, at least temporarily, with any preconceived ideas that we may have as to the existence of various ultimate moral principles. The purpose of our enquiry is to discover what ultimate principles there are, and to establish them by such reasoning as we can.

It has been well shown that by seriously engaging oneself in a form of practical discourse, such as moral discourse, one implicitly commits oneself to certain procedural principles that constitute the second-order principle of justice.[13] In particular one commits oneself to the formal principles of impartiality and fairness, which involve the notion of giving reasons for adopting one alternative rather than another. But, what has not perhaps been so well recognised is that the notions of impartiality and fairness do not make sense except in the light of some overriding aim or objective, and the reasons that one gives for differential treatment likewise cannot be relevant reasons except in the light of some overriding assumption. If moral discourse is to have point, then, and if these procedural principles are to be meaningful, there must also be some general assumption of the good for man implicit in seriously engaging in moral discourse.

The notion of moral good presupposes something ultimately advantageous for man. Specific viewpoints may have distinctive ideas as to what is advantageous: for instance, a certain kind of religious view might lead one to suppose that it is ultimately advantageous for the individual to lead a life of deprivation and suffering on this earth. But at this stage we cannot assume such a specific view and we cannot assume the existence of God. But we can note the logical contradiction involved in saying 'This is the ultimate good for man and it is in no way to his advantage'. Therefore where we consider such questions as how people ought to behave or how they ought to be treated, we are implicitly committed to some general concern for their ultimate advantage. And it is impossible to see how this concern could be compatible with a willingness to promote anxiety, frustration and generically misery, as an ultimate end. On the contrary the notion of happiness would seem to be inseparable from the idea of concern for their advantage. Even the religious fanatic who preaches worldly sorrow does so on the grounds that the individual's advantage will be thereby secured in heaven, and that advantage is presumed to include happiness.

Similarly, to be fair to people, even before we turn to actual situations, presupposes taking account of their interests. One is simply not being fair if one ignores people's interests. Naturally in specific instances people's interests may vary considerably, and if we were to assume further moral principles, such as freedom, as we are *not* doing at this stage since the premiss is that they have yet to be established, these principles would give rise to a new range of specific interests. But all we can say at this stage is that the formal notion of fairness presupposes a general notion of considering people's interests. And again, whatever people's specific interests, a general notion of interest appears to be inseparable from the idea of satisfactory enmeshment and hence happiness. Prior to the substantiation of any specific principles, a commitment to consideration of people's interests is quite incompatible with a willingness to doom them to anxiety, frustration and misery. It is manifestly not in a man's interest to be ultimately unenmeshed.

Furthermore I, and anybody else concerned as a party to this imagined moral discourse, must regard enmeshment as in my interest: it is logically impossible to desire to be ultimately unenmeshed, and clearly I will not *regard* what I do not desire in any way at all as in my interest. Consequently in so far as I am truly committed to the procedural principle of impartiality, I must intend to promote the enmeshment of all men, unless relevant grounds can be produced for distinction between them.

If some general notion of consideration of man's interests or well-being is implicit in taking moral discourse seriously, and if it is impossible to conceive of a man's well-being as being promoted by anxiety, frustration and misery as an end state, it follows that we presuppose as an ultimate objective the provision of enmeshment, and hence happiness, and that therefore any proposed moral principle will have to be examined or rejected in the light of that overriding objective.

(b)   The second argument to establish that happiness is the supreme principle is independent of the first, and is, in my view, the argument that Mill was essentially putting forward in his essay 'Utilitarianism'. The force of this argument depends upon the assumption, readily granted by the liberal-democrats, that questions of ultimate ends do not admit of proof in the normal sense of the term, i.e. a proof with the irrefutable conclusion of an empirical test. As I understand him Mill was simply arguing with a view to establishing that all men do in fact accept the principle of happiness, provided that they can be brought to understand the terminology, whereas there is no other principle of which this can be said. This does not establish that the happiness principle ought to be the supreme principle; it gives us nothing more than an intuited first principle. But it avoids the standard objection to intuitionism (namely that somebody somewhere does not in fact intuit the principle in question and that therefore one cannot legitimately claim that it just is self-evident). Mill is not proving that all men ought to desire happiness, but that all men do think that happiness ought to be desired. This is 'all the proof which the case admits of'[14] and it establishes that in the *opinion of mankind* 'happiness is good', whereas there is nothing else of which this may be said without exception. Since it is impossible for mankind to appeal beyond the opinion of mankind, there the matter must rest. Thus, in order to upset the relevance of this argument (which will be expounded in greater detail in the following paragraphs), it would be necessary either to prove the validity of some other principle as of equal significance or to disprove the validity of the happiness principle, which according to the concession in the premiss cannot be done.

In greater detail this argument is as follows: it follows from the fact that some pro-attitude or desire is necessary as motivation towards a freely chosen action or course of activity, that the individual cannot choose to abide by an ultimate principle unless he sees enmeshment, and hence happiness, bound up with its realisation. He cannot feel commitment to a principle that he presumes will lead to a situation with which he cannot enmesh. Part of what it means to sincerely assent to such a proposition as 'No man ought to have to starve' is that one has a pro-attitude or a desire for a situation in which no man does starve.

When Mill wrote that 'the sole evidence it is possible to produce that anything is desirable is that people do actually desire it', he meant two things: first, that proof as we generally understand it is not possible in the case of ultimate principles; and secondly, the point made in the previous paragraph, that no ought-statement can get off the ground if people do not desire to realise it. It may be the case, if we presuppose something like a God-figure who is the source of moral conscience, that we ought to do X, whether we like it or not. But the onus is on somebody who believes that we ought to do X to prove it, and on the assumption that the existence of God, his status as the source of our moral conscience, and the claim that we ought to do X itself, cannot be proven to our satisfaction, the fact that only one individual wants to do X, will effectively mean that it is not accepted that X ought to be done.

Mill is certainly not guilty of committing the naturalistic fallacy, as Cowan has amply shown,[15] both by citing overwhelming evidence of Mill's awareness and rejection of the fallacy, and also by providing a positive analysis of his position. That position may be summarised in three parts:

(1) If somebody thinks that X ought to be done, then he thinks that X is desirable, both in the sense that it *is* desired by him and in the sense that it is rightly desired and ought to be desired. I cannot sincerely believe that I ought to do X and yet have no desire whatsoever to do X, because implicit in sincere commitment to a moral injunction is a pro-attitude or desire towards abiding by it. (I may, of course, have conflicting desires, some of which may be stronger and even amount to intense passions; but that does not affect the argument.)

(2) But, says Mill, there is no other way of showing that something is morally desirable as an ultimate end, beyond showing that it is desired. In other words even if as a matter of metaphysical fact there is an objectively valid moral principle that says, 'Thou shalt kill the first born', one could never hope to substantiate it by a reasoned proof. All one could do to achieve acknowledgement of this principle would be either to get people to desire to kill the first born or to establish that such a practice is necessarily demanded by something that people already desire. It is quite pointless, inasmuch as it will achieve nothing, to insist that killing the first born is desirable, morally or otherwise, so long as people do *not* desire to do it.

In the same way, despite the acknowledged fact that desirable and visible belong to different categories, it is pointless inasmuch as it will achieve nothing, to insist that something *is* visible although nobody can see it. Of course, if nobody can see X, it *is* invisible, whereas it may be that, although none of us desires X, it is not morally undesirable. Mill's point is that, although we may *formally* admit this point, in fact, if none of us desires X, we shall not accept that it is morally desirable.

God may exist and may have moral demands to make of us, just as he may see things that we cannot see, but *we* cannot escape either the evidence of our own eyes or the limitations of our own desires. If an individual opts for a specific moral principle, he implicitly desires to abide by it, but he will never be able to show others that they too ought to abide by it, without persuading them that they do in fact desire to abide by it.

(3) This being the case, the only thing that will command universal assent as something that ought to be desired, is the only thing that has actual, universal assent as being desirable in a non-moral sense, namely enmeshment, and hence happiness. This we all necessarily do desire and towards this notion of enmeshment, formal though it be, we all have a pro-attitude. It is logically impossible for a man to want to be in a situation that ultimately causes him anxiety, frustration, boredom and other constituent parts of misery. We all of us use moral words such

as 'right' and 'good' with reference to things towards which we have a pro-attitude. We, therefore, in the final analysis, apply 'right' and 'good', in accordance with our view of the world as we would like it to be, which is the characteristic form of appraisal associated with happiness. Our ideal world is a world with which we believe we could fully enmesh. The moral rules that govern it would be rules that we desire to see in force. It is in the light of the notion of enmeshment, and hence happiness, that we all of us view perfection, and this ideal of enmeshment is the only principle that we all necessarily share.

If a man advocates a principle of equality or freedom as being an ultimate principle, he is essentially revealing that he would like to see an equal or free world. To establish that the world ought to be free or equal, in any effective sense, it is necessary for him to convince others that they too would like to see such a world. The desire for, or pro-attitude towards, the picture of an equal world, is a necessary condition of people's accepting it as morally desirable. Consequently the principle of happiness must be supreme, because no other principle can be embraced by the individual, save on the assumption that he believes that he can enmesh, and hence be happy, with the situation arising from the adoption of the proposed principle.

In short: the principle of happiness must be accepted as the supreme principle because enmeshment, and hence happiness, is the only thing that all men necessarily desire, and hence is the only thing that all men can accept as morally desirable; and in lieu of any formal proof to establish the validity of any principle, we must accept the universal agreement of mankind. In addition commitment to any other moral principle presupposes that adherence to it will promote the kind of situation with which the individual who commits himself may enmesh.

This is, of course, a most peculiar proof. In fact it is misleading to call it a proof, especially since the premiss was that proof in the normal manner is impossible. What we have done is given reasons such as to cause the mind to assent to the proposition that happiness is the supreme principle. It is surely reasonable to treat as the ultimate good the only thing that all men want and consider to be good, and the thing in the light of which they give their assent to other principles.

(c) I believe the two previous arguments to be sufficient to establish that we must accept the principle of happiness as the supreme principle (rather than to prove that it is). But a third argument now begins, that will continue through the next two chapters, and that is different both in kind and purpose to the previous two arguments.

The liberal-democrats acknowledge a principle of happiness as *one* ultimate principle, and that being the case, since the status of the principle of happiness as an ultimate end is common ground between them and Plato, the onus is in fact on them to establish that the principles of freedom and equality are also ultimate rather than, as I shall argue, to be interpreted in the light of the overriding principle of happiness. If the status of the principles of equality and freedom cannot be substantiated as ultimate, it goes without saying that their argument against Plato loses all its significance, since we will be left with a principle of happiness acknowledged to be ultimate by both parties to the dispute, and with two principles whose ultimate status is contested by one party and supported by the other on no good grounds.

It is therefore now necessary to turn our attention to the proposed principle of freedom.

Notes

1 Ryle, G., *Mind*, 1948.
2 *Euthydemus*, 278.
3 *Eryxias*, 393.
4 354 A.
5 Mill, J. S., *Utilitarianism*, Fontana, London, 1962 (Warnock, M., ed.), p. 289.
6 Ibid., p. 289.
7 Ibid.
8 E.g. Jean Austin.
9 Kenny, A., 'Happiness', *P.A.S.*, vol. 66 (1965–6). Reprinted in Feinberg, J., ed., *Moral Concepts*, Oxford University Press, 1969.
10 Kenny, op. cit., p. 48.
11 Ibid.
12 Cowan, op. cit., p. 117.
13 See, for instance, Peters, R. S., *Ethics and Education*, Allen & Unwin, London, 1966, p. 120ff.
14 Mill, op. cit., p. 288.
15 Cowan, op. cit.

Freedom 6

1   Plato, the liberal-democrats and freedom

It may be conceded that the citizens of the Republic are intended to be happy, and even that they will be happy. But the liberal-democrat will point out that, in order to secure this end, Plato 'denies every axiom of progressive thought and challenges all its fondest ideals' and most notably the ideal of freedom, which is condemned by Plato as an illusion that 'can be held only by idealists whose sympathies are stronger than their sense'.[1] It is undoubtedly the case that Plato does not feel that it matters, in the circumstances of the Republic, that there will be restrictions or that individuals will be discouraged from entertaining and acting on idiosyncratic opinions, arrived at independently.

However Plato is not concerned to stigmatise 'freedom' as evil; he is not arguing that the less freedom granted to the individual in any circumstances the better. Indeed he expressly denies that this is so: 'Freedom and subordination are both utterly destructive, when given excessive weight, but most beneficial in reasonable measure'.[2] This remark does not help us to decide what a 'reasonable measure' might be, it does not tell us how we are to measure, but it makes it quite clear that Plato's formal position is the same as that occupied by any theorist who believes in government and law: there are circumstances in which it is justifiable to place restrictions on the activity of individuals within a society.

When he scorns Athens, then, because there is no need 'to keep the peace when others do so, unless you feel like it',[3] it is not freedom that is the enemy, but those who argue that freedom should over-ride other considerations. It is men like Lord Lauderdale, who objected, successfully, to the introduction of a bill designed to prohibit the use of small boys as chimney sweeps, on the grounds that such matters should be left to the discretion of individual conscience, whom Plato would oppose.

Formally Plato's attitude to freedom is identical with that of John Stuart Mill. And the utilitarian view of freedom, as expounded by Mill, is very straightforward. He expressly states that he regards any liberties that he would defend as derived from the principle of utility.[4] His specific proposals are, naturally enough, geared to the utilitarian touchstone that 'mankind' should be 'the greater gainers'[5] in terms of happiness. Compulsion is quite legitimate

95

where, as with barbarians and children, it is the most efficacious means to the end, and the only reason he offers for objecting to compulsion as a means, in the case of men of maturity and civilised habits, is that he regards self-development as contributory towards men's happiness in the long term.[6]

Consequently we cannot accept the view that Mill 'offers no justification' of his view that 'all restraint, *qua* restraint, is an evil' and that 'he treats it as self-evident'.[7] It is clear that all restraint, *qua* restraint, is evil, only because as a matter of psychological fact in Mill's opinion, the consequences of restraint as such, both immediate and long term, are miserable.

Where Plato differs from Mill is in his assessment of what does contribute to happiness, most particularly, I think, because he does not recognise Mill's distinction between 'self-regarding' and 'other-regarding' actions, or at least he draws the boundaries differently. Mill puts it this way:[8]

> The sole end for which mankind are warranted, individually
> or collectively, in interfering with the liberty of action of any of
> their number, is self-protection. That the only purpose for which
> power can be rightfully exercised over any member of a civilised
> community, against his will, is to prevent harm to others.

But, clearly, the force of this remark hinges upon what we mean by 'self-protection' and 'harm to others'. It is tempting to think purely in terms of physical protection and physical harm, but the claims of the principle of utility should surely force one into accepting also psychological harm. A gang exercising themselves in Brighton on a bank holiday do not only harm the people they actually hit; they also harm, for instance, the elderly residents who become frightened, even those who merely become depressed at the way the world is going. The psychological bully in a school is every bit as harmful as the physical bully. It is in fact rather difficult to be sure that there is any meaningful distinction to be made between self- and other-regarding actions in a society. Any activity, such as drug-taking, free speech or even free thought, that is categorised as self-regarding, and hence not restricted, becomes at once a social phenomenon and as such affects, though not necessarily harms, other people, quite apart from the fact that it is difficult to imagine any of these examples not having more direct consequences which do affect the interests of others.

The question of the psychological undesirability of restraint is also more complex than it might appear. It is not in dispute that most restrictions on freedom at present absent, but which one might choose to impose upon our society, would be immediately psychologically unwelcome. But it is by no means clear that restrictions with which we are already familiar are in themselves psychologically irksome, quite apart from the question of long term benefits. The restriction on our freedom to kill, for instance, or our freedom to walk naked in the streets are not, for most of us, the lesser of two evils; we do not calculate the advantages of the restrictions and conclude that the world is happier for them; we simply do not want to kill or walk naked, and, therefore, it does not occur to us to resent the restriction. The point of this observation is that, from a utilitarian point of view, it is important that those restrictions that are considered necessary, should be accepted without resentment by those on whom they are imposed. But there also seems to be considerable evidence, that many people psychologically prefer restrictions, which they see as guiding lines that provide a secure structure for them,[9] as well as that they do not resent restrictions with which they are familiar.

Nor should we forget that neither Plato nor any other philosopher that one would wish to take seriously is arguing that the mere maximisation of restriction is in itself desirable. The claim is not that, if a particular kind of society be posited as an end, and, if it can reliably be arrived at and maintained equally well, either with or without restrictions, then it is preferable that it be achieved with restriction. It is rather that, within a community, restriction is justified by the beneficial consequences for that community, and it is being suggested that the existence of specific restrictions is not in itself psychologically unpleasant, though at the time of imposition it may seem so.

What makes Mill appear to be a champion of liberty as in itself a moral requirement, is his empirical view of the sort of thing that contributes to the general happiness, in particular his belief in individuality. In view of his philosophical position he cannot consistently believe in something such as 'individual autonomy' as good in itself; it is only good in so far as it serves the principle of utility, but he does evidently feel that as a matter of fact originality, spontaneity and individuality do contribute to the ultimate happiness of a society; a view which Plato does not share.

Mill argues that different styles of life, good and bad, in a community make it possible for new and valuable styles to be thrown up, and also provide practical tests, whereby evil styles may be seen to be such, and thus more powerfully and rationally rejected than if merely forbidden. This argument parallels his argument for freedom of thought and discussion: to stifle opinions is to risk stifling the truth, to assume infallability, and to give no opportunity for a proof of sound doctrine. Mental and moral powers are improved only by use; and strong natures are needed: 'with small men no great things can be accomplished'.

Emotionally this may sound attractive, but it is questionable whether much of it is entirely consistent with utilitarianism. The appeal for the accomplishment of great things resounds finely, but one would like to know what 'a great thing' is, and whether it is necessary for the maximisation of happiness. I do not know what sort of things Mill regards as great, but, if happiness is to be our test, there is surely no reason to suppose that any of the things one *might* regard as great achievements, artistic or scientific, have made the world better. I question whether, for example, as a result of the Mona Lisa, the *Ring*, the motor car and penicillin, people are necessarily any happier today than they were in fifth-century Greece; this is because happiness is not dependent on any necessary conditions, as we have seen. Consequently whatever attractions 'great achievements' may have for some of us, however much you or I need the motor car or the National Gallery for our happiness, there is no necessary need for these things for a happy community.

Mill's own highly individual personality seems to have led him to believe that we ought to have persons of genius in a society, and therefore 'ought to preserve the soil in which they grow. Genius can only breathe freely in an atmosphere of freedom'.[10] By 'genius', Mill seems to mean primarily 'artistic genius', and it is obviously, at best, highly debatable whether such genius contributes enough to maximise happiness against the losses incurred in other respects by the preservation of a soil fit for it to grow in; there is also the empirical question of whether it is true that genius needs an atmosphere of freedom. To argue that it does presumably involves the claim that if there is any genius in the world today, it is not to be found in the work of Shostakovich and Rostropovich. Perhaps it also implies that the work of Homer, Michelangelo and Mozart is not the work of genius, since these artists worked within the framework of relatively closed societies, even turning out their accomplishments to commission. It is a fact that free Athens produced the Parthenon, whereas regimented Sparta left so little in the way of monuments that 'future generations' may be forgiven 'for failing to appreciate the greatness she once enjoyed'.[11] But it is not a fact that Athens was therefore happier.

Clearly Mill believes that a society is better off, if people do the right thing because they understand what they are doing. But if the principle of utility is really to be 'the ultimate appeal on all ethical questions' his belief may well be incorrect. If people do the right thing (i.e. that which most effectively contributes to the general happiness) it makes no difference whether they do it by habit, or on sound and deliberate calculation, unless it can be shown that people are unhappy when they act on habit.

To stifle opinions is certainly to risk stifling the truth and one might therefore, in the interests of truth, argue that no opinion, however inflammatory, ought to be stifled. But to say this is to argue that the pursuit of truth is more important than the principle of utility, or else that the business of pursuing the truth must, on balance, contribute to happiness, which, apart from being inherently dubious, cuts no ice in the face of the Republic, which is perfectly happy. The pursuit of truth is certainly something that most philosophers, not least Plato, are drawn towards. But to argue that therefore a Hitler ought to be allowed to incite a nation by expressing his opinions is to leave the principle of utility far behind. A society or its executive must assume infallability on those issues which it regards as fundamental to its way of life. 'The claims of tolerance cannot persuade us that, though the right course is to interfere, we ought not to interfere because the right course might be wrong'.[12] Thus, incitement to overthrow the constitution is treated as reprehensible even in the most open society, although to the anarchist the truth appears in a different guise. The utilitarian, in such an open society, knowing that attempts to incite revolution will be opposed, must decide whether he thinks that allowing subversive opinions to grow, and then be thwarted by force, contributes more or less to the happiness of the community than checking their birth in the first place.

However, despite queries that one might raise about some of his actual calculations (for instance the good accruing to society from the existence of individuals of genius), there is no doubt about Mill's formal approach to the problem of freedom. A man 'must not make himself a nuisance';[13] and clearly 'nuisance' will have to be defined in terms of what offends, physically or psychologically, other members of the community, and cannot be given any specific content until the other aspects of a particular society have been filled in. 'As soon as any part of a person's conduct affects prejudicially the interests of others',[14] then the general welfare can be the test. Ultimately all political decisions are concerned with the conduct of persons in relation to one another, and are thus concerned with situations potentially prejudicial to the interests of the community. The general welfare therefore becomes the test of all political decisions.

Plato does not recognise freedom as an ultimate moral principle which may clash with the principle of happiness any more than Mill does. An ideal world, no doubt, would consist of individuals with the capability of philosopher-kings so that there would be no need for social restrictions: people would act of their own accord in a just manner, they would happily shoulder the burden of personal responsibility, and none of their actions would lead to the misery of others. But it is the premiss of statecraft and education that the world is not perfect, and that people have to be directed, to some extent, in their behaviour, if moral ideals are to be realised in practice. This being so the claims of freedom in general (as opposed perhaps to certain specific freedoms) have already been assessed as subordinate to the claims of other moral principles, in Plato's case to the utilitarian principle that society should be organised so that the greatest happiness possible should be obtained for all members of the community. If a specific proposal should militate against that end, such as Adeimantus's suggestion that the rulers be given more material reward, it is rejected and the question of whether, in rejecting the proposal, somebody's freedom is or is not infringed upon, does not arise.

When Plato speaks scornfully of freedom, then, we should understand him, not as advocating coercion for the sake of coercion, but as opposing the notion that a great degree of freedom for the individual within a community is *in itself* a laudable feature of that society. He is talking of states such as historical Athens, and the specific sorts of freedom there esteemed, when he exclaims ironically: 'In the first place are they not free? Isn't the city stuffed to the gills with liberty and freedom of speech? Isn't it true that every man is free to do as he likes?' Popper misses the point entirely when he comments that 'in the complete absence of rational arguments . . . Plato uses invective, identifying liberty with lawlessness, freedom with licence, and equality before the law with disorder'.[15] Plato is not saying that freedom *is* licence, he is saying rather that what we have in Athens is in fact disorder and lawlessness, but *they* dress it up in grand names such as freedom and liberty. He is concerned to point out that they are, indeed, relatively free in Athens to do as they please, but in fact they are not capable of making good use of that freedom. The priorities, in Plato's view, are wrong.

We should not promote individual freedom for its own sake at the expense of justice and happiness, but rather we should promote happiness and justice leaving as much freedom to the individual as is in practice compatible with ensuring these aims. It is not that the Athenians have free speech that worries Plato, but that they think that having freedom is the measure of a good society. It is true that the less need a group of people have for some kind of direction, whether via their upbringing or the rules of the group that are enforced by sanctions, the more virtuous, we may say, is the natural state of their souls, but this has nothing to do with the question of what limits should be placed on social direction, assuming that it is agreed that there is need for some degree of it. As far as Plato is concerned the latter question is answered by ruthless adherence to the principle of utility.

Consequently, for the sake of a just and happy community, Plato offers us the 'closed society' and advocates 'indoctrination' and censorship. The intention of the laws and the social organisation is 'that the citizens should be as happy as possible, and as friendly as possible to one another'.[16] And, in so far as it is empirically sound to suggest that, so long as mankind is what it is, 'there is no cessation of trouble'[17] if each individual is left free to develop as he may and to do as he wishes, Plato would feel no qualms about the restricted tribal nature of the Republic. It is in no sense, for him, a weakness, blot or necessary evil in his state, that the claims of freedom are subordinated to the claims of justice and happiness. Freedom is good where freedom leads to good results, bad where consequences are bad. Good results are defined in terms of the happiness they promote. The claims of freedom are subordinate to the claims of happiness.

For Plato and other utilitarians, then, freedom is a prima facie principle which should always be overridden by the claims of the ultimate principle of happiness. For the liberal-democrats it is in theory an ultimate principle of equal weight to the principle of happiness, with which it may clash. That this is their position is shown both by the fact that they refer to freedom, without qualification, as an aim along with happiness, and by the fact that sometimes they subordinate the claims of happiness to those of freedom and sometimes the opposite.[18]

And many other philosophers, not included in my restricted circle of liberal-democrats, feel that 'the paradox of politics is the reconciliation of liberty and obligation',[19] and incline to the view that there are various ultimate moral principles and that 'it may be regarded as certain that sometimes some of these values will be in conflict with others, but that is a painful fact which every human ideal unfortunately has to face'.[20] In point of fact the sad resignation evident in this view is not necessary to 'every human ideal'. Platonism does not involve a conflict of values. But it may be admitted that any philosophy that regards a principle of freedom as ultimate and of equal weight with other ultimate principles, must necessarily face clashes in practice, so long as human beings do not freely choose to abide by the demands of the other ultimate principles.

However, pointing out that a philosophical creed is, in practice, difficult to handle, does not invalidate it. We have to show that the status of freedom as an ultimate principle cannot be substantiated. And clearly if the principle is to be ultimate and of equal weight to the principle of happiness, an attempt at substantiation cannot be based on any reference to that other principle, for if freedom is justified by appeal to happiness then the principle of freedom is subordinate to the principle of happiness. If the principle of freedom is an ultimate principle then its status must be justified without appeal to other principles.

The principle of freedom or autonomy, stated simply, would seem to say that the individual ought to be free to think and do what he chooses to do. We cannot accept as an argument in favour of this principle that 'freedom' is a natural right of the individual. One does not deny that it may be the case, if the imagination could only grasp it, that there is an eternal and immutable moral injunction that all men ought to be free; in other words it is conceivable that this claim should be valid. But to assert that it is a natural right, in this sense, is to do no more than to repeat, with different words, one's belief that it is the case that all men ought to be free. Claiming that men have this natural right is simply reasserting the claim that the right self-evidently exists for all men; and the assertion of self-evidence does not constitute an argument to those who do not see the self-evidence. Nor does one accept the argument that freedom is a natural right, in the sense of a right derived from man's essential nature as a decision-making creature, nor yet from man's behaviour in a state of nature. Both these lines of argument involve the naturalistic fallacy: it does not follow from the fact that man is able to make decisions and act upon them, nor from the fact that long ago he may have acted entirely on his own decisions, that he ought to.

Popper suggests that 'the realm of morality proper' is one 'of norms enforced not by the state but by our own moral decisions— by our conscience'.[21] Ever since Aristotle drew a distinction between the man who acts freely and the man who acts from force of circumstances, it has been generally agreed that the agent deserves no moral credit, unless he freely chooses to act as he does. However it does not follow from this observation that we ought to allow the individual's conscience to be his only guide. It is not clear that providing people with the opportunity to earn moral praise or blame is more important than ensuring moral actions within a society. Mabbot remarks 'that a body of persons living under a perfect legislative code might be clean, they might be efficient, they might conceivably be happy, but by no stretch of Platonic Paradox could they, in virtue of their obedience to their code, be virtuous'.[22] Let us be precise: they would not deserve credit for their virtuous behaviour, but their behaviour, and hence surely themselves in some sense, by definition, would be virtuous. It seems odd to regard the individual who was brought up to believe that killing was wrong, and who accepts this view, without feeling moved to seriously examine it, and who resolutely refrains from killing, as less 'virtuous' than the individual who thought about the matter, and then accepted it: still more odd to call the individual who thinks, and then decides to kill, as more virtuous. Are we to imagine that the unreflective are necessarily less virtuous than the professional philosopher? And is a stupid man, who in his own peculiar way goes through a process of enquiry, however pathetic, before he acts, therefore virtuous?

The view, then, that the individual's conscience should be his guide in action, and that it is wrong to prevent an individual from doing what he chooses to do, which view, according to Popper, says 'nothing about a natural right to freedom' but expresses rather 'a political demand', cannot simply be accepted. We still need an argument.

Nor can 'originality' and 'initiative' be regarded as self-evidently desirable.[23] It may or may not be true, as Popper would imply, that original discoveries, or original behaviour patterns and ideas, cannot be brought to birth in a society unless it eschews all social control and destroys the concept of faith (by which is meant the notion of steadfast commitment to an opinion in the absence of rational arguments to establish the validity of that opinion); but an original idea is not necessarily a good one. If originality is in itself good, then we are faced with the proposition that an individual is better than his neighbour in so far as he finds a novel way of being different to him. Since one presumes that Popper does not advocate this view (he certainly produces no argument for it), one must conclude that he values originality, like Mill, because he believes that a society that encourages originality will in fact be likely to produce worthwhile original ideas; but in this case, since we are distinguishing between worthwhile and unworthwhile original ideas, the criteria for judging something worthwhile cannot involve the originality. Therefore freedom cannot be commended simply on the grounds that it leads to originality.

Nor is the argument that the ideal of individual autonomy is automatically approved, by those who get as far as asking themselves whether it ought to be approved or not, acceptable. It is not true that:[24]

> even for me to question whether I ought to test my beliefs and
> make my choices according to my own reasoned judgment,
> rather than in obedience to authorities, is already to have
> decided in favour of autonomy; for I am asking for reasons as
> to what I ought to do, and taking it for granted that it is I
> who will decide the merit of the answers.

It is, of course, true that in this passage 'I' am indicating a preference for a rational justification of action, rather than a justification which takes the form 'Do this, simply because it is a traditional command'. 'I', being a rational person, wish that my behaviour shall be rational; it does not follow that I think I ought never to act except after rational enquiry on my own part; and it certainly does not follow that I think that everybody else ought to act on their own decisions,

formed after rational reflection. The fact that I ask myself this
question indicates only that, as a matter of fact, I am the sort of
person who will not accept the fact that an order has been given,
as in itself an adequate reason for agreeing with the correctness of
the order.

Dearden returns to the problem of justifying autonomy as an
aim in a more recent article, conceding that we must do more than
show that some of us do exercise and believe it important for us to
exercise autonomy.[25] 'A utility value', he points out, might be
placed on autonomy, but he does not find this a sufficiently strong
thesis, and indeed for our present purposes it is not: it would concede
the point that it is not an ultimate principle of equal weight to that
of happiness, but rather desirable as a means to an end. But all his
arguments turn out to involve approving autonomy as a means to
some further end, and not as an end in itself. We are told that[26]

> what is being aimed at is the development of a kind of person
> whose thought and action in important areas of his life are to
> be explained by reference to . . . his own activity of mind. And
> in a social world where it is important to locate responsibility,
> personal autonomy will prominently attract such ascriptions of
> responsibility to the individual agent.

This comes at the end of a paragraph placed in the middle of a series
of attempts at justification and therefore looks as if it is meant to
be one. But of course it is not. It is no more than a statement of
the fact that where autonomy is highly valued the exercise of
autonomy by the individual will be approved of. Then it is said
that 'the exercise of . . . autonomy will be a source of considerable
satisfaction', and that it gives one 'pride' and 'dignity, or sense of
personal worth'. But, in so far as these claims are true, they clearly
only involve commending autonomy as a means to some further end,
and the choice of the word 'satisfaction' leaves little doubt that that
end is something like happiness. Again, we are told that 'its exercise
will be claimed as a right', but we are not told why or on what
grounds. Not altogether surprisingly this section on justification,
which was to be 'squarely faced', concludes with the remark that
'it is doubtful whether the notion of justification is in place at all
here. Rather is it the case that other things are justified or not by
reference to autonomy'.[27] But that is precisely the claim that needs
to be, and was supposed to be being, justified.

None of these arguments, then, establishes that there is a general
principle of freedom of ultimate status. There is a prima facie more
plausible argument in support of the more limited notion that people
ought to be encouraged to think for themselves, based on the point
that we, by engaging in the present form of enquiry, commit our-

selves to the approval of truth and rationality. I shall consider this argument below; for the moment we need only note that advocacy of the promotion of autonomy in this sense, is not the same thing as claiming that there is an ultimate principle of freedom such that the individual ought to be free to think and do what he chooses to do.

However, it is perhaps not surprising that we cannot find adequate substantiation of an ultimate principle of freedom, for the liberal-democrats themselves say that such substantiation is impossible. The next step, therefore, is to consider the use they make of this principle in which they have placed their faith. And here we find an even more disturbing state of affairs, for their use of the presumed principle is inconsistent.

The supposition that the principle of freedom is of ultimate status leads to the use of the word 'freedom' without qualification or explanation, a use to which both Popper and Crossman are prone. It may be legitimate for the anarchist to use 'freedom' as if it were a blank cheque, and to say simply that 'freedom' is a good thing, without any differentiation between freedom from, or freedom to do, this or that, because to him any example of the individual acting on his own initiative and independently of any external pressure from another individual or group is good. The anarchist claims to have no other criteria of moral evaluation. But the liberal-democrats are not anarchists. They have other ultimate moral principles, and further than that there are situations in which they think that it is right that the principle of freedom should be overridden by the claims of some other principle. But it cannot be the case *both* that, say, the principles of happiness and freedom are of equal weight as ultimate principles, *and* that, in cases of a clash between the principles, there may be occasions on which one principle *ought* to override the other. For that 'ought' would need substantiation, and substantiation could only come from the actual supremacy of one of the principles or from appeal to some other higher principle. If the claims of happiness and freedom clash on a certain occasion, and if the two principles are really of equal weight and ultimate significance, then there is nothing to choose between considering the demands of one principle or the other.

Consequently if the liberal-democrats are really committed to some general principle of freedom as being of ultimate status, they can never justify any of the specific restrictions that they do regard as morally necessary. At best, they can argue that there are reasons for the restriction, based on some other principle, as well as reasons against it, based on the principle of freedom. But they have no way of evaluating these reasons, no way of deciding which principle ought to carry the day. Nor, conversely, can they substantiate that any particular freedoms ought to be preserved, if it can be shown that restriction of those freedoms would promote the claims of some other of their ultimate principles, such as happiness.

Of course many philosophers who share a faith in a plurality of ultimate principles are often to be found debating, in specific instances, what weight ought to be put on their various principles in coming to decisions. What, it may be asked, is the 'logic' of such debates?

The answer, alas, is all too clear. There is no 'logic' in such debates, and the fact that some sincerely presume there is does not establish that there is. One might suggest that deciding between the claims of conflicting ultimate principles is a matter of judgment. But on what criteria would one distinguish between sound and unsound judgment? In the light of what, would one judge between what are supposed to be one's ultimate principles?

It is inescapable, however tiresome, that if these principles are ultimate and of equal weight, there is no way of establishing that the claims of one ought to override the claims of another. From which it follows that the liberal-democrats are inconsistent to claim that some freedoms ought to be upheld and that some ought to be sacrificed in the light of other principles, and from which it also follows that they have no grounds on which to claim that Plato is wrong, if it can be shown that he consistently adheres to the principle of happiness, which they also recognise, and only restricts freedom to that end.

We see, then, that no argument has been produced for a general principle of freedom of ultimate status, and that the liberal-democrats inconsistently sometimes assume that the claims of freedom must override other principles, most notably in their attack on Plato, and sometimes assume that the principle of freedom must be overridden, neither of which assumptions could be true if there really is a plurality of principles of equal weight and ultimate status.

But the final point to be made is that as far as one can judge from their cryptic remarks on the subject, when it comes down to specific examples, the liberal-democrats justify certain restrictions by reference to a principle of happiness. For instance, Popper talks of 'the protection of that freedom which does not harm other citizens' as being the 'fundamental purpose of the state',[28] and he admits the propriety of restricting that freedom which does 'harm other citizens'. The particular wording of this formula may give the impression that freedom is of crucial importance, but what the formula actually involves is that there is something more important than freedom, namely whatever is involved in 'the prevention of harm to others'. Crossman's formula for explaining the limitations of freedom is the claim 'that of course you must stop people acting in ways which disturb the freedom of others . . . but, as far as possible, you must leave them free'[29] to make their own decisions. This formula seems prima facie less obviously to involve reference to another principle as superior to the principle of freedom, though again, if that is really so we are still faced with the inconsistency of claiming that 'you *must* leave them free' and yet that the principle of happiness is of equal weight.

But, in fact, even this second formula surely involves reference to a principle of happiness as overriding. For the formula is vacuous until we define 'the freedom of others'; unless this phrase is more precisely delineated, virtually anything could be interpreted as disturbing my freedom: the man playing his gramophone next door, the man driving his car along the road outside my house, both disturb my freedom to think in peace, for instance. If on the other hand we try to distinguish between freedoms, we are back where we started. On what grounds do you decide that people shall not be free to disturb freedom X of others, but shall be entitled to disturb freedom Y? Presumably by appeal to one of one's ultimate principles, one of which clearly cannot be the principle of freedom, since one is arguing that freedom may justifiably be overridden. Since the other presumed ultimate principles of the liberal-democrats are the principles of happiness and equality, and since, as will be shown,[30] the principle of equality must be taken in close conjunction with and as subordinate to the principle of happiness it seems that the liberal-democrats, effectively regard the principle of happiness as overriding the principle of freedom. And this, in any case, is the natural interpretation of the claim that only 'that freedom which does not harm other citizens' should be protected. For there seems no good reason to confine the notion of harm to the sphere of physical hurt. To make a man miserable is surely to harm him.

It would therefore seem that the liberal-democrats, in view of what they have to say about the justifiability of restricting freedom on certain occasions and in view of the absence of an argument to substantiate the claim that the principle of freedom is an ultimate principle, have no grounds for talking as if it were one, nor for condemning Plato for subordinating freedom to happiness, nor for moving beyond this recent formulation of the principle of freedom: 'Reasons must always be given for interfering with people, not for allowing them to do what they want';[31] 'the onus of justification must always rest on the would-be restrainer'.[32]

This formulation is purely formal, as its authors recognise, and its justification is involved in 'the criteria defining the sphere of moral discourse'. It makes the principle of freedom a prima facie principle, which is exactly what it is for Plato, but a prima facie principle, by definition, is not an ultimate principle: it is a principle which it may be necessary to override. And indeed involved in this formal analysis of the principle of freedom is the assumption that something else is more important than freedom, for if nothing else is *more* important, the reasons given for a specific restraint can never be compelling. Since it is conceded that happiness is an ultimate principle, it must override freedom.

2 Freedom of action, expression and thought

There is a tendency to assume that there must be more restrictions on the activity of citizens of the Republic than on the citizens of most other states. This does not necessarily follow from the mere fact that Plato adheres ruthlessly to the idea that the principle of happiness must override the principle of freedom. And indeed in looking for examples of specific restrictions, we find that few are actually mentioned. As an illustration of these justifiable restrictions I shall take one that has most excited Plato's enemies.

This is the restriction on the freedom of the Guardians to have sexual intercourse with whom they wish. Instead they are to mate only with those alloted to them at certain times by the rulers, who make the allocations in accordance with the aim of making the offspring of the union 'as perfect as possible'[33] and of keeping the birth-rate constant.

It is important to note that he is not in fact restricting sexual activity *per se*, but only the procreation of children,[34] for he removes all restriction from those who are beyond the age at which they are likely to bear children. In modern conditions, therefore, the use of contraception would render the precise details of the arrangement unnecessary. However, it is with the principle that we are concerned: if it were the case that one could so control mating as to ensure that no physically or mentally handicapped children should be born, would it be wrong to do so?

It sounds reasonable, prima facie, to say that the sphere of sexual activity ought to be outside the competence of the state. But the matter surely looks less clear cut when we consider the following points: according to psychologists people with an IQ of under seventy are completely incapable of coming to grips with our industrial and materialistic society; they live out their lives as cabbages, miserable and fearful, protected from reality by the four walls of an institution. According to some geneticians, no less than 80 per cent of our IQ is due to hereditary and not to environmental factors, and we are in a position to predict the birth of at least some of those who will be born with IQ's of under seventy. Finally some statisticians are convinced that within fifty years the population figures will be insupportable. If these three assumptions are correct, would it still seem so obviously wrong to prevent the birth of children with IQ's of under seventy?

Restriction on the individual's liberty to choose his partner in sexual union may startle us, but is it different in principle to restrictions on the liberty to kill, the liberty to undress in the street or the liberty to marry one's sister? In the last case the rationalisation of a restriction, that no doubt started out as a taboo, is that the offspring of such a union would be mentally weak; in every respect, save that society insists that brother and sister ought never to mate even with contraception, this is similar to the proposed restriction on the mating of parents who would produce children with chronically low IQ's.

Crossman comments scornfully on Plato's sexual norms: 'the really responsible citizen must not simply produce children to satisfy a whim or to please someone'. This is certainly Plato's view. Crossman's view is that sexual union is a self-regarding activity, and therefore outside the sphere of state interference,[35] whereas Plato does not distinguish between self- and other-regarding activities. Crossman is right: Plato does not consider sexual union, resulting in the production of children, as self-regarding, and it is difficult to see how Crossman could seriously maintain that it is. An increase in the birth-rate, an increase in the number of physically or mentally deformed, clearly affects the community, and does so in considerable degree.

The situation is simply this: Plato sees long-term advantage for the community in ensuring healthy and intelligent children. He therefore seeks to implement the means to this end in the Republic, and naturally his citizens will come to accept the conventions, as readily as any other society accepts its sexual conventions. This procedure is precisely the same as that followed to justify any other restriction. In order to discredit this, there are three possibilities only open to one: to take the anarchical view that no restrictions are justified; to argue that the means do not secure the end or that the end is undesirable; or to argue that freedom to copulate with whom one chooses, when one chooses, is an inalienable right. Liberal-democrats will not take the first way out. They may feel, and possibly rightly, that this is a storm in a teacup, since the means will not really serve the end; they cannot consistently object to the end, which is ultimately happiness. But undoubtedly what Popper and Crossman would like to say is that sexual freedom ought never to be interfered with; and this is most implausible: if it is a natural right, the onus is on them to convince us that it is. And in reply to the suggestion that sexual activity, when it leads to children, is 'self-regarding', or cannot 'harm' others, even in theory, we say simply that this is patently not so.

All other restrictions on free activity in the Republic are justified, in the same manner, by reference to the claims of happiness. The liberal-democrats therefore have no case against Plato's restrictions on freedom of action, provided that it can be shown that these restrictions are necessary for the promotion of happiness. But the Republic also restricts freedom of expression by censorship, and we therefore have to consider whether this is justifiable.

The censorship in the Republic is of a specific nature. Plato is not censoring on aesthetic criteria. His admiration for Homer as a great poet is explicitly acknowledged.[36] The censorship is designed to prevent the promotion of undesirable behavioural characteristics and attitudes through example. 'We admit that there are men and women who are mad and bad, but we cannot have them represented in poetry or drama',[37] 'for we soon reap the fruits of literature in life'.[38] And likewise musical modes which promote undesirable behaviour must be censored.

There is no obvious reason to agree that Plato's assumption 'that we tend to become like characters in the books which we admire, will hardly do'.[39] Plato's view is prima facie as tenable as Aristotle's contrary view that literature works cathartically and rids us of the urge to behave as we see the heroes of literature behave. In fact it seems at least questionable to argue that the mass media are merely following slavishly behind the enormous increase in figures for violent crime, abortion and illegitimacy, in their portrayal of violence and sexual permissiveness. If people are not suggestible to the influence of fictional characters, it is difficult, for instance, to see how much of advertising has any effect.

However, the empirical assumptions cannot be properly tested here: we must work on the hypothesis that people are influenced in their development by the values embodied in literature that they admire (while conceding, of course, that if the empirical assumption were to be invalidated, the case and the need for censorship would disappear). But it must not be forgotten that Homer was not simply a television play of the week to the Greeks. He was, as has often been observed, the bible of the Greeks, a repository of wisdom and example, that the individual was called on to admire. There can be no underrating the didactic nature of Greek poetry, from the theological and moral ground-plan laid down by Homer and Hesiod, via the gnomic utterances of Theognis, through the political verses of Solon and the critical verses of Xenophanes, to the waspish comedies of Aristophanes: 'the poet's job is to teach'.[40] And the musical modes of a poet like Tyrtaeus were admired precisely because they were supposed to be martial and inspiring, and just the thing for rousing the spirit as battle was joined.

The nub of this issue then is quite simply whether it is justifiable to censor examples of undesirable behaviour in literature (or, in modern terms, in the mass media), on the assumption that they inspire similar behaviour in the audience. And, of course, the question of what behaviour is undesirable must be kept quite distinct from the question of whether censorship can in principle be justified.

It follows from what has been said above that it is insufficient to condemn censorship merely on the grounds that it is censorship or that censorship by definition involves a restriction of freedom. One is therefore somewhat disconcerted by the fact that the sum total of Popper's contribution to this matter is three references to the fact that there is censorship, which, like Russell, he describes as 'rigid'. [41]

A standard defence of freedom of expression, in speech and writing, is that which we have already noticed in reference to Mill, the essence of which is that the existence of free speech makes it more likely that original and worthwhile ideas will be thrown up. Thus John Strachey writes: 'The whole intellectual life of the community depends, in my opinion, on there being the widest practical degree of freedom in this respect'. [42]

But this desire to prevent intellectual atrophy in the community is met in the Republic by the existence of the philosopher-kings whose interest in life is precisely intellectual enquiry. Furthermore, there is apparently no censorship of prose works that present intellectual arguments, but only of works that persuade or tempt the audience to undesirable behaviour by means of other than rational argument. [43] In other words it is the presentation of Achilles as at one and the same time a man to be admired and a man who behaves in an undesirable fashion that is objected to (or as a man who behaves undesirably and will in fact provoke emulation), and not the presentation of a thesis that attempts to argue that certain undesirable activities are not in fact undesirable.

It will be noted that Strachey refers to the 'widest practical degree of freedom in this respect'. He does not offer us any guidance as to how wide a degree might be practical, but he continues:

> It is perfectly true that in all communities there must be things people are not free to say or write. For example, no civilised community would tolerate an incitement in speech or writing to murder some particular individual; therefore, freedom of speech is a question of degree.

Now, of course, it is not a question of degree. It is a question of principle and justification. If it is once admitted that there must be things people are not free to say, then it becomes pertinent to enquire what things and for what reasons. Strachey's example of incitement to murder cannot be left to stand as self-evident. And if we pursue the matter it surely becomes clear that, essentially, we cannot allow incitement to murder, because we do not tolerate murder.

If it is accepted that the principle of freedom is not an ultimate principle, but that freedom of action may be restricted for some other end, it is difficult to see why freedom of expression should not be curbed for the same end. If a man may legitimately be restrained from performing an action which 'harms' others, then presumably he may be restrained from the act of speaking or writing, in so far as that 'harms' others. As already mentioned, what Popper means by 'harm' is not made explicit, but in general we may say that a person's view of what constitutes 'harm' can only be decided by reference to his other principles; and if this is not accepted, if rather 'harm' be understood in some restricted, possibly exclusively physical sense, those, such as the liberal-democrats, who also believe in the validity of other ultimate principles, cannot coherently argue, *both* that claims of conflicting principles cannot be judged, *and* that our judgment is wrong.

Expressing opinions, whether in speech or writing, can constitute the performance of what Mill called an other-regarding act; as such it may justifiably be restricted. When restriction of free expression is justified can only be decided by reference to the other values of society.

Selfish behaviour harms the community; Plato does not want individuals to grow up as selfish people, and he therefore restricts those who would continually hold before the community examples of selfishness that are to be regarded as commendable.[44] Censorship, considered as a restriction on certain types of speech or writing, namely those that promote enthusiasm for anti-social behaviour, seems no different in principle to restriction on other forms of other-regarding activity. If it is legitimate to restrict actions that harm the community, there seems to be no reason why one should not also restrict speech or writing that either harms the community directly or causes action that is harmful.

However, the real snub given to freedom by Plato is not contained in the laws restricting freedom of action or in the restriction of free expression, for it is to be assumed that few will come to oppose the laws or values of the community anyway. And the reason for this is that the citizens are going to be lulled into the acceptance of certain beliefs and attitudes from the start. Involved here are censorship again, considered primarily as a refusal to allow the individual to experience the promotion of certain ideas and values, and the indoctrination myth of the earth-born.

For the sake of ensuring happiness, the whole ethos of the Republic is designed to foster in the individual a sympathy for, and an approval of, the society and its values. Consequently Plato shows scant regard for the liberal-democratic conception of rationality, self-development, individualism and personal responsibility as educational aims. He does not recognise a restricted principle of autonomy, namely the principle that all men should hold only those beliefs and opinions that they have reasoned out for themselves, as being of ultimate status, any more than he recognises a general principle of autonomy or freedom. This is the fundamental point at issue between Plato and his critics, and it is of course possible that although consideration of happiness may override freedom in some spheres, nonetheless freedom of thought is something that we must recognise as being of such status that we may never legitimately infringe this freedom.

The arrangements of the Republic are such that all citizens in their early years will be brought up to accept the values of society and to abide by those conventions of society that are deemed to be morally desirable. At a later date some, the philosopher-kings who by definition are trained for, adept in and interested in such enquiry, will examine the basis and justification of these beliefs; the rest will receive no encouragement to do so, and the lack of emphasis on enquiry into such matters in society as a whole, maintained partly by censorship and partly by the fact that everybody has grown up with similar assumptions, will mean that there will be no stimulus to do so.

It should be recognised, therefore, that if this state of affairs is to be shown to be morally unacceptable, it will not be sufficient simply to establish that those who have a meaningful contribution to make and who want to make it should be allowed to enquire into the justification of society's values, particularly the ultimate values from which all others are derived. For formally this is what happens in the Republic, and the fact that Plato may be wrong in his assumption that all the philosopher-kings will agree with him that happiness is the supreme principle, so that there will be no dissension amongst those who control the ethos of society, is irrelevant. The question of whether the values that Plato would have society embody *are* desirable is quite distinct from the question of whether a society may legitimately inculcate adherence to those values that it does regard as desirable. The former question is one with which this whole book is concerned; the latter is the one on which we are now concentrating. And it is clear that in order to show that the Republic is unacceptable on this account it will have to be shown that all men ought to examine and justify for themselves the ultimate principles, and the derivative values, to which they and society as a whole are committed, whether they want to or not, and whatever their ability in such a task. We should recognise from the outset that this is a strong claim and considerably more imposing than the mere predeliction in favour of people who behave in a reasonable rather than an unreasonable manner or who can argue intelligently rather than expostulate absurdly, with which it is often confused.

The arrangements of the Republic are seen to raise two distinct questions: (a) is it wrong for children to be brought up to believe in certain values? and (b) is it wrong to allow some to continue to believe in those values, as adults, without having examined their justification? To both questions I shall return a negative answer, arrived at by means of an examination of the concept of 'indoctrination'.

3 Indoctrination

Although it is impossible to dispense with the word 'indoctrination', since it is much used in educational theory today, and since it is often applied to the *Republic* by critics, it is the attempt to discover what if anything is an inherently bad method, aim or content in a situation of potential influence that should be concentrated on. We can therefore dispense with the view of such men as Green,[45] who regards the holding of a belief without evidence as the hallmark of indoctrination, not because this view is 'false', but because on this view virtually everybody could be said to be indoctrinated and in a great many cases it would be impossible for this to be otherwise. One has neither the time, nor the means nor the ability to furnish oneself with the evidence necessary to establish all one's beliefs. And if this must, at least in some cases, be so, it is pointless to insist that it ought not to be so. It is also difficult to see how, on this view, one could insist that people ought not to indoctrinate, since, once again, it is often impossible to avoid fostering beliefs in others without providing evidence. A teacher with a strong charismatic personality may well cause his pupils either to share his beliefs or more simply to believe that he and his conduct are admirable, without intending to do so at all. Furthermore the liberal-democrats, with whom we are still primarily concerned, certainly do not dispute that in the case of young children who are not capable of understanding the evidence, we are obliged, to some extent at least, to foster the holding of beliefs without evidence. If children are to be dissuaded from indulging in murder, as they are on liberal-democratic terms since murder certainly falls within the obscure rubric that demands a restriction of activity that interferes with the freedom of others, then, in most instances, we shall be obliged to inculcate the belief that it is wrong before we can hope to provide the child with 'evidence' that it can grasp. We are concerned to discover whether there are things that we ought not to do when we are educating people. Green's analysis of 'indoctrination' draws attention to an inevitable feature of virtually everybody's life at some stage.

Some[46] wish to define 'indoctrination' in terms of certain techniques or methods of creating a particular mental outlook which are regarded as, in all circumstances, immoral. They are not primarily concerned with brutal methods, such as the use of rubber truncheons or torture, for it may readily be admitted that this sort of method is obnoxious *qua* activity in itself and not essential *qua* method of inculcation of beliefs. Rather, those who wish to define 'indoctrination' in terms of method, are concerned to object to the use of any non-rational techniques of persuasion, whether inherently brutal or not, popularly summarised as 'brainwashing'.

Let us assume, first, what is almost certainly not the case, that 'brainwashing' in the comic-strip sense of altering a man's beliefs at the throw of a switch were possible. Would it necessarily be wrong? As it is, we do countenance tampering with the brain, in the most literal sense, for our doctors are allowed to practice leucotomy, 'the cutting of white matter between the pre-frontal lobe and the thalamus in order to modify behaviour in certain mental cases'. Is this necessarily wrong?

It is not difficult to imagine the brainwashing switch being under the control of an evil and insane Professor Moriarty, and to throw up one's hands in horror at the thought of all that this might involve. But it is also possible to construct emotively more attractive examples: for instance, if it were possible at the throw of a switch to persuade a Hitler, who is about to exterminate a segment of mankind on what we regard as wholly absurd grounds, but who has shown himself impervious to rational argument, to change his mind, would it be wrong to throw the switch? Can one differentiate between the legitimacy of such brainwashing and the legitimacy of fighting against a Hitler on the strength of one's beliefs, or would a man who felt that we had no right on the strength of our beliefs to tamper with Hitler's beliefs be obliged, if he is to be consistent, to oppose also the idea of fighting on the strength of our beliefs?

It is surely evident, even at this stage, that one cannot answer these questions without appeal to one's ultimate moral principles. Those who approve leucotomy are implicitly placing the claims of something like the principle of utility before some offshoot of the principle of liberty, such as a respect for the sovereignty of the individual. And those who approve leucotomy, therefore, cannot consistently simply dismiss the idea of brainwashing Hitler as obviously objectionable; they would have to establish that such a practice would in some way militate against the claims of happiness. Conversely those who regard leucotomy and brainwashing as necessarily absolutely unjustifiable would be committing themselves to the view that something like the sanctity of the individual must override the claims of happiness.

All I wish to bring out here is that one's view of what constitutes indoctrination, in the sense of morally objectionable teaching or influence, is necessarily linked to one's other values. In point of fact, however, it is doubtful whether brainwashing in the throw of a switch sense is really feasible at the present time. White appositely quotes Schein's study of the *Chinese Indoctrination Program for Prisoners of War in Korea*, to support his contention that the term brainwashing 'does not refer to a new and awe-inspiring process of social control, but to a whole battery of techniques, many used since antiquity, to enforce belief: punishment, reward, group discussion, lectures, social isolation, interrogations, forced confessions, self criticisms'. And he concludes that 'it is wrong, therefore, to identify indoctrination with a process'.[47]

He is obviously correct in arguing that, if a combination of techniques such as he lists constitutes brainwashing, and if we wish to confine 'indoctrination' to use as a term of condemnation, we cannot regard it as marked out by the process above. But we need to go further than this and ask whether the use of any non-rational technique of persuasion to enforce belief must be wrong. The terms to concentrate on in the above list are reward and punishment, since such things as lectures may involve a rational justification for a belief, and such things as social isolation may be regarded as particular examples of techniques that are objectionable because brutal.

It would seem to me to be impossible to insist that the use of reward and punishment to enforce belief must be obnoxious simply because they are non-rational techniques of persuasion, and likewise impossible to insist that any other non-rational technique, such as example, approval or rebuke, is necessarily objectionable *qua* its non-rationality. First one may legitimately doubt whether any of those who decry the use of non-rational techniques are entirely consistent or sincere, since a father or teacher who never showed approval and never rebuked would be an interesting phenomenon. But secondly, and much more importantly, one could not sensibly argue for the elimination of non-rational techniques, since, as was pointed out in our consideration of Green's analysis of 'indoctrination', one cannot possibly avoid the influence of non-rational persuasion on any, such as young children in particular, who are not supremely rational. Even if one never praised or rebuked, never punished or rewarded, one would necessarily constitute an example that would impinge on the child. And even if the teacher managed to be such a faceless example, the child is bound to be subject to the praise, blame, approval, reward and punishment of his fellow children and the other members of society. A myriad of facts are liable to constitute a non-rational influence on the child: a broken home, the existence of a dominant mother, a childhood spent in the country, the forces of law and so on.

This being the case, to insist that the deliberate use of non-rational techniques of persuasion by such people as teachers is illegitimate, is not to insist that children shall only be subject to rational persuasion but to insist that they shall be subject to non-rational influence on a chance basis or at random.

The difference between the open and closed societies in this respect is therefore not one of kind. The closed society tends to ensure that all non-rational techniques point in the same direction and foster beliefs that are compatible with the ethos of society. But if this constitutes indoctrination the open society also indoctrinates, for a battery of influences, which we may summarise as social pressure, is brought to bear upon the child to persuade him both of the desirability of our way of life in general, and the worthiness of our values, notably freedom, and the limits of our tolerance in particular. The open society differs from the closed society in this respect only in as much as it tends to enforce belief in a smaller number of propositions, because it is committed to a small number of fixed beliefs.

None of this amounts to saying that it is particularly desirable that one should make extensive use of non-rational techniques in the upbringing of children. But it does amount to saying that where rational argument will not convince, as may be the case with young children or with the potential suicide overlooking the top of the Post Office Tower, the use of non-rational techniques of persuasion may be justified. The onus is on those who would argue that persuading a young child that it ought not to kick the girl next door, by means of exhibiting parental displeasure, is unacceptable, because it is a non-rational technique, to prove their point. And it is difficult to see how they can do this in view of the fact that, if the child is not susceptible to rational argument, it is to be presumed that his belief in the desirability of kicking the girl is itself the product of non-rational influence; indeed for the parent to refrain from expressing displeasure is itself a further non-rational influence on the child.

There seems no reason then to rule out all non-rational techniques of persuasion, as always unjustifiable, *qua* the fact that they are non-rational. And, if we wish to confine the use of the word 'indoctrination' to a morally objectionable activity, the concept therefore cannot be defined in terms of method or technique.

The favourite contender for the title of the essence of indoctrination amongst philosophers is the content. It is not certain methods that are necessarily repugnant, runs the argument, but the inculcation of certain types of opinion or belief. Flew[48] has suggested that indoctrination is marked by the implanting of certain beliefs which may be described as ideological beliefs; only beliefs which are not known to be true, and which belong to an ideology, can be indoctrinated. Atkinson[49] and Wilson,[50] likewise, see the inculcation of beliefs for which there is 'no publicly acceptable evidence' as morally objectionable. But who is to decide whether the belief being inculcated can be justified? Once again one's whole philosophical position would seem to be involved here. As Hare[51] points out, in his rescue bid on behalf of Wilson's lamentably weak position, the latter's transition from 'publicly acceptable evidence' to beliefs 'which are seen by every sane and sensible person to be agreeable and necessary', is quite inadequate. 'For who are to count as sane and sensible people?'

The suggestion that it is morally wrong to inculcate a belief, that cannot be known to be true or false, if it is part of an ideology is a very odd manoeuvre. The question of what an ideology is, of course, raises itself; I would agree with White that an ideology is, at least, a system of beliefs, and, with Corbett,[52] that further features of an ideology are that the beliefs involved 'taken together, should have important implications for a wide range of conduct', and that some of them 'should concern the general nature of man and of the world he lives in'. Communism, Nazism and Catholicism are thus clearly ideologies; but so, as Corbett realises, but e.g. Wilson apparently does not, is democratic theory an ideology. It may be a great deal less systematic, even coherent, than Nazism, but it nonetheless involves a system of inter-related ideas which concern the general nature of man, and the world he lives in, and have important implications for a wide range of conduct.

Now certainly the Nazis inculcated (by non-rational means) beliefs which cannot be proved to be true, and which formed part of a system, most notably the belief that the Aryans were born to rule the world; likewise the Catholics teach that only Catholics shall enjoy God's grace in the fullness of time as a lynch pin to a whole system of ideas that has obvious repercussions on life. But Wilson's belief that it is wrong to brainwash people to believe in communism is itself merely part of the liberal-democratic ideology: a system of ideas based on the unsubstantiated lynch-pin that 'Freedom is a necessary condition for social and individual progress, for the expansion and development of a personality or a society'.[53]

Naturally if one knows what this means (what for instance is the 'progress' of an individual or society?), and believes it, one is going to object to the inculcation of ideas that do not seem to conform with this particular ideology. But if one is a Catholic, who believes that the road to 'progress' is God's road, one is going to regard belief in God as of fundamental importance. 'We' says Wilson, 'value the human personality and do not want it to be diminished'. But we want to know what valuing the human personality means. Is it any more than a restatement of his objection to the habit of persuading people to believe in God or communism? What is needed is a convincing account of what constitutes diminishing the human personality, in such a way as to make it clear that it ought not to be done.

If, therefore, we drop the proviso that a belief must be ideological for it to be wrong to inculcate adherence to it, we are left, on this view of indoctrination, with the simple claim that it is wrong to inculcate belief in propositions that are not known to be true or false.

The suggestion that it is morally objectionable to inculcate belief in propositions which are not known to be true or false, or for which there is no publicly acceptable evidence, or which we do not even quite know how we would set about proving, throws into relief that question which continually besets us when we attempt to get to grips with the liberal-democrats. Do moral propositions fall into this category, or do they not? For it is only the inculcation of moral norms that Plato advocates and that I wish to defend.

Consider, for instance, at this crucial juncture, the contortions of Russell. He has argued, with considerable intensity, that it is objectionable and unjustifiable to inculcate belief in religious propositions, on the grounds that they are not known to be true. With the actual argument about religious propositions we are not here concerned. But since Russell regards ultimate moral values, from which specific norms are derived, as likewise not being 'matters as to which argument is possible',[54] it should follow that, as far as Russell is concerned, it is equally objectionable to inculcate belief in moral norms. And yet, wholly inconsistently, and also inconsistently with his strictures on Plato, Russell, in his educational writings, as has been pointed out, offers us an almost Platonic programme of conditioning to the moral norms of society, even concluding that 'a certain amount of uncompensated propaganda is necessary for the minimum of social cohesion'.[55] We are not to confine ourselves, for instance, to talking *about* kindliness or to rational arguments in its favour, but must promote a tendency to kindliness and hence a belief in its desirability by example.[56] The conclusion, of course, is one with which I fully concur. But in what direction is the Platonist to turn when Plato's most virulent critics come up with Platonic proposals that they have arrived at by inconsistent and contradictory reasoning?

However, Russell's inconsistency aside, we do not accept that

Freedom

no argument is possible and that one cannot reason about ultimate
values, not even on the assumption that Russell meant that one
cannot justify adherence to ultimate moral principles. (Obviously
it would be absurd to claim that one cannot reason at all in any way
about ultimate values; but we are saying more than this.)

It has been conceded that the truth of moral propositions cannot
be established with the dazzling effect of an empirical proof, and it
must also be acknowledged that other apparently equally intelligent
people do not agree that the Platonic value code is established as
commanding our assent. Nonetheless, while willingly keeping our
eye open for further liberal-democratic defences, I must claim to be
engaged in the task of showing that it is true that one ought to show
impartial consideration for all people's happiness, and that it is not
true that one ought to adhere to a principle of freedom in the manner
that the liberal-democrats do. I may be wrong, my argument may
contain fallacies, but in principle I am busy establishing the truth
of certain moral principles in the manner appropriate to the case.
How does one judge that an empirical test proves an empirical
proposition? One observes, and *one is convinced*. Conceivably one
might observe and not be convinced: how long did it take the Red
Indians to realise that it was true that guns killed people who stood
in the line of fire, and not merely an example of the infernal white
man's trading trickery? How does one judge that an argument
establishes a moral proposition? One follows it, and *one is convinced*.
The unfortunate fact is that the truth of anything rests *for us* on
conviction about some kind of proof. (N.B. The claim is *not* that
believing makes it true, but that our assent to the truth of it involves
our being convinced.)

If, however, the previous paragraph is regarded as unconvincing
and if the liberal-democrats insist that moral propositions are
amongst those that are not known to be true or false, it is my belief
that their case is severely weakened, not strengthened. If 'killing
people is wrong' or 'freedom is desirable' are merely conventional
norms, dependent for their adoption on the favourable attitude
towards them expressed by a community, and, if the community
is necessarily responsible for the non-rational influences that will
come to bear on children, it can hardly avoid influencing them
towards acceptance of these norms. To argue that our norms may
be invalid, and that therefore we ought to expose children to contrary influences, to redress the balance, is absurd, because, on the
present assumptions, our norms *cannot* be invalid: they are neither
valid nor invalid—they are simply norms that we approve. To
deliberately introduce influences that may destroy approval of
the norms in the next generation, is not to play fair and give that
generation a chance of making up its own mind—it is to interfere

as deliberately with the children as those who would advocate only influences that support the conventional norms.

We therefore reject the view that it must be morally wrong to inculcate belief in moral norms, that are not known to be true or false, on the following grounds:

(a) If the truth of ultimate moral propositions *cannot* be known, then one's adherence to certain specific propositions is ultimately a matter of taste or guesswork. Since the individual's taste and the direction of his guesses are the product of non-rational influences, such as examples he witnesses, the conduct of people he admires, the pressure of peer-groups, the fear of disapproval, the experiences of his childhood, or a search for affection, rather than rational proof, it would be absurd to regard inculcating adherence to norms as objectionable. In theory the view would lead to the conclusion that since such beliefs should not be inculcated by non-rational means, and since that is the only way they can arise, nobody ought to have any moral beliefs. In fact, of course, since one cannot bring children up in a vacuum, it would lead to beliefs being formed by chance and the random pressures of society, which would be worse from a utilitarian point of view, and no better from the point of view of those who object to the inducement of belief in propositions that are not known to be true or false.

(b) The true antithesis of believing that 'one ought to do X' is not believing that 'one ought not to do X', but *not* believing that 'one ought to do X', or believing that 'one is entitled to do X or not, as the mood has one'. To fail to foster a belief in the child that he ought to be kind is, therefore, to foster belief in the proposition that it does not matter whether he is kind or not. This proposition would be equally unproven, on the premiss, and therefore equally unworthy to be believed in. Since one or other proposition has to be believed in, we are being asked to avoid doing what cannot avoid being done.

The conclusion to be drawn from the previous pages is that it is not necessarily objectionable to bring up young children to believe in the values of society by means of non-rational techniques, whether the status of the principles on which those values are based is provable or not. This gives us a negative answer to the first of the the two questions we set out to consider. But the second question— is it wrong to allow some to continue to believe in those values, as adults, without having examined their justification?—has still to be answered. And this brings us on to White's definition of indoctrination in terms of intention, which is a refinement of Hare's argument that it is the 'aim' involved that might turn teaching into indoctrination.

In my view the intentional analysis of indoctrination is to be preferred to others, because, I think, it gives the most plausible account of what people in general might be thought to object to. It is simply not the case that people in general, who would claim to object to indoctrination, object to the use of non-rational techniques of persuasion in respect of social values with their young children, whatever the ultimate justification of those values. And it is surely much more plausible to argue that what people in general might most readily be thought to object to is that one should intend that people 'should believe that "p" [a proposition] is true, in such a way that nothing will shake this belief'.[57] The great advantage of this analysis is that, unlike the others we have considered, it avoids the problem caused by the fact that it is impossible in the case of young children to avoid the assumption of values as a result of non-rational influence.

But the question of whether we can argue that it is necessarily wrong to inculcate the belief that 'p' is true in such a way that nothing will shake this belief, as opposed to admitting that most people in calling this 'indoctrination' feel that it is wrong, is entirely separate. I have to accept some analysis, since the word exists, even if I cannot accept the pejorative overtones. What we have to consider, then, is whether it is necessarily wrong to inculcate belief in moral propositions in such a way that some individuals at least will cling to these beliefs unreflectingly.

The contention that a belief must not be implanted so that nothing will shake it has certain oddities. At the time of inculcating or developing the belief one must obviously want it to stick. There is no conceivable point in getting the child to believe that it is wrong to kick the girl next door, if it is entirely acceptable that he should go home, reject the belief, and give her a good kick. Once one has accepted that the belief inculcated is supposed to last for at least a period of time—and indeed it would scarcely be a belief in any meaningful sense, if it did not last for some time—one has implicitly accepted that there are reasons that justify the inculcation of a belief in such a way that it shall be firmly held. Consequently we have to understand the 'intentional' analysis of 'indoctrination' as accepting that beliefs may legitimately be induced in the young child in such a way that they are held with conviction, provided that the child may later come to assess the plausibility of the belief for himself. And most liberal-democrats would go further and say not only that he should be able to, but that he ought to.

At this point we have to consider what arguments the liberal-democrats can produce to justify the assertion that the individual ought to be brought to examine and assess the strength of his own ultimate beliefs (for they are 'his own' beliefs, however he came by them). On the face of it this demand is a gross interference with the privacy and freedom of the individual, that refuses to allow him to rest comfortably in the faith of those beliefs that he has grown up with. Can this interference be justified?

Two arguments may be put forward, the first dependent on the fact that all parties to this dispute are committed to rationality, the second on the fact that they are committed to truth. We shall consider both, in turn.

There are, of course, some very pertinent reasons for advocating a stress on 'rationality' in one particular sense. If by 'rationality' we mean to summarise such procedural qualities as consistency, impartiality, coherence and relevance, then it is clearly desirable that every individual should be encouraged to be as 'rational' as possible about the matters he discusses, particularly in a democracy where every individual has an important role to play and the prospects for the community look that little bit more hopeful, if some of the electorate are capable of avoiding self-contradiction. In Crossman's muted words: 'It is no use giving a man a vote unless he can use it'.[58]

It should be clear to any reader of Plato that he is a staunch champion of 'rationality' in the sense of consistency, impartiality, etc. The *Republic* is perhaps the most consistent and logical work ever written, and that it is impartial I shall argue in the next chapter. But it is quite another matter to insist that *all* people ought at some time or another to examine and question *all* the ideas, opinions and values that they happen to hold or come across. And it is this latter claim that would have to be made to upset Plato. For, of course, there is no reason to suppose that the citizens of the Republic do not 'make [their] own reasoned judgment'[59] about most things. All they are not encouraged to do is to worry about establishing by their own reasoned judgment the ultimate values or assumptions in the light of which they do their other reasoning. Why and on what grounds do the liberal-democrats assert that all men ought to do this?

From the premiss, which I accept, that it is desirable that thought be 'rational' in the sense of consistent, impartial, etc., one cannot move to the conclusion that people who think about more things are morally superior to those who think about less; consequently one cannot move from this premiss to the conclusion that the individual ought to question as many of his assumptions as possible. Conceivably one might argue empirically that the more things one enquires into, the more practice one has, the more rational in the sense of consistent, impartial, etc., one becomes. But, even if this argument could be empirically validated, it still would not show that one ought to enquire into the justification of one's ultimate values: there are plenty of other things to practise on.

The liberal-democrats confuse an approval of rational, as opposed to irrational behaviour and argument, with an approval of the exercise of pursuing the rational justification of things. As one who approves of rationality, I cannot consistently approve of the individual who holds contradictory opinions or whose arguments appear to be irrational. But it is quite consistent for me to approve of the relatively unreflective individual, provided that he does not have opinions which strike me as irrational and that when he does argue or act he does so in a rational manner.

Let us imagine that two children, one intelligent and one relatively unintelligent, have reached a certain age with an attitude of affection towards others and a belief in the proposition that one ought not to kick other people. How could one substantiate that they ought to question the attitude and ask themselves whether they have good grounds for having it? They feel affectionate, and that is all there is to it. However, the attitude presumably gives rise to certain behavioural tendencies, such as the refusal to kick people, and in turn gives rise to the question 'Ought they to refrain from kicking other people?' This brings us to the second argument put forward by the liberal-democrats in favour of the idea that all people ought to examine all their opinions. For it may legitimately be pointed out that if we say that such propositions ought not to be questioned, we are either showing no concern for truth, or assuming that the truth is as we see it, neither of which conclusions is acceptable to the philosopher. We desire that society should continue to question.

But this desire is met by the Republic where the philosopher-kings continue to question, just as they continue to make sure that the society is grounded on rational principles, the fact that Plato thinks they will continue to accept his cardinal principles being irrelevant; for nothing can stop them rejecting them if they choose to do so. The more intelligent of the two children may therefore be encouraged to enquire into the justification of the moral injunction, which is to say no less than that he may undertake the pursuit of a branch of philosophy. But we cannot even say that he *ought* to do this, because it does not follow from the fact that we approve of truth, that we approve of everyone enquiring into the truth of each and every thing. And are we to say that the less intelligent boy ought to be encouraged to question his conviction? Is he necessarily able to do so in any meaningful sense?

If the liberal-democrats are to establish that it is wrong for any individual to accept the values of society unreflectively, they need to do two things: they need, if they are to make use of our admitted commitment to truth and rationality, to establish that all men can make a meaningful contribution to the search for true and rational principles, and that the search cannot succeed unless all men do contribute to it. And, of course, before they could hope to establish either they would need to clear up the ambiguities in their view of the status of ultimate principles. For if one takes the view that moral norms are essentially a matter of subjective assent without the possibility of ultimate rational justification, it follows, in the first place, that the demand for substantiation of the truth of ultimate principles is pointless, and in the second place, incidentally, that objection to the refusal of a society to impose this pointless exercise on its citizens, would itself be merely an expression of taste without significance to others who do not share it.

If, on the other hand, as we believe, ultimate values may be in some significant sense more or less reasonable, one presumably has ways of judging this reasonableness and hence ways of judging people's competence to make reasonable contributions to this enquiry.

What, then, are we to say that the criteria for a meaningful contribution are? The liberal-democrats tend to lay stress on a distinction between such things as the sphere of medicine and the sphere of moral propositions, and argue that whereas some people's contributions to a discussion on cardiac arrests may be judged irrelevant, this is not the case with discussions on moral principles where anybody might come up with a significant suggestion. Certainly in a discussion on ethics anybody might come up with a suggestion such as that X is good or that we ought to do Y. But if it comes to that I might come up with a good idea for dealing with cardiac arrests, albeit it would be a shot in the dark based on no knowledge. And the problem in the ethical sphere is surely not a dearth of proposed goods or injunctions; it is rather the substantiation of any that have been or might be proposed. A person making a meaningful contribution would have to do more than utter random suggestions; he would need to argue in support of a given suggestion and understand and meet objections.

Clearly the sort of criteria for establishing whether somebody is competent to contribute to such an enquiry are the very things that the liberal-democrats have been urging on us as valuable: consistency, an eye for relevance, concern for truth, avoidance of false premises (some of which may be factual), and impartiality. And those are the very qualities that Plato demands in his philosopher-kings.[60] No doubt it is often difficult to judge whether an individual lacks these qualities or whether we are misunderstanding him, no doubt also they are very broad and need more elucidation if they are to be of much practical use. But for our present purposes all we need to point out is that it is manifestly empirically the case that some people are inconsistent, partial, irrelevant and disinterested in the truth when they argue or discuss. Certainly we shall wish to discourage them from these tendencies when they are engaged in discussion, but our immediate point is that it is an empirical fact that such people do not make a meaningful contribution to the search for the truth about ultimate principles, and therefore the liberal-democrats cannot maintain that all men can make a meaningful contribution.

It may be argued that although it is obviously the case that some individuals are incapable of making a meaningful contribution as things are, nonetheless there is no necessary reason why this should be so, and we might reasonably aim to make all people proficient in this matter. I feel that we are entitled to have very strong doubts about the empirical likelihood of all men becoming proficient, especially since, if we were to pursue this as an aim, besides ensuring that all were rational, impartial, and concerned for the truth, we should have to ensure familiarity with, and understanding of, the nature of philosophical debate on ethical matters (for such debate is, after all, carried on with what we may call its distinctive jargon) and interest in the enquiry. But even if the empirical possibility could be established, which one doubts, this still would not show that we ought to make everybody join in on this search, for our desire to find the truth only leads to the conclusion that everybody ought to partake in it, if it can be established that the truth cannot be found without the participation of everybody. And this seems a wholly ludicrous suggestion, especially as a counter-suggestion to an arrangement whereby those who are already engaged in enquiring into this matter, the philosopher-kings, are by definition as well-equipped for the task, in terms of interest, concentration, and rationality, as the society in question can hope any man will be. Furthermore, this whole preoccupation with getting everybody in on the search for truth in the moral sphere presupposes that there is a truth to be found, which is quite in-inconsistent with the liberal-democratic objections to Plato on the grounds that he thinks he knows the truth in a sphere where it cannot be known. If he cannot know, how are we to know when one of the liberal-democratic recruits has hit upon the truth? And if we cannot judge that, why is his contribution supposed to be so useful?

We reject, then, the suggestion that all men might be brought to make a meaningful contribution to the search for the truth about ultimate values, in the absence of empirical evidence for this view, and that all men can do so equally as things are, in view of the clear empirical evidence against this view. And in any case we reject the suggestion that the truth is more likely to be found if more people are searching for it. Consequently, despite our own commitment to truth and rationality (understood as consistency, impartiality, etc.), we reject the claim that we are therefore committed to enlisting all in the search for rational justification of ultimate principles. We see no good grounds for agreeing that all men ought to examine the justification of their beliefs, and therefore we deny the claim that it must be wrong to bring up children with beliefs that they continue to hold staunchly without examining them for themselves, and return a negative answer to the second of the two questions we asked above.

Nothing that has been said by the liberal-democrats supports the contention that there is a moral obligation on us to bring up all children in such a way as to encourage them to assume that their moral beliefs have not been substantiated, and that therefore they must work out for themselves whether they think that there is good reason for abiding by them. Nothing has been said to substantiate the claim that it is wrong for a child to be allowed to grow up simply believing that the little girl next door ought not to be kicked. The statement that it would seem more reasonable to bring the child up to appreciate the grounds for the ultimate beliefs in question is without foundation, although formally this is what happens in the Republic to those who are capable of understanding the philosophical argument. But there is no reason why all who could understand the argument, should have to study it. The claim that it is more reasonable that they should, plays upon the ambiguity in the term 'reasonable'; reasonable people respond to reasoning and act in a manner that can be justified by reasoning. But one is not more reasonable because one does more active reasoning; one can behave reasonably without understanding the reasons that make one's behaviour reasonable. It is no more reasonable to insist that people understand why not kicking people is such a good idea, than it is to insist that people understand how moon-rockets work.

Attempts to validate a limited principle of autonomy (i.e. the claim that all people ought to think out the substantiation of all their beliefs) by reference to rationality and truth do not lead to this conclusion. And all other liberal-democratic arguments for a general principle of autonomy, in so far as they succeed in convincing us that autonomy can be desirable, are dependent for their force on some other principle, most notably the principle of happiness. We therefore conclude that freedom of thought, like other freedoms, may legitimately be restricted.

4 Plato and indoctrination

Those, such as Plato, who wish to indoctrinate, wish to do so for a reason. We therefore finally need to consider what reasons may actually justify indoctrination.

Let us suppose that 'p' be something which is demonstrably false, for instance that the taking of drugs involves certain death within a month. But suppose also that the truth is that one in ten drug takers do die, two in ten become incapacitated, and yet no amount of repeating these true and dire warnings seems to discourage people from taking the risk, and thus bringing misery to their friends and relatives (and perhaps themselves), and confusion and stultification to the national economy and hence way of life of the community. In those unlikely circumstances the Platonist would argue that it was justifiable, assuming it was possible, to set about convincing everybody that the original (false) proposition was true in such a way that nothing would shake the belief, so that, even if presented with a case of someone who had taken drugs for some months before and was still alive, people would simply refuse to believe that he had taken drugs. And, of course, in so arguing the Platonist makes it clear that the claims of happiness override other considerations, in this case a premium on truth and objection to indoctrination.

The point is that liberal-democrats are committed to a principle of happiness, and despite the difficulties we have experienced in analysing the concept, it is at least clear that misery plays no part in it. What one begins to wonder is whether the claims of happiness are ever going to be allowed to achieve anything. Why is it, if happiness is an ultimate principle not inferior to any other, that it *must* be wrong to indoctrinate for the sake of happiness?

The model cases of indoctrination selected by Wilson—communism, Catholicism—indicate that what is really objected to is a situation in which people are not free to form their own beliefs either from the beginning or at any rate at a suitable later juncture. This is what all absolute opponents of indoctrination, whether they pin their analysis to content, method or aim or some combination, object to. But there are two objections to their objection: one is that this involves the assumption that this freedom overrides the claims of happiness (or else that it contributes to it, which we have rejected), and this those who believe in a principle of happiness of *equal* weight to a principle of freedom cannot maintain. The other is that it is a nonsense to talk of people literally forming their own beliefs and opinions. And once one holds a belief that cannot be proven or disproven, it is a nonsense to talk of weighing up its truth for oneself; and if it can be proven true or false, the question is whether it *is* true or false, not whether the individual can understand that it is true or false.

Hare refers to a man who says that he is 'absolutely determined not to influence his child's moral growth in any way'[61] lest he diminish its human personality. One can only feel sorry for any child so neglected, and Hare himself agrees that this is 'obviously absurd . . . we cannot help influencing our children; the only question is, how, and in what direction'.

The answer is obviously in the direction of one's ultimate beliefs, which, for both Plato and the liberal-democrats, include happiness. Thus we should influence our children in the direction of believing in the promotion of happiness and of holding those beliefs that will enhance happiness; and, for the purpose of enmeshment, that will involve taking account of the society in which he lives and other beliefs, if any, that are regarded by the society as morally essential. If the liberal-democrats wish also to influence our children in the direction of believing in the promotion of freedom, they need to substantiate, as they have failed to do, that freedom is an independent ultimate moral principle of equal weight to the principle of happiness. And of course they also need to do that, or at least to substantiate an ultimate principle of freedom of thought, if they are to produce significant objection to our intention of influencing children in the direction of the happiness principle with the aim that this influence shall remain effective. So long as they acknowledge happiness as an ultimate principle they cannot establish that one ought not to indoctrinate for its sake; and so long as they cannot substantiate a principle of autonomy without reference to other principles they cannot object to indoctrination for any end deemed desirable.

The question of how we should influence our children is answered by finding a method that works and which is not morally repugnant. Happiness being the supreme moral principle, methods that involve cruelty are objectionable, for instance. But such methods as example and censored material that reinforces example are, in so far as they are efficacious, entirely acceptable.

Plato tells his citizens a myth that will persuade them that some were born to rule, being fashioned with an admixture of gold, others to be Guardians, those imbued with silver, the rest, of iron and brass, to form the largest group.[62] Behind the myth he is saying that some are qualified by their nature to undergo the upbringing that will fit them to rule well (which means justly, and with the happiness of the whole community in mind as the end), others to be farmers and producers; in addition the myth will foster a sense of unity and brotherhood by stressing that they are all of common stock.[63]

I do not see how we can avoid calling this 'indoctrination', regardless of our own preferred analysis of that term. Plato's intention is confessedly to tell a story that will 'persuade'[64] and he wonders whether he can hope to 'get them to believe';[65] the purpose of getting them to believe would be completely nullified if it were not also the intention that nothing should shake their belief. The beliefs being inculcated are also ideological in the sense outlined above; nor could the content, being literally fabulous, be regarded as belonging to that corpus of propositions for the truth or falsehood of which there is publicly acceptable evidence. The method is not specified, but the use of the word 'persuasion' coupled with the nature of the content and the conclusion to be drawn from the myth, make it clear that we are dealing with non-rational techniques.

One thing however we should note: despite the fact that Popper refers to the myth as Plato's 'greatest propaganda lie',[66] Crossman as 'a convenient falsehood',[67] and Russell as 'elaborate lying to persuade the population that there are biological differences between the upper and lower classes',[68] it is not a lie in any meaningful sense. It must be admitted that the word 'lie' in this context arises out of Plato's own introduction of the myth as a 'necessary lie' and a 'lie in respect of a worthy end'.[69]

The fact remains that the myth is not a lie. It is called a *pseudos* by Plato because that word is far less restricted in meaning than the English word 'lie'.[70] For us the word 'lie' is very narrow in meaning: it cannot really mean other than an unjustifiable false statement made with intent to deceive, and if we wish to suggest that a certain lie is justified we have to qualify the word either explicitly or by calling it 'white' or 'innocent'. By contrast the Greek word *pseudos* simply denotes an absence of a truth quotient and may as easily be applied to a fable or myth as to what we would call a falsehood or lie.

But the crucial point is that, although the question of the truth or falsehood of an allegorical fable cannot really arise, the idea that Plato wishes to get across to his citizens by this means is in fact true. The aim is to prevent those who by background, training and aptitude belong to one group, from thinking that they could as well belong to another group, or that they have a right to. One cannot object that there are no distinctions to be made between the members of the three groups, because there are by definition. The groups arise by classification according to three different sets of criteria. If one argues that citizens in one group have a right to belong to another, the answer is that they certainly do not have a legal right in this society and if the claim is that they have a moral right that claim needs substantiation. But how would one substantiate the claim that I have a right, for instance, to be a farmer or a policeman, except on the general grounds that I have a right to be whatever I want to be? Besides the fact that this general principle of freedom has been found to be without substantiation, even the liberal-democrats do not really think that if a man wants to be a policeman he ought to be able to be one, regardless of his abilities and character.

That there are difficulties in seeing how (in practice) there is
going to be very much transference between Plato's groups is
admitted.[71] But the essential principle of Plato's arrangements is
not therefore invalidated: that is that people are born with different
potential, and that in a community different people are going to
have to do different things, and that therefore people ought to be
educated with a view to these two factors. The sensible course is to
provide them in adult life with a way of life that suits the aptitudes
and abilities that have been developed out of their potential.
Education is therefore a process of developing the actual, with a
view to the appropriate ultimate, nature of the individual.

Now, of course, none of this justifies Plato's particular society
nor the ways of life he allots to his various groups. All we have
pointed out is that his principles are that education should be fitted
to the needs of the individual both now (the needs of his nature),
and for the future (the needs of his way of life). His belief is that,
at birth, one can see whether a child is suited for one type of upbringing or another. (Not, N.B., whether a child is actually suited
to belong as an adult to one group or another, because that can only
come about through the all-important reinforcement of upbringing).
Our belief is that it will take longer than that to see whether a child
is by nature suited to the development of 'a philosophic disposition,
energy, acuteness, and strength of mind and body',[72] which are
essential for those who would watch over the interests of the community. But that one can distinguish between the slothful disposition, and the acute, the philosophic and the coarse, I do not see that
one can deny.

Plato is therefore in the position of having classified people
into one of three groups by straightforward criteria which he regards
as justifiable. One group is going to rule because it contains those
best suited to rule: the criterion used for allotting individuals to
this group was fitness to rule. Consequently the education of this
group will also be suited to the end of producing good rulers. The
situation is similar in respect of the other two groups. Details of
the education of the largest group are not given for three reasons:
(a) Their education is essentially to be differentiated by the fact
that it does not contain the lengthy and intense intellectual programme demanded, in varied degree, from the other two groups:
firstly because by definition these people are not suited to the
education, and it is not suited to their adult way of life; secondly,
because they will not wish, nor be able, to continue their education
until the age of fifty, as the future rulers must. (b) One presumes
that since these people will lead lives akin to the average Athenian
of Plato's time, as small-time farmers, artisans, etc., their education
will be similar to that in force in Athens, save only that Homer

will have been censored and they, the citizens, will have imbibed the myth. By our standards this education is minimal; there is nothing to stop us expanding and enriching it provided we do not ignore the nature of the pupils and their future role in life. (c) Plato does not think the details of their education need concern him as much as the details of the education of his two other groups. This annoys Popper, as does Plato's remark that 'the community suffers nothing very terrible if its cobblers are bad and become degenerate',[73] and what Popper sees as Plato's refusal to legislate for people of the largest group, and for their petty problems. The passage cited by Popper for this last accusation does not support it.[74] The refusal is not to legislate for the petty problems of any particular class; it is a refusal to 'legislate for minor matters . . . such as keeping one's hair tidy . . . [because] laws and regulations won't either produce them or maintain them'. Popper's mistake in general on this point is to confuse the fact that Plato does not think certain details to be part of his brief (laws on hair), and regards certain points as less important to the correct running of society, with the idea that Plato doesn't care. It is surely obvious that corruption in positions of importance to the state is more critical to the well-being of the state, and hence its members, than corruption in those whose behaviour does not affect the state as a whole. That is what Plato means and says.[75]

All this being the case it follows, as I have said, that the belief that Plato wishes to instil is true. The second part of the myth which attempts to foster a sense of unity by postulating a common mother to all the citizens on Earth itself, may or may not be regarded as putting across a truth, depending entirely on whether one believes in any unity between men, *qua* men. It is odd that this part of the myth has been overlooked by the critics, except in so far as they can use it to reinforce their claim that Plato is busy constructing a sentiment of *Republik über alles*. It is, of course, an undoubted fact that a sense of national unity can be turned into a sense of national superiority, and from there one may advance to a position of literal attempts at national supremacy. But Plato's society, again, it must be admitted, unrealistically from a modern point of view, is expressly designed to be self-sufficient and without access to the rest of the world. The principle of fostering unity is therefore to be seen as fostering the unity of all who are involved in contact with one another; an extension of this idea leads one to the notion of fostering unity between a larger community, first (historically speaking) a country, then, one hopes, a world community. Anyway, one can hardly object to the fostering of national unity on the grounds that it may turn sour, for national disunity already is sour. On the face of it, the picture of rulers and ruled regarding each other as brothers, not to mention each individual thinking in this way of his neighbour, is precisely the ideal we wish to realise. Behind the myth Plato is in fact arguing that (a) People are different in certain respects (b) These respects make a difference to the sort of thing they are most suited to do (c) Nonetheless these differences are not relevant criteria for regarding people as worthy of more or less consideration as people.[76]

These points being established, it only remains to enquire whether the telling of this myth, with the intention that it shall promote a belief that will not be forsaken, is offensive.

The answer is that it is not, as we have seen. If it is asked why it is not *explained* to the citizens that all men are deserving of equal consideration, why happiness is the supreme principle, why some are better suited to joinery than adjudicature and why one ought to obey the laws of the community, the immediate answer is that we are dealing with children under ten who would not understand the rational argument, nor perhaps be interested in it.[77] If it be asked why, when they become adult, all are not encouraged to examine these beliefs for themselves, the answer is the same: some people are not very good at examining such beliefs, and some people are not interested in so doing. If this were not so, indeed if it *is* not the case that some people are unable to make good use of, and to understand rational justifications, so far as the case allows of them, then there would be no need of the myth. The rational justification, in the form of the *Republic*, is there waiting to be read by those who have the ability and the interest to read it. All that is being denied is that it is society's moral obligation to insist that the individual who is not capable of understanding, and who has not the patience or desire to read the *Republic*, should nonetheless do so. All that is being denied is that the liberal-democrats have any right to control our schools in such a way as to ensure that we do not believe things if we ourselves cannot prove them in a scientific manner.

It is being done in the interests of happiness, on the grounds that those who have to live within a society that makes demands that they do not believe in, cannot enmesh with that society, and that a society that does not aim at promoting happiness, at the expense of freedom where necessary, cannot ensure happiness. Moral beliefs are beliefs upon which one acts, that is why there is no point in having them, unless one is truly committed to them and has a belief that amounts to conviction.

5 Conclusion

The premium placed on freedom today has, needless to say, many causes. There is the psychological point that, having arrived at a point at which we question impositions on our freedom from without, we begin to simply dislike being told what to do; the advances of intellectual pursuit of truth have so successfully shaken our unquestioning belief in the validity of first principles and the assumptions of convention, that there seems little reason to accept somebody else's opinion in preference to our own: there may or may not be a distinction between the wise and foolish, the cogent argument and the illogical, but the foolish and illogical are not generally the first to recognise their shortcomings. In the meantime, who are they to follow the unprovable first principles of others? The cult of Romanticism with its stress, in the personal field, on the power and reality of the individual's feeling, which rapidly becomes a stress on the importance of that feeling as a guide for action, has also contributed to the high evaluation of individualism; and in a wider sphere the swashbuckling hero of the high seas, recently metamorphosised into the 'loner' of pop-culture, has emphasised the glory of the independent agent. The attraction of the image has also, no doubt, been increased by the failures, perhaps hardly unexpected, of various governments, institutions and bureaucratic groups.

But, whatever the reasons, the ideal of a world of autonomous beings, a world in which the individual is free 'to do his own thing', is now widely held. The odd feature of this ideal is the use that is made of it in practice. There is no compelling reason why we should not believe that Plato also shared this ideal, if by 'ideal' we mean an image of what a perfect world would be like. An ideal world would presumably contain ideal people, and consequently it would be a world in which people spontaneously and cheerfully chose to behave in whatever manner the dreamer believes to be important. For Plato it would be a world in which people were all sufficiently perfect to be able to live together harmoniously. He does not believe that the details of the various individuals' ways of life are important, provided that there is no conflict. His *Republic* is based upon the empirical assumption that unless certain things are done, and unless they are co-ordinated by a group whose sole concern is to do 'what is in the interests of the whole community',[78] people will in fact behave selfishly and unjustly. So far as the ideal goes, a world in which people behave justly and unselfishly of their own accord, there is no dispute. The question is one of practicability: without control how will people behave? And to what extent can we hope, by promoting a considerable degree of freedom for the individual in society now, to move ever more surely to the realisation of the ideal? More especially to what extent can we hope to promote the ideal by opting for more freedom in education? The rules and proposals of the *Republic* are not laid down in the belief that certain people do not count or that they have no right to consideration, but in the belief that they will guard against the innate undesirable tendencies in man's nature.[79] The liberal-democrats would have a case against Plato if they could establish the empirical claim that without deliberately initiating children into certain values, but instead with deliberate promulgation of the idea that each individual should question and decide norms of conduct for himself, and with as few rules and restrictions as possible, society will produce individuals who will choose to behave in a desirable manner, which is to say at least, from the liberal-democratic point of view, in accord with the principles of happiness and equality. And they must bear in mind that evidence that some people may do this is not enough, for rules and restrictions seldom arise to meet a situation in which all would otherwise act in an undesirable manner, but rather to coerce a minority. If even a few grow up with the intention of ignoring the interests of others if they can get away with it, the ideal is soured and we need some form of restriction. We can only say that the evidence for this idealism is sadly lacking.

What the liberal-democrats do not have a case for is the blanket use they make of 'freedom', so that whenever they find a proposal distasteful they imagine it to be sufficient to discredit it to say that it restricts freedom. Full stop. And in this connection we should also note a tendency they have to use a number of other terms, generally without any attempt at elucidation or justification, as if they were self-evident goods. Examples, taken from Popper, are: self-development, self-determination, personal responsibility, independence, 'the voice of conscience',[80] 'intellectual freedom . . . with which one must not lightly interfere',[81] and individualism.

The notion of 'self-development' is logically odd-man-out in this list, since the notion of development presupposes that we focus on the (at least relatively) undeveloped, which is to say the young child. But it is inconceivable that the young child should literally develop itself in a complex social milieu. The mere fact of putting a child in school, whatever the nature of the school, is a deliberate control of influences on the individual, and since the child develops in response to non-rational influences, we are developing him along some lines rather than others. One does not interfere with a child's development any less, because, for instance, one places him in a school where there is a minimum of regulation and authority. One merely influences him in a different way. One does not leave him to form his own attitudes and values, one merely abdicates a certain degree of responsibility for the formation of those attitudes to chance. But development in accordance with random influences is not self-development. Or, rather, we should perhaps say that it is, and that

K   135 the only sense that can be made of the term is to take it as chance-development.

Self-determination (and indeed self-development, applied to the older child) is not a patently absurd notion, since obviously it is to be understood as the principle of each individual reasoning out his own convictions. But at once we see that it, and all the other slogans listed above, are not distinctive and self-evident goods, any more than censorship and indoctrination are distinctive and self-evident evils, but are dependent for their prescriptive value on the substantiation of a certain view of freedom.

It is consequently quite insufficient for Popper to 'argue' that 'individualism', in the sense of 'the free and independent action of the individual', is desirable simply by referring to 'the emancipation of the individual'[82] as evidently desirable and opposed by Plato. He also talks vaguely of 'a happy versatility and self-reliance'[83] and contrasts Plato's ideal that 'the individual should subserve the interest of the whole', in the sense that the individual should not put his own interests before those of the mass of his fellow citizens, should they conflict. Popper tries to suggest that Plato wrongly identifies 'individualism' with 'egoism', and he offers a chart to show that the two need not be identified.[84] Of course they need not. Though if the individual is to be encouraged to ignore the interests of the community, that in itself is egoistic. Finally Popper talks of 'the rights of human individuals', which once again begs the question.

What are these rights? Where is their justification? All that is clear is that the prescriptive element in 'individualism' is dependent on the substantiation of a principle of autonomy or freedom.

Substantiation for a principle of freedom of ultimate status has not been produced. We therefore have no reason to treat the claims of freedom as of equal weight to those of happiness, and, in any case, on liberal-democratic terms it could not be wrong to put happiness before freedom logically, and they often seem to claim that we ought to do just that. A limited principle of autonomy, involving the claim that no individual ought to be allowed to accept ultimate values as true on trust, is also without substantiation.

We must therefore accept that the principle of freedom can only be understood as involving the formal claim that reasons must be given for interfering with the freedom of others. Whether those reasons are acceptable must be decided in the light of our ultimate moral principles or principle, one of which may not be the principle of freedom. This is, in fact, what the liberal-democrats do sometimes. This is what Plato does consistently.

Notes

1 Crossman, op. cit.
2 Seventh Letter, 354.
3 557 E.
4 Mill, *On Liberty*, in *Utilitarianism*, chapter 1. 'It is proper to state that I forgo any advantage which could be derived to my argument from the idea of abstract right, as a thing independent of utility. I regard utility as the ultimate appeal on all ethical questions' p. 136.
5 Ibid., p. 138.
6 Ibid., p. 135ff.
7 Benn, S. I. and Peters, R. S., *Social Principles and the Democratic State*, Allen & Unwin, London, 1959, p. 220.
8 Mill, *On Liberty*, p. 135.
9 Cf. Fromm, op. cit.
10 Mill, *On Liberty*, p. 194.
11 Thucydides, 1.10.
12 Benn and Peters, op. cit., p. 228.
13 Mill, *On Liberty*, p. 184.
14 Ibid., p. 205.
15 Popper, op. cit., p. 42. 557 B.
16 *Laws*, 743.
17 *Laws*, 701.
18 'Freedom' is 'an aim of our civilisation', Popper, op. cit., p. 1. 'Freedom' is an 'ideal of progressive thought', Crossman, op. cit., p. 84.
19 Mabbot, J. D., *The State and the Citizen*, Hutchinson, London, 2nd edn, 1967, p. 14.
20 Dearden, R. F., *The Philosophy of Primary Education*, Routledge & Kegan Paul, London, 1968, p. 47.
21 Op. cit., p. 113.
22 Mabbot, op. cit., p. 63.
23 Popper, op. cit., p. 34ff.
24 Dearden, *The Philosophy of Primary Education*, p. 46.
25 Dearden, R. F., 'Autonomy and education' in Dearden, Hirst and Peters, op. cit., p. 448ff.
26 Ibid., p. 460.
27 Ibid., p. 461.
28 Popper, op. cit., p. 110.
29 Crossman, op. cit., p. 101.
30 See chapter 7.
31 Peters, R. S., *Ethics and Education*, p. 180.
32 Benn and Peters, op. cit., p. 221.
33 459 E.
34 461 B.
35 Crossman, op. cit., chapter 7. (Quotation p. 118.)
36 387 B.
37 396 A. For censorship proposals, see 377ff and, above, chapter 2.

38 395 D.

39 Crombie, I., *An Examination of Plato's Doctrines*, Routledge & Kegan Paul, London, 1962, p. 91.

40 Aristophanes, *Frogs*, 1009, 1030ff, 1420. Cf. Plato's own repeated appeals to Homer as an authority in the *Republic*, even after the censorship proposals, e.g. 404 C, 441 B, 468 D. Cf. also Cephalus's reference to Pindar, 331 A; Polemarchus's use of Simonides, 331 E; Glaucon's appeal to Aeschylus, 361 E; and Adeimantus's claim that parents 'cite the poets' for moral law, 364 C.

41 Popper, op. cit., pp. 53, 86, 132.

42 Strachey, J., *The Challenge of Democracy*, Encounter Pamphlet, 10.

43 This at any rate would appear to be the implication of 607ff., where we are told that it is the 'honeyed muse of lyric and epic', which is specifically contrasted with philosophy, that is to be censored. And lovers of poetry are to be free 'to plead her cause in prose'.

44 'Shall we tell stories so that children take into their minds opinions for the most part contrary to those we shall think desirable when they grow up?' 377 B.

45 Green, T. F., 'The topology of the teaching concept', *Studies in Philosophy and Education*, vol. III, no. 4.

46 E.g. Sargant, W., *Battle For the Mind*, Pan Books, London, 1959.

47 White, J. P., 'Indoctrination' in Peters, R. S., ed., *The Concept of Education*, Allen & Unwin, London, 1967, p. 187.

48 Flew, A., 'What is indoctrination?' *Studies in Philosophy and Education*, IV. 3. 1966.

49 Atkinson, R., in R. D. Archambault, ed., *Philosophical Analysis and Education*, Routledge & Kegan Paul, London, 1968.

50 Wilson, J., in Hollins, T., ed., *Aims in Education*, Manchester University Press, 1964.

51 Hare, R. M., in Hollins, op. cit.

52 Corbett, P., *Ideologies*, Hutchinson, London, 1965.

53 Wilson, op. cit., p. 33.

54 Russell, *Education and the Social Order*, pp. 128, 129.

55 Ibid., p. 133.

56 Ibid., p. 25.

57 White, op. cit., p. 179.

58 Crossman, op. cit., p. 99.

59 Dearden, *The Philosophy of Primary Education*, p. 46.

60 See chapters 2, 3 and 7. See also 375 A ff., 412 B ff., 455 B and 474ff.

61 Hare, op. cit.

62 414 D ff.

63 414 E.

64 414 B.

65 415 D.

66 Popper, op. cit., p. 139.

67 Crossman, op. cit., pp. 82, 83.

68 Russell, 'Philosophy and Politics', p. 117.

69 414 B ff.

70 Pindar, for instance (*Pythian Odes* 2. 37), uses the phrase *pseudos gluku* in reference to the 'sweet delusion' (i.e. the phantom) that Zeus unwittingly embraces. Cf. Plato's use at *Gorgias* 505 and *Euthydemus* 272 B.

71 See chapter 7.

72 376 C.

73 421.

74 425 B.

75 421.

76 (c) will be established in chapter 7.

77 540 E.

78 412 C ff.

79 'Mankind must have laws, and conform to them, or their life would be as bad as that of the most savage beast', *Laws*, 875.

80 Popper, op. cit., p. 113.

81 Ibid., p. 131.

82 Ibid., p. 101.

83 Ibid., p. 102. The phrase is part of Popper's translation of Pericles's funeral speech.

84 Ibid., p. 100.

7 Equality

1 The principle of equality

The third key principle in the liberal-democratic vocabulary is the principle of equality. It is largely by reference to this that they argue that the *Republic* is unjust in a distributive sense. Popper claims that 'Equalitarianism was his [Plato's] arch enemy' and 'he was out to destroy it'.[1] Russell says that 'we have come to associate justice with equality, while for Plato it has no such implication'; his definition of justice 'makes it possible to have inequalities of power and privilege without injustice'.[2]

In support of their view that Plato ignores the claims of equality the liberal-democrats might seem to gain a prima facie plausibility by citing Plato's categorical assertion in the *Laws* that 'equal treatment of unequals must beget inequity'[3] and his derision of democracy in the *Republic* on the grounds that it 'distributes equality to equals and unequals alike'.[4] They would also, of course, point to the *Republic* as an example of the unequal distribution they condemn.

What does the principle of equality involve? What does it mean to say that all men are equal or that all men ought to be treated equally? We tread well-trodden ground here, and there can be few who regard the statement that all men are equal as a straightforward descriptive truth; all men are not equal without qualification: some are shorter, some are more beautiful, some are more clever, some are more generous, etc. Likewise, few will interpret the demand that all men should be treated equally as meaning that in all respects the same things should be done for and to each individual. Most egalitarians would accept Plato's contention that it is acceptable, and therefore not to be seen as a heinous contravention of the equality principle, to give a larger amount of meat to a full-grown man than to a new-born baby.[5]

At one point Popper glosses the principle by saying that 'Equalitarianism proper is the demand that the citizens of the state should be treated impartially'.[6] We may say at once that we accept this identification of the principle of equality with the principle of impartiality. It is, in fact, the only interpretation of the principle of equality that seems acceptable. But it should be noted that if this is really what 'equalitarianism proper' demands, then appeal to the principle of equality does not necessarily discredit Plato

140

(although as we shall see it does effectively discredit the liberal-democrats), since impartial treatment of people, or an impartial distribution of goods, does not necessarily involve exactly similar treatment or an exactly similar distribution. Consequently pointing out the differences between the treatment of people and the allocation of goods they receive in the *Republic*, is not in itself sufficient to show that Plato ignores the claims of equality.

The principle of impartiality is equivalent, not to the claim that all people should be treated the same in all respects, but to the claim that people should be treated the same except where relevant criteria for differentiation can be produced. I do not see that this principle can be formally 'proved' (i.e. one cannot 'prove' that all men ought to abide by the principle). But, as has been shown,[7] one's own commitment to the principle is involved in one's seriously engaging in rational discourse. The rules of rational discourse involve the backing up of a point, or the making of a distinction, by means of relevant reasons, rather than at random. The great value of the principle of impartiality is that all those who are concerned with rational discussion of the broad issues with which we are concerned, are committed to it. It is common ground. But, on the other hand, it is a purely formal principle giving us no indication of what, in any particular case, are relevant grounds for discrimination, and carrying with it no specific consequences about the distribution of rights, goods, advantages, burdens, etc. It is not the principle of impartiality itself, for instance, that tells us that we should give more milk to new-born children than to certain other people; that calculation is based, broadly speaking, on assessment of the needs of various people in relation to the properties of milk, *and* in the light of certain ultimate values.

Popper offers a second gloss on the principle of equality, which is that we must provide 'an equal distribution of the burden of citizenship, i.e. of those limitations of freedom which are necessary in social life . . . and an equal share in the advantages'.[8] He does not make it clear precisely what he means by this, but the interesting point is that, though it might mean several things, it only seems acceptable on the assumption that we reject what is almost certainly the liberal-democratic interpretation, and understand it to mean something that Plato would certainly accept and that he subserves in his organisation of the Republic.

'An equal distribution of the burden of citizenship . . . and an equal share in the advantages' might mean four distinct things. First, it might mean that in the case of any specific advantage or burden we should distribute it equally in the sense that we should give the same amount or degree of it to all; secondly that, again in the case of a specific advantage or burden, we should distribute it

Equality

so as to achieve an end result in respect of that advantage or burden
that involves an equal amount or degree for all; thirdly that in
distributing advantages and burdens we should give the same overall amount or degree of either to all citizens; and, fourthly, that we
should aim to achieve an end result that is equal in the overall
amount of advantage and burden given to each citizen.

(a)   The first proposal (or possibly the third) would appear to be
the one advocated by Popper, since it is the one most obviously
ignored by the *Republic*, to which he is denying the aim of an equal
distribution of advantage and burden, and since he quotes,[9]
apparently with approval, Aristotle's definition of democratic justice
as involving 'the application of the principle of arithmetic equality'
—that is to say distribution on a one for one basis.

Whether this is what he meant or not, this notion of equal
distribution is to be rejected for reasons indicated above in our
consideration of impartiality. For a schoolmaster to allot extra work
on a one for one basis, or for milk to be distributed on a one for one
basis to grown men, nursing mothers and new-born babies, would
appear to be simply irresponsible.

We know that this is Plato's view, since he has given us the
similar example about the distribution of meat,[10] and, on the face
of it, it is this principle of giving everybody exactly the same share
of everything, regardless of their particular needs or abilities, that
he is attacking when he stigmatises democracy as 'an anarchic
form of society which treats all men as equal whether they are equal
or not'.[11] Provided that we are thinking in terms of specific distribution of specific things, this remark amounts to no more than
the argument that it is absurd to give the same share or amount
of X to all people, in cases where the individuals concerned are
different in respects regarded as relevant to the distribution of X.

And it is difficult to see how anyone, whatever his political or
philosophical persuasion, could justify a denial of this principle.
If there can be no criteria to justify distribution of anything, except
on a one for one basis, then the liberal-democrat would be involved
in deploring the provision of resources and special schools to the
educationally subnormal, a graduated tax system, the paying of
old age pensions, legal aid—in short any distribution that treats
people as having different claims.

(b)   Some of the same argument can be made against the
suggestion that in distributing any specific advantage or burden
we should aim to equalise rather than give the same amount. In
some instances this seems a sensible procedure. For example it
may be felt that an equal distribution of the burden of taxation
should involve taking account of the different amounts of money
that people start with and trying to produce an end situation of

equality in respect of money. But this involves the assumption that people ought to have the same amount of money. The question then arises as to whether people ought to have the same amount of everything, and on what grounds one justifies the claim that they ought to have the same amount of any particular thing. It seems no more plausible to suggest that people ought all to *end up* with the same amount of milk, or pupils with extra work, than it did to suggest that they should all be *given* the same amount. What is clearly being ignored in both this and the first proposal is that people have different needs in respect of some things, and the principle of impartiality demanded that we should take account of these needs, where they were considered to be relevant.

(c)   The third proposal is also to be rejected on grounds partially involved in the rejection of the first. Giving the same overall amount of advantage, even if certain specific things are distributed differently, to all people, regardless of the fact that some start off with decidedly less advantage, does not strike us as a satisfactory way of meeting the demands of equality. It involves treating all people overall in the same way, despite the fact that considered overall some have more need of the deliberate provision of advantage by the community than others. Thus, even if we accept that in considering the allocation of any specific advantage, say a tax concession, it is preferable to consider the overall advantages enjoyed by an individual or group, such as free housing or free travel, as well as their income, rather than simply their income, before deciding who shall receive the concession, there still seem some, such as the blind or the old, who would be decidedly worse off in respect of advantage overall if they were merely allotted the same amount of advantage overall as other more able-bodied groups. On the face of it their greater need is a relevant criterion for a greater overall distribution of advantage, just as Popper acknowledges in a specific instance that the need of financial assistance for education in the case of the poor is a relevant criterion for the provision of it.[12]

(d)   The fourth demand is that the community should be so organised that the end result is that each citizen should have the same amount of advantage as his neighbour. This does not mean that all should have the same advantages, or that any specific advantage should be distributed equally to all men. A proposal that is equally advantageous to both me and my neighbour might involve something different for both of us.

The demand for an equal end result of advantages is still effectively a formal demand, since it has to be filled in with an account of what various people do consider as their advantage, which, as we saw in our analysis of happiness, can vary considerably. But it draws attention to something that is implicit in the notion of equal consideration and the principle of impartiality, and that is that one is concerned equally for the ultimate happiness of each man and determined to allocate impartially with a view to maximising happiness. Now, of course, one could impartially maximise misery, but in the examples we used, and in the examples used by other philosophers, it is tacitly assumed that we are concerned with an impartial distribution under the aegis of happiness. For, if this were not so, it would not be true that an impartial distribution of milk or extra work in schools demanded the sort of distribution we outlined. If we wanted to be impartial with an eye to misery, for example, we should insist that the baby ate a large raw steak and the grown man nothing, that the adult men drank all the milk, leaving the nursing mothers and babies nothing, and that all children be set extra work.

In other words the way we talk about the principle of impartiality presupposes that we imagine all to be equally entitled to happiness, and therefore that all should have the same overall amount of advantage, if we understand advantage to mean 'that which the individual requires for his happiness'. Nor can we see any reason to object to this assumption, since none of the criteria sometimes advanced as good reasons for discrimination in specific cases of distribution, such as intelligence, strength or interest seem good grounds for allowing an individual a greater share of advantage overall.

At this juncture then we arrive at the conclusion that both the liberal-democrats and Plato are committed to a principle of equality, in the sense of a principle of impartiality, with the broad intention of aiming at equal happiness for all. The suggestion that the principle of equality must necessarily demand an arithmetic distribution of goods and advantages has been rejected. In order to establish that Plato fails to abide by the claims of equality, it is therefore now necessary for the liberal-democrats to show either that he distributes certain specific things on irrelevant and unacceptable criteria, or that there are certain things for which there are no relevant criteria for distribution, so that they ought to be distributed arithmetically, or that he fails to provide an overall equal amount of advantage or happiness.

Popper offers another gloss on 'the equalitarian principle proper' which brings in this matter of specific criteria and raises the question of privilege which, according to Russell, Plato distributes unequally.[13] It also raises an issue that is central to the liberal-democratic claim that the *Republic* is fundamentally unjust, namely the suggestion that it is 'based on the most rigid class distinction . . . a caste state'.[14] That is to say a state in which one of the criteria for distribution is birth, whereas the principle of equality demands that 'birth, family connection or wealth must not influence those who administer the law. In other words it does not recognise any "natural" privileges, although certain privileges may be conferred by the citizens upon those they trust'.[15]

With this demand we are in full concurrence. But, as will now be argued, Plato does not distribute anything on the basis of these criteria. The Republic is not a class state in the damaging sense intended.

2 Class and power

The Republic is obviously a class society in the sense that it is possible to point to distinct classes, categories or groups of individuals within the community, each of which pursues a way of life that is peculiar to itself. It is usual to talk of the three classes of the rulers or philosopher-kings, the auxiliaries and the workers, although the most marked distinction is between the rulers and auxiliaries taken as one group, and the rest of the population taken as another. Clearly, however, it is possible to point to any society and make classifications such that it will be seen to contain separate groups; in our own society one may make a sociologically descriptive distinction between the 'working class' and the 'managerial class'; this possibility of classification remains in the case of any society that involves a degree of specialist activity and retains diverse characters amongst its population.

We are concerned here with the suggestion that the Republic is a class society in the sense that the way of life or role in the community allotted to each individual is dictated by the parentage of that individual; in other words that the criterion whereby the individual is allotted to one of the three main classes in the state is the criterion of blood, heredity or race.

On the face of it the charge that the Republic is a class society in this sense is adequately denied by Plato himself, since he explicitly argues that justice itself demands the adoption of the principle 'that each man should perform that one role in society for which his nature is best adapted';[16] thus aptitude, and not birth, is the criterion to be employed. Nor is there any obscurity, in theory, about the meaning of 'aptitude'. (I adopt the term 'aptitude', in place of Plato's 'nature', simply because it is the term generally used today. But by the term 'aptitude' I intend to refer both to ability and interest, although this is not usually conveyed by the term. The reason for this is that when the adult in the Republic takes up the role to which he is suited by 'nature', as a result of the educational process, he is presumed to have both ability and interest in respect of that role.) Of course in practice one cannot judge the individual's aptitude for a specific task until one has assessed the nature of the task itself; the criteria of selection must be relevant to the task in hand, a point to which Plato gives recognition when he ridicules the idea that bald-headedness is likely to be a relevant criterion for anybody's aptitude for any task.[17] But, in general, we may say that, if a person has aptitude for a specific task, he should have an interest in performing that task, he should pick up an understanding of it easily, he should so grasp the nature of it that he readily sees for himself more about it after a little instruction and does not forget what he has already been taught, and he should not be physically incapacitated for it.[18] The nature of the basic division between the Guardians and the rest means that the community is called upon to make a judgment between those who have the aptitude to undergo a lengthy and rigorous education with a strong intellectual flavour, while living an ascetic kind of life, and those who, by contrast, are suited rather to a manner of living more usual in our experience and what we may call a technical training.

However, it is still possible that the arrangements of the Republic are designed to create a master race, in the sense of a self-perpetuating clique. The problem in the Republic, which is primarily the cause of the charge of racialism and a class society, is simply this: does Plato in fact intend to allow transference from one group to another on the basis of aptitude? It is not seriously denied that he says that aptitude is the criterion of selection, but it may be questioned whether it meaningfully can be. First, however, we must deal with Popper's claim that in any case Plato did not seriously mean that aptitude should be the criterion and that he actually withdraws the provision.

Popper says:[19]

> The stronger the feeling that the ruled are different and an altogether inferior race, the stronger will be the sense of unity among the rulers. We arrive in this way at the fundamental principle . . . that there must be no mingling between the classes: 'Any meddling or changing over from one class to another', says Plato, 'is a great crime against the city'.

In a note to the text Popper adds that, although 'when first speaking about these matters in 415A ff, Plato speaks as though a rise from the lower to the upper classes were permissible . . . in 434 B-D [quoted by Popper above], and, even more clearly in 547A, this permission is, in effect withdrawn'. But in point of fact the passage translated by Popper does not refer at all to the question of an individual born of parents in the largest group, who nonetheless has an aptitude for the role of ruler; it refers to an individual whose aptitude is for a role in the largest group, and argues that if such an individual be placed amongst the rulers, that will bring ruin to the state. In other words the passage adds nothing to Plato's fundamental principle that aptitude is the criterion on which to ascribe social functions. The passage reads in full:

> But I imagine that when one who is by nature an artisan or some kind of money-maker, tempted and incited by wealth or popular support or physical strength or some such advantage, tries to enter the group of auxiliaries, or when one of the auxiliaries tries to take over ruling, for which he is not suited, or when the same man undertakes all these functions at once, then, I take it, you too believe that this kind of substitution and diversity of activity is the ruin of a state.

Likewise the other passage cited by Popper (547A) adds nothing to his case, for it is about the dangers of indiscriminate breeding between citizens of one group and another. Certainly, one may object to the practice of any state control over who should have sexual intercourse with whom; but that is a separate question and has nothing to do with the claim that the society is a caste or racialist society, in the sense that the individual's social role is decided by his birth. There is in fact no evidence that Plato ever formally goes back on his original remarks, made in connection with the introduction of the myth that explains to all citizens, in symbolic form, that those whose aptitude is for ruling must rule, those whose aptitude is for the auxiliary's life must act as such, and those whose aptitude is for the life of a farmer or craftsman, should be such. There he says that, if children are born to parents of the ruling group with iron or brass in their make-up (i.e. if their aptitude is membership of the largest group in some capacity):

> then to each such child must be assigned the social role suitable to his nature and he must be transferred to the group of artisans and farmers . . . and again if parents belonging to the largest group should unexpectedly produce a child with gold or silver in his make-up [i.e. with an aptitude for the auxiliary or ruling group] they shall honour such, and bid them go on to the office of guardian or auxiliary.

We may conclude with Levinson that 'it is Plato's serious purpose to fit each individual's capacity to the social function he is to perform. This being the case, it would be impossible for Plato to fix permanently the status of any child on the basis of his pedigree'.[20]

However there is a much more serious, because less obviously false, criticism that may be made of the *Republic*, and that is that whatever Plato's intention, in practice it must turn into a matter of selection by birth rather than aptitude. Levinson adds that 'as any given child grew older it would become increasingly difficult for him to make up his deficiencies in training' and Rankin, after a sober review of those elements in the *Republic* designed to habituate the individual to his role, concludes that a contradiction remains: 'Plato wanted mobility of talent within society, but these assimilative tendencies in his society are against it . . . people become what they do. They become what they perceive. They are therefore liable to be fixed in the group in which they were born'.[21]

Plato does not make it very clear in the *Republic* at what age he assumes that misclassification will become apparent, and transference take place. On the two occasions on which he actually enunciates the principle of transference he talks of the possibility of a child being born with iron or whatever in his soul, as if he thought that the matter could be detected at birth. On the other hand, when dealing with the eugenic proposals for the Guardians, and talking about the disposal of various children born in contravention of the eugenic laws, all of whom are to be dealt with at birth, it is noticeable that he does not include those who are mentally incapable of the Guardian's way of life: he refers only to those children whose character is supposed to be a foregone conclusion from the nature of the manner of their conception, and children who are born physically defective, a matter which can obviously be judged at once. Furthermore the *Timaeus*, summarising the *Republic*, says that 'the rulers were to keep an eye on the children as they grew up and promote again any who deserved it, and demote into the places of the promoted any in their own ranks who seemed unworthy of their position'.[22] It seems clear, therefore, that in theory Plato intends that there should be a permanent watch kept out for individuals whose aptitude in fact demands a transference one way or the other; for as we have said there is in reality only one division, that between the Guardians—i.e. rulers and auxiliaries—and the largest group. The rulers are merely selected from the Guardians 'on the basis of examinations which test their intellectual and moral qualities'.[23]

But the problem raised by Rankin is far from resolved. Plato evidently believes in hereditary factors moulding the persona of the individual, or else he would not have elaborated his eugenic proposals and could not contemplate transference at all; on the other hand the ethos of the *Republic* and the attention shown to educational matters indicates his profound belief in the influence of environment and upbringing. Can he really hope to find a moment, at which he can both judge that the individual child has the sort of innate qualities necessary for the rigorous intellectual training and austere life of the Guardians, and also remove that child from the bosom of a family and place him, without causing him to undergo psychological harm, in the communal world of the Guardians? Up to what age can you let the child grow convinced that he is 'bronze', before you inform him that he is 'silver'?

I do not see any way to answer these questions. I suspect that Plato sincerely thought it was possible to make transferences, to judge that they were necessary, and yet to maintain a belief in the rightness of their role amongst all people, even those who are about to be transfered, up to the point of their transference. He may have been right; but it remains difficult to see how, except in exceptional cases, one is supposed to detect in, for example, the son of a farmer, who has been successfully brought up to enjoy his family life and to acquire the rudiments of a farmer's education, a child who is in fact suited to communal life, austere conditions and a hard intellectual climb.

I therefore conclude that in practice the two main groups in the *Republic* will be self-perpetuating; but to admit this is not to concede anything to critics who see it as a caste state or the embodiment of racialism, for what they wanted to establish was that birth was the criterion of allotment to a group, and this they have failed to do. Aptitude, by which is meant both ability and inclination, is still the criterion. The individual is not born with a specific aptitude, rather the aptitude of each one of us is the product of the external influences that play upon us while we develop, combined, perhaps, with some innate tendencies; to disentangle the natural tendencies and the effects of external influence seems, in our present state of knowledge, an impossible task. We judge whether the individual is performing that function for which he has an aptitude, at any given time, by assessing his interest and ability in respect of that function. If in any case a citizen in the Republic is not performing that function to which he is most suited, it is clearly stated that he will be transferred; but such is the design of the Republic, with its emphasis on bringing people up to suit the function for which they are, at the given time, being trained, that, in practice, few will need a transfer. Perhaps Rankin was wrong to say that 'Plato wanted mobility of talent within his society', for that implies that Plato wanted to see people born in one group and moved to another; but he did not necessarily want this. All he required was that people should do that for which they are by nature most suited. As Rankin says 'People become what they do'; their nature is developed by what they do and see. People are 'liable to be fixed in the group in which they were born', only because their nature is liable to develop in such a way as to make their aptitude demand membership of that group. The 'assimilative tendencies' in the Republic, therefore, do not in fact contradict Plato's aim of a society in which aptitude is the criterion; they are a very important contribution to that end.

There is therefore absolutely no evidence to support the contention that the Republic is a class society in which advantages or anything else are distributed by reference to the criteria of birth or family connection; nor is wealth anywhere referred to as a criterion for distribution. The fundamental criterion is aptitude, which involves capability and interest, and such things as material possessions are distributed to the largest group rather than the rulers precisely on the assumption that they will need and want them, and not on the grounds that they are born to working class parents.

Having failed to establish that Plato offends the principle of equality by being partial and distributing on the unacceptable criteria of birth and wealth, the liberal-democrat may next suggest that certain things at any rate ought to be distributed on a strict arithmetic, or one for one principle. They are not, however, noted for their advocacy of one for one distribution, particularly in the sphere of wealth and the many many things that are dependent on it. There is, in fact, only one thing that they seem to think everybody ought to have the same amount of and that is power. Russell, characteristically, puts this bluntly, and criticises Plato's view of justice on the grounds that it involves inequalities of power.[24] Popper demands equality of political privilege, and Crossman complains that Plato ignores 'the right to self-government'.[25]

It is obviously inadequate for Crossman simply to state that there is this right. A right only makes sense within a framework, political, social, moral, that justifies it, and before meekly accepting this right we should require Crossman to explain whence it comes and what justifies it. But certainly it is true that Plato ignores it, or rather does not accept it, just as it is true that he does not grant equal political power. The reasons for this distinction are very straightforward.

He sees the task of the ruler as demanding certain characteristics on the part of the individual entrusted with the job. It would be best for me to admit here and now that in applying Plato's philosophy to any actual society such as our own I recognise that there may be empirical difficulty in establishing that any individual has the required characteristics; and this fact alone might lead one to a prudential defence of some form of democracy. But here I am only concerned with the formal statement that it must be wrong for Plato to have advocated unequal political power. This is to be rejected, for, given the requirements necessary for a ruler, Plato's criteria for distinction in this respect are obviously relevant to the thing being distributed. The characteristics required in a ruler by Plato are:

(a)   A ruler ought to be of a high intellectual calibre; specifically, even if we reject the notion of the possibility of knowing the
Good, he ought to be trained as a moral philosopher. He ought
to be rational, in the sense of impartial, consistent, etc. He must
understand the difference between relevant and irrelevant criteria
on a formal level, so that he cannot abandon himself to making
decisions about, say, people's right to happiness, on the basis of
differences in colour of skins, parentage or brain power. All this
is implicit in the emphasis that Plato places upon their education
and the details of their higher education. It is also implicit in the
methods and arguments that he himself uses in the *Republic*.

(b)   A ruler, besides being intellectually strong, must be concerned about moral claims. Plato's whole attack on demagogues
is based on the supposition that they are concerned with popularity
and success, rather than the claims of morality.

(c)   A ruler must not stand to gain anything at the expense of
others, from the fact of ruling.[26]

(d)   A ruler ought to look to the happiness of the whole
community.

If one accepts these injunctions it would follow, as a matter of
course, that only certain people ought to rule, and almost certainly
that rulers ought not to be elected by popular vote, since the majority
of people would neither be in a position to make an informed
judgment about candidates for office in relation to these requirements, nor, probably, would think to do so. But what is more
disturbing is that those who demand that government officers
ought to be elected by popular vote are committed to saying that it
does not matter if rulers are unintelligent, immoral or amoral,
motivated by personal loyalties or interests and unconcerned about
the happiness of the whole community. In other words by altering
the method whereby the ruler is elected, we effectively alter our
view of the nature of ruling.

In short, the demand that all citizens should have a vote of
equal validity involves acceptance of the view that it is relatively
unimportant to lay down qualifications for ruling. The non-
democrat would argue, on the other hand, that ruling ought to be a
qualified activity and that consequently the right to vote ought to
be restricted to those who have some understanding of the qualifications involved.[27]

There is no point in pressing this argument further, at this
juncture, since a lot must depend upon the overall nature of a given
society. We shall end this section simply by asking what the justification is, in a democracy, for not allowing sixteen-year-olds to vote,
if it is admitted that the question of whether a vote is more or less
informed does not arise? For it is simply not true that people under

sixteen are incapable of voting, if there are no criteria for sound political judgment. If it be said that there should be *some* criteria, then formally Plato's discrimination between those fit to make political decisions and those unfit, has been shown to be acceptable.

3 Equality of opportunity

There is one further interpretation of the principle of equality that must be considered, since it is the interpretation most prevalent in liberal-democratic societies. This is the view that the principle of equality demands equality of opportunity.

The argument runs: although one cannot distribute all roles, goods, rights, and other advantages absolutely equally, nor in such a way as to ensure an equal allocation at the end of the distribution, for a variety of reasons, one can and should provide an equal opportunity for all persons to acquire such things. This doctrine is frequently appealed to with reference to education, and it is claimed that education must provide this equality of opportunity. People are born with varying disadvantages due to no fault of their own. It does not seem equitable that a child should be doomed to deprivation, just because he is the son of poor parents who cannot afford to educate him. Consequently society ought to see that he is provided with an education that redresses the imbalance of disadvantage and that fits him out with an equal opportunity.

The doctrine can be interpreted, more specifically, to mean not that an equal opportunity should be provided for all persons to obtain various advantages, and that therefore education should seek to fit people out with an equal opportunity, but simply that all people should be given an equal opportunity of receiving education. This injunction would be directed against certain criteria, such as wealth and birth, that have as a matter of historical fact been used to ensure that some have less opportunity than others, or indeed no opportunity, of receiving education. Another way of expressing it is to say that all should have equal opportunities for the development of their capacities and interests.

With this limited interpretation of 'equality of opportunity' there is no need to quarrel, but two points must be made. First the demand involved might just as well be expressed by saying that equal educational provision should be made for all ('equal' of course not necessarily meaning the 'same', but the 'same amount'), which in educational terms would mean something like ensuring the availability of similar resources, of a certain standard of teacher, and of a certain standard of school buildings, etc., for all children. In other words the claim is that there are no relevant criteria for distinguishing between children in respect of the distribution of education. And it would be as well to formulate the demand in some such way, rather than by using the slogan 'equality of opportunity', in order to distinguish this specific injunction from the broader doctrine of equality of opportunity that will be examined presently. Secondly it is only possible to insist that all should receive equal educational provision because 'education', until it is subdivided and defined in various specialist ways, is an unlimited good. That is to say the fact that you are being educated, does not in itself prevent anybody else from also being educated. (Once 'education' is tied down to a more or less specific content certain types of education may become limited by reason of such factors as the ability of the pupil, and the availability of teachers. But the demand we are here concerned with is not a specific demand such as that all should learn to plough and appreciate Shakespeare; it is merely the demand that the state should ensure that all, equally, may be provided with an education that is desirable.) With unlimited goods, then, we may say that there is no obvious reason why equal provision should not be made for all.

It is with the notion of equality of opportunity understood as meaning that the principle of equality is satisfied, if we provide people with an equal opportunity to obtain various goods that are limited, that we are here concerned.

If one talks of an opportunity, it must be an opportunity *for* something, and clearly what is in view here is broadly speaking an opportunity to prosper within society, or an opportunity to acquire various generally desired 'goods', in which term we include roles, rights and material advantages. Equally clearly, implicit in the plea for equal opportunity is an admission that whatever the opportunity is for is ultimately going to be distributed unequally. For, if this were not the case, there would be no need to talk of 'opportunities': one would simply distribute whatever was in question 'equally'. Besides we are dealing with goods that are limited in various ways, and the doctrine arises out of the premiss that we cannot distribute such goods equally.

Goods may be limited by definition, as positions of management are, or contingently, as university education is, or fortuitously as material wealth is. It is not necessarily true, as has been suggested, that goods that are limited by definition or contingently 'are goods which not all the people who desire them can have';[28] indeed the Republic is specifically designed to achieve the equivalent of a situation in which those who are not able to be managers, do not desire to be such. However, in our own society it may be admitted as an empirical truth that not all who desire to be managers or to go to university are able to do so. The question therefore is whether, for us, the provision of equal opportunity is desirable in relation to such goods, limited by definition or contingently. And the answer is that the idea does not make sense.

The objection to advocating equal opportunity for people to become managers is that by definition in the final analysis the opportunities provided turn out to have been unequal. If it is suggested that on some occasions, at least, two applicants for a managerial post might be said to have been provided with a genuinely equal opportunity, inasmuch as they were both equally deserving of the job, one must counter by asking why it is supposed to be desirable to equip two people for a role that only one can fulfil, so that the rejected candidate is disappointed and frustrated at his arbitrary rejection? Given that, say, only one in ten people can be a manager, and that, for whatever contingent reason, only one in twenty can go to university, it is absurd to talk of equal opportunity in relation to such things. What can be said is that all should have equal educational provision made for them, since education is not a limited good, so that it can be established who is most suitable for the demands involved in a university education and for the role of manager.

The case however is different if we understand equality of opportunity to mean the provision of an equal opportunity to acquire limited goods such as wealth and all it brings with it. The first point that must be made is that in fact equal opportunity to acquire goods that are fortuitously limited is not provided in the very societies, such as our own, that proclaim it. For we tie our distribution of wealth to certain roles, with the result that those who emerge from the education process with greater opportunities for certain roles also thereby obtain greater wealth.

But the second and more important point is that, although wealth is limited, it is not so limited that it could not be distributed in arithmetically equal quantities. What is required of the advocates of equality of opportunity is a convincing criterion for discriminating between people in respect of wealth. Plato offered the reasonable criterion of certain people's disinterest in wealth. If A does not want wealth and B does, it would seem as ludicrously doctrinaire to insist that they have equal amounts of wealth as it would be to insist that all people should have an equal number of books. In our society most people want wealth and what it provides; why, then, should we talk of giving them an equal opportunity to get it, rather than of providing equal amounts of it?

If equality of opportunity is to be distinguished in any way from the equal provision of what the opportunity is for, it must imply an equal opportunity to compete for what it is acknowledged not all will acquire an equal amount of. But if people ought to have an equal opportunity to acquire wealth that is presumably because there are no good grounds for giving some more than others, in which case we surely ought to provide all with an equal amount. People do not want to be merely provided with a better handicap, or a different handicap, than that with which they were born in order to fight for advantages; they want an equal share of the advantages (not a race to run), as is implicitly admitted in the effort to provide them with an equal opportunity to compete. Any attempt to compensate the individual's birthright of handicaps surely betrays an uneasy feeling that nobody in fact has more right to advantages that everyone wants than anyone else.

We conclude that the provision of equal opportunity in respect of wealth and associated material advantages, rather than an arithmetically equal distribution, is implicitly self-condemned, and in respect of roles, which cannot be arithmetically distributed, is meaningless and contributory to frustration and disappointment. Those who advocate the distribution of roles in accordance with the results of an attempt to provide equal opportunity for all, would also seem to be committed to the view that some roles are inferior to others. For obviously one would not strive to educate all children, including the sons of manual labourers, in such a way as to attempt to provide them with an equal opportunity to be managers, unless one felt that being a manager was better than being a manual labourer. Perhaps it is some such feeling that causes Plato's liberal-democratic critics to feel that his largest group, which includes manual labourers, are just so much 'human cattle'.

But what is wrong with being a manual labourer?[29] Why is it so important to take positive steps to create a desire in the child and an ability to be something other than a manual worker? We know what is wrong with it in our liberal-democratic society: the non-manual roles are more advantageous. But this is so because they carry more material advantage and because we attempt to indoctrinate our children with the idea that manual jobs are inferior intrinsically: we encourage them to 'better themselves', especially by showing academic expertise and moving out of the manual class. This solves no problems at all: we still need and have manual labourers, but they are liable to be relatively dissatisfied with their jobs since they have been encouraged to aim at something 'higher', and, not surprisingly, they are somewhat aggrieved at the rate of pay for the job. If it were to be seriously maintained that a manual labourer's job was intrinsically inferior, then some suggestions as to how we could do without them, rather than new kinds of lotteries to select them, would be called for.

But there are no grounds whatsoever for regarding one job as intrinsically inferior to another. It is the doctrine of equal opportunity applied to roles and wealth that produces the idea of a hierarchy of worth. By divorcing wealth from roles, by promoting respect in all citizens for all roles that contribute to the efficient functioning of society, and by ensuring that people take on roles to which they are suited, Plato both dissolves the need to worry about who is a manager and who is not, and also puts an effective end to the disdain which liberal-democrats seem to evince for non-intellectual manual workers.

From the premiss that if left to themselves, with no compensation for the disadvantages of birth, some individuals will never be in the running for certain coveted roles, and from the premiss that virtually everybody would like a slice of the national wealth, the liberal-democrat, meekly accepting that certain roles carry with them a greater slice of the wealth and hence advantages, moves to the conclusion that all ought to be given an equal opportunity, via education, to compete for the coveted roles. What does this mean in practice? It means that instead of running from birth in a handicap race, we run from a later starting line in a handicap race. Education is used to alter the odds. Equality of opportunity amounts to the demand that all children should go to school. The liberal-democrat thus does nothing in fact to alter the admitted inequality of distribution of wealth; he reinforces the idea in our community that some jobs are inferior to others; he tries to avoid bringing up the child to enmesh with the role he may well have to take on; he adds external rewards to those roles that he has persistently advertised as desirable in themselves. The whole policy is calculated to promote frustration, envy and disappointment. We are offered a game to play, instead of a rational system of distributing goods, whether they be unlimited or limited by nature, contingently or fortuitously.

If the doctrine of equality of opportunity is so unsatisfactory, why, it may be asked, did it ever arise? The answer is that it arises to meet the problem caused by liberal-democratic emphasis on freedom. Equality of opportunity is a substitute for the more natural interpretation of the principle of equality as demanding positive equal treatment or distribution in at least some respect. The liberal-democrats acknowledge a principle of equality, but they recognise, obviously correctly, that one cannot literally distribute roles equally, and they feel that to distribute material goods equally, which need not involve the same things being given to all and does not therefore involve a drab uniformity, but merely requires the same amount of material advantage for all who want it, would run counter to the claims of freedom: societies that do aim at equal distribution of wealth do need to indulge in restriction and coercion, and will continue to need to do so so long as even a minority of individuals cannot be persuaded to refrain from accumulating a disproportionate share of advantage for themselves of their own free will. It is not clear, as has to be repeatedly stressed, why the principle of freedom should be presumed to override the principle of equality in this particular instance, when it does not, for example, in the case of equal educational provision for all. But it is clear that in practice it does. And 'equality of opportunity' purports to serve both masters, by indicating equal concern for all and yet leaving all relatively free. But, of course, it is only equal concern up to a point. And perhaps the most uncanny knack of the liberal-democrats is their ability to determine what this point should be, without even having to use a system of evaluation. The cripple is cared for; the unemployed are given a dole; the poor are given tax rebates. But just as we wonder why equal treatment for all ended at the end of schooling, we wonder why equalising shares of wealth is a process begun, carried up to a certain point, and then dropped. Is there some way of judging a minimum that a man needs? Needs for what? For his happiness or for his survival? Can one define a 'need' without any reference to ultimate values?

Once the principle of freedom has endorsed the existence of a society in which people compete for roles, we naturally see rewards becoming attached to roles, and we are inevitably faced with a disproportionate distribution of goods, including an unequal distribution of rights if we compare rights by reference to their effective power. Furthermore a society built upon a competitive economy, unlike communism or Plato's Republic, inevitably stresses, via advertising and the subtle influence of one's neighbours' envy, the importance of material wealth, so that the dissatisfaction felt by those whose 'equal opportunity' somehow fails to attain equal recognition is compounded.

Naturally a society with a competitive economy can try to maintain equal rights and equal political power, if it chooses to. It may, for instance, insist that a man's wealth be ignored in a court of law, insist that the same laws apply to all citizens, provide free legal aid for the poor, provide a free medical service and free education, and insist that one man has one vote. But in the first place, so long as wealth remains the potent means that it is, it is doubtful whether these provisions can hope to provide a true equality in respect of their aim. The rich man may plausibly be said to have the advantage in being able to buy the most able defence counsel available, the time of good doctors, the services of better teachers. He can more easily afford to get divorced or to guarantee himself a seat in a railway carriage. One might even suggest that in practice the standing and way of life he can acquire might make a material difference to his treatment at the hands of a judge or jury. Wealth has been known to render somewhat void the idea that each man has effectively his one independent vote. In the second place, if it is justifiable for the rich to gain the effective advantages they do gain (which, of course, we dispute), it is not clear how one would justify refusing them such advantages as we have been considering in this paragraph. If it is justifiable for the rich to be able to eat incomparably better than the poor, why is it not also justifiable for them to have incomparably better medical services, and why do we therefore pour so much money into the National Health Service? There is nothing in liberal-democratic philosophy to explain why the distribution of education and health services should be conducted in a manner different to the distribution of other advantages.

We arrive at the conclusion that liberal-democratic society, as it is known to us, and liberal-democratic theory, in so far as it insists that the demands of freedom may on occasion override the claims of other principles, fails to ensure equality in any acceptable sense.

First, distribution is not impartial. For where wealth is not equally distributed, distribution of many other goods is effectively decided by the criterion of wealth, despite the fact that it was specifically ruled out by Popper as a legitimate criterion for any distribution.[30] And we agree with him in feeling that no argument has ever yet been produced to show that it is an acceptable criterion. Nor is the case improved if we say, as perhaps we should, that the criterion of distribution in the liberal-democratic society is not wealth, which is merely a currency for exchange, but merit.

In point of fact, unless merit is defined in some such way as 'ability to make money', it would not be strictly true to say that advantages in the liberal-democratic society are awarded according to merit. But on the assumption that merit, in the more usual and general sense of worth, desert or ability in respect of the role in question, is on the whole the criterion of allocation of jobs and hence of the wealth involved with the job, we need to know why some specific ability is a reasonable criterion for discriminating between people in respect of advantages. Why should being born with a certain ability be any more acceptable as a reason for enjoying advantages over one's fellow men than being born of certain parents? Or why should developing a certain talent be more acceptable as a reason than growing one's hair long?

One appreciates that a meritocracy may be a relatively efficient society, since, in theory, it is capable people who rise to control every facet of life, and, furthermore merit seems a prima facie reasonable criterion for the allocation of jobs and one which, in the light of one's ultimate principles, may prove to be justified. But this does not make it a reasonable criterion for the distribution of advantages. Until such time as grounds are produced for saying that merit is a reasonable criterion for discriminating between people in respect of advantages, we must consider that liberal-democratic demands lead to partial distribution in many respects.

Secondly, as we have seen, the liberal-democrats do not in practice ensure the equal rights and equal political power that they demand. Thirdly, they cannot claim to be able to distribute an equal amount of advantage to all citizens, whether we understand this to mean an arithmetically equal amount of specific advantages or overall advantage, or an amount that produces an equal end situation in specific instances or overall. Fourthly, because of the unequal distribution of generally desired advantages, they are unable to provide equal happiness for all.

An open society cannot subserve the principle of equality in any meaningful sense, because the demands of equality are such that, to ensure that they are continually met, it is necessary for there to be continual control and adjustment of the forces that produce inequality. This the liberal-democrat cannot bring himself to advocate because to do so would be to subordinate the principle of freedom to some other principle.

The open society by giving people the freedom to compete for coveted roles and the freedom to acquire varying amounts of advantage, and by failing to make all roles equally attractive to somebody, and by failing to ensure acceptance of the norms of society, is quite incapable of meeting the demands of the principle of equality in any acceptable sense. It certainly cannot provide equal happiness, since it necessarily fosters disappointment, frustration and envy. The liberal-democrats want each individual to develop as chance may have it, at least up to a point, but of course his possibilities of happiness will also be dependent on chance: the more 'open' society is, the less chance there is of guaranteeing that a square hole will be found for a square man.

4 Plato and equality

We have examined various liberal-democratic interpretations of the principle of equality. Of these we reject the view that the claims of equality could be said to be met by doing one's best to compensate for inequalities at birth, via education, and then leaving all equally free to compete for various goods. If such a situation were desirable its defence would rest on the claims of freedom, and, if it were to be regarded as the *only* justifiable way of organising the distribution of the goods in question, it would involve the assumption that the principle of freedom was actually superior to that of happiness. We also reject the suggestion that the principle of equality necessarily demands that citizens ought to have equal political power, while reserving judgment as to the possibility of approving such an equal distribution for utilitarian reasons. And we reject the view that distribution in every instance should necessarily be arithmetically equal.

However we, like the liberal-democrats, respect the principle of impartiality. The principle states that discrimination between persons may only be practised on relevant criteria. But criteria only become relevant in the light of one's ultimate values. Since we have argued that there is not an ultimate value 'freedom', and since in considering what the demands of equality are, as we are now doing, one cannot appeal to that principle, it follows that we must assess relevant criteria for discrimination in the light of the remaining principle of the liberal-democratic triad, namely happiness. Thus the principle of equality demands that we treat all people impartially with a view to their happiness. Furthermore one can think of no good grounds for discriminating between people in respect of happiness, and the onus is on those who think otherwise to produce them. This claim also ties in with our agreement with Popper that all citizens should have an equal amount of advantage, if that means that all citizens should end up with an overall equal amount. For one defines and quantifies advantage, by reference to the satisfaction or enmeshment of the individual. If A is happy being a hermit and is able to be one, and B is happy being prime minister with access to gramophone records and is able to be such, both have what they regard as their advantage: both are happy.

It is to be presumed that, whether Popper meant this or not when he demanded an equal distribution of advantages, the liberal-democrats, who do recognise a principle of happiness, will approve of the aim of providing equal happiness for all, in view of the difficulty of seeing what criteria could be produced that would be relevant to discriminating between people in respect of happiness. Furthermore it may be argued that acceptance of the aim of equal happiness is involved in formal acceptance of the principle of impartiality or equal consideration for all. For if one ignores people's individual wants or desires and people's individual natures, one is not being impartial but indiscriminate, and if one takes account of people's differing desires and natures, and tries to meet their requirements one is promoting enmeshment, which is to say happiness. If one ignores the question of people's happiness one could not be showing equal consideration; one would not be showing consideration for them at all.

It seems then that equal happiness is due to all. Happiness is at least one thing that we should attempt to ensure that all have arithmetically equal shares of.

Plato can now be seen to be abiding by the only acceptable interpretation of the principle of equality. He is providing equal happiness and discriminating between people in respect of roles, rights and material advantages only on relevant criteria. It is certainly true that he treats different people differently, granting to some a communistic way of life and to others private families and property, to some one kind of educational curriculum, to others another, and to some a role as ruler, to some a role as Guardian, to some a role as farmer and to some a role as shoemaker, carpenter, builder and so on. When he talks of treating unequals unequally,[31] he is referring to precisely this procedure of allotting different roles and different amounts of specific goods to different people, and is contrasting it with the opposite procedure of distributing everything arithmetically equally to all persons, regardless of the difference that may exist between them. He may be taken to mean that, at least in some instances, there will be relevant criteria for discriminating between people in respect of the distribution of a particular thing. Likewise when he advocates geometric distribution in contrast to arithmetic distribution, he draws attention to the fact that in so far as people have different wants, needs and abilities, a one for one distribution will often be inapposite. Geometric distribution, taking account of differences between people, attempts to achieve an end result of equality, by giving different amounts to people, in respect of those things where an end result of equality is desired.

But although the *Republic* presents a spectacular picture of people being treated differently, and also ending up enjoying very different advantages, there can be no doubt either that Plato believed in equal happiness for all and in the principle of impartiality, or that the *Republic* provides an example of such impartiality in distribution and the enjoyment of equal happiness by all.

It is true that Plato does not use the phrase 'equal happiness' in the *Republic*, but we have seen that he repeatedly says that he is concerned to promote the happiness of all, and it seems legitimate to assume that he did not mean what he neither says nor does, namely to promote the happiness of all to different degrees. Certainly when in the *Gorgias* Socrates is made to add, as a postscript to his discourse on happiness, the comment that Callicles 'has failed to observe the great power of geometrical equality amongst men', it is clear from the context that he means the potency of a principle of geometric distribution to effect equal harmony and satisfaction for all within a society.

His recognition of the principle of impartiality is evident in his use of the painting of a statue as an analogy, when he concludes that one's principle in painting should not be to give 'the most beautiful pigments to the most beautiful parts' but rather to give each part 'what is proper to each part'.[32] This is nothing other than a rejection of such distributive principles as 'one for one' or 'like to like' in favour of the principle of discriminating in the light of relevant criteria for so doing.

The same view is explicitly expressed in the rejection of bald-headedness as a likely criterion for the distribution of anything, already referred to, and in the claim that femininity, *qua* femininity, is an irrelevant criterion to the distribution of the role of ruler.

The question therefore is, regardless of what he says, is Plato impartial, are his criteria for discrimination acceptable, and does he ensure equal happiness?

Since happiness involves enmeshment and is dependent on a harmony between the individual's aspirations and his situation, between what he wants to do, wants to have, how he wants to behave on the one hand and what he is able to do, able to have and how he is free to behave on the other, it is necessary in respect of limited goods, such as social roles, that the criteria for distribution should be ability and interest. The individual cannot enmesh with a role that he is unable to perform or disinterested in performing. In respect of unlimited goods it is necessary that distribution should be arithmetically equal amongst those who desire the goods in question, unless it can be shown, which seems empirically unlikely, that certain people desire more of it than others. In other words, the aim of equal happiness demands distribution according to men's desires, needs and abilities.

These are precisely the criteria that Plato observes in distribution. Roles are distributed according to aptitude, or to use Plato's phrase according to the nature of the individual; ways of life are distributed in accordance with people's needs, hence the largest group, presumed to be unable to enmesh with the rigorous communism of the other two groups, have private families; and material advantages are divorced totally from roles and distributed according to the needs and wants of people, so that luxury is reserved for the largest group who can only find happiness in such things, and not for the Guardians who do not derive any particular enjoyment from them. It is not specifically stated by Plato that the distribution of wealth and material advantage amongst the largest group will involve providing them with an arithmetically equal amount of such advantage, but it must be presumed that this will be the case, in default of any criteria for distinguishing between the individual members of the group in respect of the happiness which they, with their particular nature, will derive from the enjoyment of it. Plato makes it quite clear in his review of existing societies, in which we may presume it to be empirically true that most people require wealth equally much, that he abhors the idea of an unequal distribution of wealth amongst people who all require it for their happiness. The timarchy differs from the ideal state in that the Guardians become enamoured of wealth and use their power to reduce 'the subjects whom they once ruled as free men and friends . . . to the status of serfs.'[33] And an oligarchy is described as having one overwhelming flaw: 'it inevitably splits society into two factions, the rich and the poor'.[34] This is only acceptable where, as in the Republic, the poor are those who do not want wealth.

It is, of course, the case that this provision of equal happiness is only achieved as a result of the education provided, which, by dint of indoctrination, censorship and the discovery, reinforcement and even creation of aptitude, ensures enmeshment. The demands involved in the norms of society are acceptable to all, and cause no frustration, only because all citizens are brought up to approve them and to habitually act in accordance with them; the roles satisfy because care is taken to develop embryonic interests and abilities towards the role to which they point, to discourage the development of interest and ability in other roles which the individual could not satisfactorily perform, or could not also perform at the same time, and to create in all citizens a respectful recognition of the value of all roles; and the lack of material wealth only does not make the Guardians miserable because they are brought up in such a way that their characters enmesh with austerity rather than luxury.

All that can be said of this is that such conditioning is necessary, if all are to be equally happy, and that is its justification, since happiness is the supreme principle.

The logical order of Plato's thought on this subject is thus as follows:

(a) A just society will be organised on rational principles; discrimination will only take place where relevant grounds for it can be produced.

(b) There are no relevant grounds, prima facie, for discrimination in respect of happiness.

(c) Despite the differences felt by many to exist between moral knowledge and other forms of knowledge, grounds can be produced for discrimination in respect of ruling. If society is to stabilise its rational foundations then it is necessary that rulers should be rational and that they should have integrity. Some are by nature more prone to undergoing the sort of education designed to foster rationality and intellectual rather than physical desires, some are even by nature more prone to being disinterestedly fair and rational. These should therefore be educated with a view to their ultimate role as rulers. Regardless of the status of moral knowledge this kind of distinction, very similar to the distinction one might make between those who are and who are not suited to being judges over and above the question of the knowledge of the law, is possible and appropriate.

(d) In order to preserve the stability of this state, and, therefore, by definition, its happiness and rational basis, the citizens must be developed in such a way as to suit them to the society and to protect them from irrational doubts; the cobbler, for instance, must not be encouraged to think that he could as well farm or rule, although he has never even considered the question of what farming or ruling involves, still less understood the arts in question, or proved himself correct. Consequently we influence the citizen to believe in the virtue and validity of his state and its norms.

5 Justice

The liberal-democrats regard the Republic as fundamentally unjust. Popper contrasts its 'totalitarian justice' with the 'humanitarian' justice of the open society.[35] Russell, besides objecting to Plato's view of justice on the false grounds that for him it has no implication of equality, argues that for Plato 'the city is just when trader, auxiliary and Guardian each does his own job without interfering with that of other classes'.[36] There are inequalities of power and privilege, we are told, and this 'perfect state is . . . an aristocracy in which a hereditary caste of cultured gentlemen care with paternal solicitude for the toiling masses'.[37] or, in stronger terms, it is 'a caste state' in which there is no consideration for the mass of 'human cattle'.[38]

We have seen that it is not a caste state in the objectionable sense of a state in which distribution of various goods is determined by the irrelevant criterion of one's parentage; the Guardians are only a group perpetuated by heredity on the empirical assumption that hereditary factors are significant in the development of the individual's character. Plato may have laid too much emphasis on heredity, and he may have been wrong to do so. But he certainly did not assume it to be all powerful, as is clear from his equally strong emphasis on environment and his formal statement that if a child does not take after his parents in terms of ability and interest he shall be transferred to that group to which his aptitude is suited. Besides Plato can hardly be presumed to have believed in the over-riding significance of heredity in view of his acquaintanceship with the worthiness of the stone-mason Socrates and the folly of his own aristocratic uncles. We may add, incidentally, that the description of the ascetic philosopher-kings, whose life seems devoid of cultural artefacts, as 'cultured gentlemen', is quite inappropriate.

There are no inequalities of privilege, although various advantages are not distributed to all citizens. Instead of insisting on a one for one distribution of all goods, Plato, recognising that a good awaiting distribution is only an advantage to those who want it, distributes each good arithmetically equally amongst those to whom it does constitute an advantage. One such thing is political power, which Plato has deliberately rendered unappealing to members of the largest group since they are by definition relatively lacking in the particular talents demanded of a ruler; the reason that these talents are demanded of the rulers is that, only if rulers have them, can the state hope to avoid decisions that are prejudicial to its welfare, which are empirically likely to be made if rulers are motivated by such factors as private greed or personal popularity, if they fail to keep the end of happiness in view, or if they are simply not very good at calculating means to ends.

It is misleading for Russell to summarise Plato's view of justice by saying that 'the city is just when trader, auxiliary and Guardian, each does his own job without interfering with that of other classes' and to categorise this as the precept 'that everybody should mind his own business'.[39]

The stress of Russell's summary is entirely wrong: the mere fact that a dustman remembers that he is a dustman and does not seek to meddle in affairs of state does not, in Plato's view, constitute justice. His claim that 'taken in a certain sense the principle of each individual doing what is properly his to do appears to be justice'[40] implies rather that it is unjust that the dustman should be a dustman in the first place, unless being a dustman involves the sort of way of life to which he is suited and with which he can enmesh. His celebrated censure of 'the doing of many things'[41] is quite obviously a condemnation of the actual practice of democratic Athens, where the individual might be soldier, farmer and politician within the space of a week, without any reference to competence, qualifications or interest which might make him more or less suited to any of these roles.

According to Plato a farmer or a soldier or a politician is a better farmer, soldier or politician if he has inclinations, abilities, and training directed to the role in question. He is working from two premises, one empirical and the other logical: the empirical premiss is that not all individuals are either desirous of or capable of turning their hand with equal success to any social role. The logical premiss is that if the role of soldier or farmer is distinctive in any respect, then criteria relevant to deciding who will make a good soldier or farmer must involve reference to what is distinctive to the role in question. Consequently in the interest of happiness or enmeshment inclinations are taken account of, and, in the interests of efficiency, abilities are taken account of, which may be summarised by saying that each individual should adopt the role 'for which he is by nature most suited',[42] 'nature' meaning *his* nature, which is the product of hereditary and environmental factors.[43] Furthermore efficiency in the state will itself contribute to happiness, most particularly if the rulers are able and efficient at ruling in such a way as to promote happiness.

The Republic is a just society because it ensures equal happiness for all citizens, which we must demand in lieu of the production of relevant grounds for discriminating between people in this respect. It is just because, in the light of this aim, its specific distributions of roles, material advantages and rights are based on the relevant criteria of needs and wants and abilities; it is impartial and gives equal consideration to all. It is just because it guarantees that an irrelevant criterion such as birth or specific talent shall not govern the distribution of material advantages, and that an irrelevant criterion such as wealth shall not govern the distribution of power or effective rights.

To establish that it is an unjust society it would be necessary to argue that being born of certain parents or being blessed with certain talents are good grounds for enjoying more material advantage, that having more wealth is a relevant reason for enjoying more power, or that equal happiness for all ought not to override certain other aims.

The liberal-democrats are not concerned to make positive noises of support for the first two lines of argument, but they are concerned to point out that Plato's aim can only be achieved at the cost of a certain amount of freedom. The state controls the distribution of wealth and roles, thereby denying the individual freedom to compete for and to acquire what he can: it indoctrinates and censors, thereby denying the individual the freedom to acquire beliefs, attitudes and ideas, as chance influence and his own reasoning ability dictate, and the freedom to say and do what he chooses where and when he chooses.

But this state of affairs can only be condemned as unjust if it can be established that such freedoms override the claims of equal happiness for all. And the liberal-democrats cannot establish this, partly because they do not entirely believe it—there are limits, for instance, to the freedom they are prepared to grant to the individual to do and say as he chooses—partly because in attempting to substantiate objections to a specific restriction such as censorship they can do no more than appeal to a broad principle of freedom which they themselves are prepared to ignore in some instances, and partly because they too are formally committed to a principle of happiness which, although they will not explicitly claim that it is overriding in its claims, they regard as of equal weight with the principle of freedom, and it therefore cannot be wrong, on their terms, given the clash of principles, to opt for adherence to the principle of happiness. And when we recall that in any case some of their 'demands' could only be justified on the assumption that the principle of happiness overrides the principle of freedom, it is clear that they have cut the ground from beneath their own feet. But we would go further than this and say that any society, such as our own, which, because of commitment to an incoherent principle of freedom, or for any other reason, fails to ensure equal happiness for all is fundamentally unjust. For it has been argued, and implicitly acknowledged by liberal-democratic theory, that there are no good grounds for discriminating between people in this respect.

The reason for the liberal-democratic abhorrence of the Republic in respect of equality is their assumption that certain things such as wealth and power, which Plato fails to share arithmetically equally amongst all, are necessary for each man's happiness equally. This is not so; there are no necessary conditions for happiness. The paradox is that, while criticising Plato for failing to give the same to all in a society where all do not want the same, their philosophy, because of its selective adherence to the principle of freedom, also ensures that wealth and power shall not be arithmetically equally distributed and that all shall not have the same; but because of that same philosophy the open society is the sort of place where it matters that all do not receive the same, since, broadly speaking, all want the same.

The Republic is effectively based upon the principle of utility. Though Plato talks in terms of knowing that this or that is right by dint of an intellectual climb up to the world of ideas where one comes face to face with goodness, it cannot be denied that what he himself saw when he got there was that happiness is desirable, and the only thing desirable, as an end.

Notes

1 Popper, op. cit., p. 93.
2 Russell, *The History of Western Philosophy*, p. 135.
3 *Laws*, 757 A.
4 558 C.
5 Cf. 338 C.
6 Popper, op. cit., p. 95.
7 E.g. Benn and Peters, op. cit.
8 Popper, op. cit., p. 89.
9 Ibid., p. 92.
10 338 C.
11 558 C.
12 Popper, op. cit., p. 131.
13 Russell, *History of Western Philosophy*, p. 135.
14 Popper, op. cit., p. 46.
15 Ibid., p. 95.
16 374 C. Cf. 370 B, 423 D.

17 454 C.
18 I am not being prescriptive here. I am not attempting to define 'aptitude', but merely using it as shorthand for Plato's criteria for distribution of roles. At 455 B he refers to all the above points as part of what he means by being 'naturally gifted' for something, apart from 'having an interest'. But clearly, empirically, having some interest would be necessary if the other points were to be met. Plato does make it clear that he also looks to interest.
19 Popper, op. cit., p. 48.
20 Levinson, op. cit., p. 537.
21 Rankin, H. D., *Plato and the Individual*, Methuen, London, 1964, p. 76.
22 *Timaeus*, 19.
23 Wild, op. cit., p. 27.
24 Russell, *History of Western Philosophy*, p. 135.
25 Crossman, op. cit., p. 83.
26 521.
27 This does not assume that a popular vote *could not* be an informed one, though empirically one might incline to that view. It assumes that in so far as no consideration is given to the possibility of it being an uninformed one, which it obviously might be, the question of its being informed or otherwise is not considered important.
28 Williams, B., 'The idea of equality', in Laslett and Runciman, op. cit., 2nd series, 1969, p. 124.
29 Cf., for instance, Rubinstein, D. and Stoneman, C., *Education for Democracy*, Penguin, Harmondsworth, 1970, p. 23. 'At the age of eleven or even earlier, many of our children have their future as manual workers determined'.
30 Popper, op. cit., p. 95.
31 558 C. *Laws*, 757 A.
32 420 C.
33 547 C.
34 551 D.
35 Popper, op. cit., chapter 6.
36 Russell, *History of Western Philosophy*, p. 134.
37 Crossman, op. cit., p. 84.
38 The terms are Popper's, op. cit., pp. 46, 47.
39 Russell, *History of Western Philosophy*, p. 134.
40 433 B.
41 433 A.
42 433 A.
43 But this does not involve the Naturalistic Fallacy, since the argument is not that a man ought to be X, because his nature is X. It is rather that since his nature is X, he will be most happy being X.

Education   8

1 Introduction

There are certain things that can be said about the practical
consequences for education that follow from an acceptance of utilitarianism, and in this final chapter I shall attempt to outline them.

The first thing to be noted is that educationalists have tended
to associate the placing of a premium on happiness with the so-
called progressive wing of education. Thus Dearden quotes Bantock's
assertion that[1]

> a supine acquiescence in the notion that happiness is the
> ultimate value has led us to underestimate the importance of
> achievement, even at a temporary loss of personal content.
> Child-centred education has been much imbued with the
> desire for happiness.

Certainly progressive educators, such as Lane, Kilpatrick and
Neill, have made frequent appeals to happiness, and it is not
altogether surprising that Dearden implicitly accepts Bantock's
identification. But, although it may be true that child-centred
theorists see themselves as attempting to ensure that 'every stage of
life should be lived for its own sake as happily . . . as possible',[2] and,
therefore, so far as the school years are concerned, as transforming
schools from 'sombre places in which laughter called for immediate
investigation' to places marked by 'an happy atmosphere',[3] it is
by no means clear that they are necessarily advocating the sort of
education that is in fact demanded by a reasoned 'acquiescence in
the notion that happiness is the supreme value'.

The term 'child-centred' I find as vague and vacuous as most
other educational slogans, but, if we understand it to mean something like a situation in which what goes on is decided primarily by
reference to 'what was valued by the child', in contrast to a situation
in which what goes on is decided primarily by reference to what
certain adults think ought to be valued, as P. S. Wilson intimates we
should,[4] there seems no obvious reason to assume that child-centred
education is demanded by a utilitarian ethic. (I pass over in silence
the question of what precisely the distinction is between a situation
in which adults decide that this and that ought to be valued, and a
situation in which adults decide that what the child values ought to
be valued.)

To say that happiness is the supreme value is *not* to commit oneself to the view that at any given point in time any individual should do what makes him feel happy. On the contrary, as I have repeatedly stressed, to commit oneself to happiness as the supreme principle, backed by a distributive principle of impartiality, is to commit oneself to a world in which people are able to pursue happiness without infringing upon the pursuit of happiness by others; it is to commit oneself to a way of looking at the world in respect of evaluation and assessment, and hence to arrive at rules and norms of behaviour and to pick out various activities which are presumed to facilitate the general maintenance of happiness, and which are, for that reason, moral rules and norms or worthwhile activities.

Now it is, of course, logically conceivable that child-centred education should both provide immediate happiness and promote the long-term overall happiness of the community to a greater extent than any other kind of education. That is to say, a community in which the educative process is fundamentally tied to the criterion of the individual child's expressed values and interests might, as a matter of fact, be one in which people in general were happy and did not impinge upon each other's happiness. If this were so, that would be the justification of child-centred education. But if it were true that such an education had such a result, it would only be a contingent truth.

There is not, as far as I know, any evidence to support the view that child-centred education will promote happiness any more than a variety of kinds of education might; there is no evidence that if all education were conducted along the lines deployed at Summerhill, for instance, the community will be the happier for it. Therefore we certainly cannot conclude that child-centred education or a relatively free educational situation are demanded or justified by the claims of the principle of happiness. But, more than this, surely what we have said about the concept of happiness and what has been revealed, through consideration of the *Republic*, about the features necessary to a state that is concerned with the impartial distribution of happiness, must lead us to the conclusion that if we wish to make a *deliberate attempt* to promote happiness, rather than simply leave the matter to chance, we certainly cannot accept a child-centred view of education? For, to adopt an extreme child-centred approach, although it *might* conceivably result in happiness, is, in default of any evidence that it will, effectively to subordinate the claims of happiness to something like the claims of individualism, personal sovereignty, autonomy or some similar variant of freedom, and to entrust the hope of happiness to the mercy of chance. An individual, depending on his character, *might* be happy doing anything. A community concerned with the happiness of all individuals *must* take steps to see that happiness is only found in certain situations. A child, whose education is pivoted upon his own expressed desires (or who is encouraged to partake in activities that he values, which must mean activities that he has a strong motivation towards, which is to say, again, activities that he particularly desires to partake in) may very well be more enmeshed with what goes on, and hence happier, than a child whose education is pivoted upon the desires of adults. But, if that is a plausible generalisation about the relative happiness experienced by children while involved at a specific point of time in distinctive educational situations, consider now the limitations or reservations that have to be added:

(a) As has been said, the claim that all men necessarily pursue their enmeshment, or choose that course of action which, of those available, seems to them most likely to promote enmeshment between themselves and the activity in question, does not mean that people may not make mistakes. This applies no less to children, and is to say no more than what is obviously true: children may decide to do one thing rather than another, although, had they done the other they might have been more enmeshed and hence happier. Here I am thinking only of the immediate present: the child, for instance, might observe other children playing cricket and decide that he would prefer to opt out of this boring looking game and to continue playing in the sandpit. It is conceivable that he is simply wrong, and that, had he joined in the cricket, he would have been happier. (Clearly, in view of what I have said above, I am not making a qualitative distinction. I mean that he might have been more fully enmeshed, perhaps for a greater period of time.) If we ought to promote happiness, then surely education ought to be concerned to initiate children into activities that may provide a great degree of enmeshment.

(b) Much more significant, however, is the point that even if we assume that the child is not mistaken at the time, he may nonetheless make a grave miscalculation in respect of his long-term happiness. Again, this is a frequent possibility with adults; how much more likely is it to occur with young children who lack the information, the foresight and the cognitive ability to make long-term calculations. It well may be that the child now will enmesh less with a cricket situation than a sandpit situation, but to be initiated into cricket now may lead at a later date to the possibility of a great deal of happiness being derived from a game that the individual might never approach if not originally initiated into it. A more telling example would obviously be the suggestion that although learning to read might be an activity with which the child is less enmeshed than playing in the sandpit, in the long run the ability to read easily and fluently may open the door to numerous activities with which the individual may enmesh more completely than he can with the limited range of activities open to one who cannot read or write. To put the matter at its simplest: it is possible to introduce people to activities that they themselves would not have embraced which may turn out to provide more happiness, measured by intensity or duration of enmeshment or their potential for continued enmeshment provision, than those activities that they choose to embrace for themselves. I certainly do not want to endorse Mill's peculiar, and obviously inadequate, argument to the effect that the 'higher' pleasures, such as those of the intellect, must be more valuable qualitatively than the 'lower' pleasures, such as those of sex, because those who have experienced both are the only people in a position to judge, and they say that they are. In the first place the fact that only some are in a position to judge does not necessitate that their judgment will be correct; in the second place it is by no means clear that it is true that all who can experience both 'higher' and 'lower' pleasures would say this (even if we define 'experiencing a higher pleasure' as 'taking pleasure in' rather than simply indulging in the activity in question, as we should surely have to do); thirdly, since people are different, there is nothing absolute about such claims. For Mill, being Mill, it may be true that intellectual pleasure is superior to sexual pleasure; for others, not being Mill, it may not be true. Nonetheless there are two points implicit in his argument here with which we may readily agree: (1) there are criteria for assessing, say, the study of literature as a better source of happiness than sexual activity—namely that it is a more stable source, that it is more varied and involves more aspects of the personality, and that through it other sources of happiness may be to some extent opened up. (None of this is to say that the individual will necessarily be more happy studying literature, nor that the happiness he experiences while doing so is in some way of a superior quality. It is to say only that, given happiness as the end, it may be for those who can enmesh with such study, a better way to pursue happiness.) (2) Some people may not be in a position to even consider this possibility. If we ought to promote happiness, then we ought, in so far as we are able, to initiate children into activities and impart skills to them that are likely to serve this end, using our experience and knowledge to provide the long-term considerations that children are in a relatively weak position to provide for themselves.

(c) So far I have considered merely the individual and his own happiness, and if that were all there were to be considered then the reader might well argue that I am on relatively weak ground, since although people might find more happiness or a more stable source of happiness in cricket or literature than in sandpits, it follows from all I have said in chapters 3 and 4 that if individuals do *feel* happy playing in sandpits that is prima facie a good reason for leaving them there. Prima facie. But, of course, we cannot only consider the individual and his happiness in isolation. If happiness is our aim, then a happy society is necessary, which means that ways of acquiring happiness must not conflict, that rules of conduct must promote the equal happiness of all, and that the maintenance of happiness in the future must be looked to.

The individual therefore needs to be brought up to enmesh with the rule-bound situation. That is to say not only must there be rules that promote happiness, but, ideally, every individual must enmesh with the situation that makes these demands on him. Any activity, therefore, which, while it might provide happiness for some taking part in it, nonetheless militates (whether directly or indirectly) against the happiness of others must be ruled out. But not only must we rule out activities that are, for instance, cruel, for this reason; we must also attempt to ensure that, since people will not be allowed to be cruel and will be restrained from being so by sanctions of various kinds, they do not wish to be cruel. For only if they do not desire to be cruel can they fully enmesh with a situation that prevents them from being so. Another limitation on the child's freedom to determine the pattern of his own education must therefore arise on these grounds.

(d) But the child does not only have to abide by rules as an adult; in a more general sense, the situation with which he needs to enmesh for his happiness is determined in despite of his wishes. I do not want to argue, as Neill has accused those who are sceptical of his educational views of arguing, that life is an unpleasant rat-race in which people are pushed around by forces bigger than themselves and that therefore, in the interests of enmeshment, education ought to promote a character that will accept this situation. If life is an unpleasant rat-race, then it ought not to be, on grounds that I have amply demonstrated in the course of this book. But there are certain features that any conceivable society will exhibit and with these it is necessary that the individual should be able to enmesh. For example, it will be necessary for the individual to have a job; the ultimate aim of enmeshment therefore demands that attention be given in education to the question of equipping the individual to find enmeshment with some job that is available to him.

(e) Finally it cannot be forgotten that if happiness is all that matters, then this must be an ongoing process—we have to think of the future for this and subsequent generations—and, if we wish to be practical, which, despite rumours to the contrary even philosophers sometimes wish to be, we have to face the fact that we are trying to promote happiness in a community which is part of a wider world and which is governed by various practical considerations. It is at this point, it seems to me, that the various educational objectives often put forward, such as developing skills and competences, promoting knowledge and autonomy, or initiation into forms of knowledge, come into the reckoning.

The only trouble with the *Republic* is that it is impracticable. This is no objection, provided that it is realised that it is only, as it claims to be, a *paradeigma poleos agathes*,[5] or a formal presentation of the embodiment of certain principles. The specific proposals that Plato makes may all of them be dismissed for one reason or another without doing mischief to Plato's intentions. Thus his proposed censorship of Homer is irrelevant to a world in which Homer does not represent what he represented to the Greeks; it is the principle that censorship may be justified by the claims of happiness that matters. The proposed limitations on sexual activity are rendered irrelevant by technological advances; it is the question of to what extent births can be controlled and manipulated and whether they should be that matters. The notion of rule by philosopher-kings may be seen as acceptable in theory, but unacceptable in practice, because although we can formally distinguish between desirable and undesirable rulers, on Plato's criteria, we cannot be so sure that we can distinguish between them in practice, and we certainly cannot be sure that absolute power will not corrupt absolutely. More generally a self-sufficient, inward-looking community such as the Republic simply could not survive in the world as we know it.

Thus, although a community might be happy for a short while on almost any terms, provided that education had promoted enmeshment, if we wish to be realistic, the continued existence of a happy community will depend upon the maintenance of a high level of competence and expertise in various spheres, most obviously the scientific sphere. Scientific enquiry, and the pursuit of knowledge and competence in various other spheres, thus become worthwhile activities, not because there is any inherent value in such activities, but because they are necessary as a means to the maintenance of a happy community in a world that is in danger of being beyond our control.

The above remarks merely constitute general observations (that will be expanded below) designed to indicate that there are various considerations, tied to the supremacy of happiness, that make it quite clear that any view of education that puts the emphasis on what the child 'chooses' to do (whatever 'chooses' is supposed to mean in reference to five-year-olds), is simply abandoning its responsibility in respect of the claims of happiness. Child-centred enthusiasts must therefore be seen as curious optimists or as advocates of some principle, presumably freedom, that is of more weight than happiness, or as liberal-democrats, benignly but hopelessly juggling around with freedom and happiness.

Plato's principles are, I stress, compatible with the notion of a representative democracy such as our own. To say as much is merely to repeat the point that the rule of the philosopher-kings, as outlined in the *Republic*, embodies merely the formal claim that some are more fit to rule than others, because they are more concerned for the general welfare and less for private profit or honour than others,[6] because they are more adept at appreciating and serving the demands of morality than others, and because they are more proficient at seeing how the moral ends of a community may truly be served than others. But, while holding this view, one might consistently argue that, in practice, to determine who are philosopher-kings is extremely difficult and that there is an enormous risk involved in entrusting absolute power to any limited clique, particularly if that clique is effectively self-perpetuating. Therefore, one might reasonably conclude, the aim of promoting happiness might in practice be better served by some form of representative democracy (taking Mill's assumption that people are often better able to make a sound selection of representatives than a sound decision on any specific issue), and a better way to achieve the objective of having right reason enthroned over government (right reason meaning adherence to utilitarian principles) might in practice be to insist that chosen representatives be truly divorced from private interest and compelled to undergo some training specifically related to the requirements demanded of statesmen.

But Plato's principles are not compatible with many actual features of our democracy. Broadly speaking all those features that lead to anxiety, frustration, tension, envy and all other concepts logically opposed to happiness, up to and including actual opposition to the demands of society, and that are supposedly justified by appeal to a principle of freedom, are objectionable. Thus the competitive basis of our society is unacceptable, since competition necessarily only serves its purpose, if some desire what they cannot have. The distribution of rewards, decided in our society by a combination of specific ability and power, is unacceptable, in so far as the rewards in question are desired by all. The distribution of jobs, in so far as it is governed by supply and demand rather than the aptitude of individuals is unacceptable. And the promotion of exemplars of patterns of behaviour that are denied to the individual, in so far as this promotion fosters a tendency towards such patterns of behaviour, is unacceptable.

Faced with this open society, which is fundamentally unjust because its manner of distribution is largely random and because it fails to aim at ensuring equal happiness for all, what would Plato do today? Presumably, now as then, he would eschew violence and revolution. The objection to violence is that it causes immediate unhappiness and involves the assumption that one knows that one is right and that further discussion with others with a different point of view is a waste of time. Plato does not say this, of course, and it may seem paradoxical to claim that the progenitor of the philosopher-kings would have any qualms about knowing that he was right. He was certainly convinced that he was right, but we cannot avoid recognising that his whole life is devoted to the aim of convincing others that he is right rather than enforcing his conviction.

Clearly he would seek to convince us first of the soundness of his philosophy, which task has been attempted in the preceding pages, and secondly that the end must be achieved via education. That is the significance of the ending to Book 7 where we are told that the institution of the Republic is to be begun 'by sending away into the country all citizens over the age of ten; having thus removed the children from the influence of their parents' present way of life, they can be brought up according to the methods and rules which we have described'. The point is repeated elsewhere that the first step is the important one and the educational provisions of a state dictate the nature of that state.[7]

Popper is therefore correct when he says that Plato's educational aim is 'exactly the same' as his political aim.[8] That aim is the creation of a community in which the individuals shall live together on fair terms, in happiness and harmony. Within this aim there is no *a priori* reason why education should not involve many other features, such as the promotion of culture or the development of the intellect. But this aim is overriding, and the substantiation of its claims now clear.

It is astonishing in itself that Popper finds this identification of a political and educational aim 'astonishing'. We cannot take seriously the suggestion that a community might have some fundamental aim, such as the provision of happiness for all, and not intend that education within the community should contribute to that end. Since political aims, political methods and political practice on the one hand, and educational aims, methods and practice on the other, are both judged and valued by reference to ethical values, a state or community that exhibits or enshrines certain values is bound to value educational activity that enshrines these same values and to seek to see that they are appreciated and observed.

Nor is the practice of liberal-democratic states in fact any different in this respect to that of totalitarian states. For all Popper's horror of the thought, the liberal-democratic political aim of a society that maximises free and independent activity, even at the expense of the claims of happiness, is ideally reflected in a similar educational aim. Hence the emphasis on rationality in the sense of the spontaneous probing of principles as an aim of education,[9] the claim that we ought not to allow an uncritical and easy belief in God,[10] and, more broadly, the rejection of a utilitarian view of education in favour of a classical view.[11] The justification of the classical view, considering education 'in its own character, as the development of thinking or criticism',[12] is itself dependent on the ethical substantiation necessary for the justification of the liberal-democratic state.

The reason that it is necessary to write 'ideally reflected' is that, sadly, the liberal-democrats are not even consistent. Thus Crossman amazingly concedes that we ought to let the state deliberately mould the minds of children;[13] the concession is amazing because it seems at such a variance with the usual liberal-democratic emphasis on individuality, but it is not, of course, actually contradictory with liberal-democratism, since all that Crossman needs to do to explain his position here is to arbitrarily lay stress on the principle of happiness. Popper, on the other hand, though reticent about what he really thinks ought to be done in the name of education, objects that Crossman's view that 'it is madness to allow the minds of children to be moulded by individual taste and force of circumstance' is alien to the spirit of liberal-democratism; but then it is not at all clear how, while building up the claims of freedom and objecting to state interference, Popper can consistently justify his demand for state education or the provision of funds so that the individual's incapacity to pay should not debar him from study. Characteristically Popper is content to leave the matter on the level of a statement of his point of view: 'This, I believe, belongs to the state's protective functions'.[14] Beyond that he is content to take refuge in the Manfred syndrome:[15]

> *A certain amount* of state control in education ... is necessary, if the young are to be protected from a neglect which would make them unable to defend their freedom, and the state should see that all educational facilities are available to everybody. But *too much* state control in educational matters is a fatal danger to freedom, since it must lead to indoctrination (Italics mine).

What does Popper *mean*? How much control is too much control? By what criteria does one decide? We have seen that, whatever view is taken of 'indoctrination', those who object to it do so because it involves a restriction of freedom. But this does not help us to discover when and why it is wrong to restrict what freedom. The formula 'protection from neglect which would render one unable to defend one's freedom' is beguiling, but what does it mean? Is it different from Popper's other formula 'the protection of that freedom which does not harm other people'? If it is not, then, as I have already argued, superficial reference to freedom is obscuring the fact that formally the claims of freedom have been declared subordinate to the claims of avoiding harm, which can only meaningfully be explicated in terms of promoting happiness. If it is different, why is it different? Why is Popper making use of two distinct formulae? Besides which surely one has to offer some explication of what *freedom* the individual should be in a position to defend, unless Popper is willing to go the whole way and say that all that ultimately matters is that the individual should be free to do whatever he chooses to do.

As for Russell, his contortions are nothing short of a shambles. He refers to the importance of 'creating the habits which will give happiness and usefulness in later life'[16] and remarks that the 'preservation of a civilised community demands ... some method of causing children to behave in a manner which is not natural to them',[17] thereby, on the face of it, placing himself firmly in the Platonic utilitarian camp. But, of course, Russell would never so classify himself, and the demand that we 'create' and 'cause' changes in the individual child with a view to the preservation of a happy community, therefore sticks out as an arbitrary fiat, since its *justification* would seem to be dependent upon the view that the principle of happiness is supreme. Because Russell will not accept this, but remains committed to an independent principle of freedom that may override the claims of happiness, he too reverts to the Manfred syndrome, recommending specific courses of action in the educational sphere and then demanding that adherence to that course of action be qualified in the name of freedom—naturally without being able to say to what extent the qualification should apply: 'A sense of citizenship, of social co-operation', he tells us, for instance, 'is therefore ... necessary ... but it remains important that this should be secured without *too great* a diminution of individual judgment and individual initiative'[18] (my italics.) And he offers (on the same page, incidentally) the wholly Platonic view that 'if a man's life is to be satisfactory ... it requires two kinds of harmony: an internal harmony of intelligence, emotion and will, and an external harmony with the wills of others'; but he then adds that 'the matter of external harmony with the wills of others is ... not capable of a complete solution' because 'it is difficult to suppress competition completely without destroying individuality'.[19]

Amateur psychology seems to be a constitutional disease amongst freedom fighters, but even if we accept this particular psychological claim about the need for competition as well founded, we still need to know on what grounds Russell thinks that we are entitled to create any attitudes that promote external harmony, if the claims of individuality can legitimately stand in the way of the aim of that harmony.

Every state, assuming that it is in control of itself, imposes its own values on its children both indirectly (in the way it organises distribution, in the way its teachers behave, etc.), and directly (in the things we say, the behaviour we punish, etc.), with more or less success. The fact that a state seems to impose little, because its value code allows of contradictory evaluations, because it leaves much of education to private influence, and because its teachers have considerable freedom, shows only that one of its values *is* freedom, which, naturally enough, is enshrined in or imposed on the society, whether its members like it or not.

Therefore, in order to arrive at a juster society, by a steady if slow means, we must modify out approach to education. But, in saying we must use education as a means to this end, we are not implicitly slighting the concept, as we might be felt to be slighting the inherent value of a piece of mud, if we saw its use only as a means to the end of blocking a gap in a wall. Education is not like a piece of mud; it must necessarily result in something, it must bring something about, on any analysis, and it is in that sense that we regard it as a means to an end. The task of deciding what ought to be done, in order to achieve what end is equivalent to filling in one's concept of education. The decision to turn to the educational process in order to realise one's ideal, and the application of one's moral philosophy to the sphere of education are ultimately one and the same thing.

2   Application of Platonic principles to education

Application of Plato's utilitarian principles to the sphere of education gives us three basic principles, of which the latter two are to some degree dependent on the first. They are:

(a)   The aim of education is to produce sociable and happy citizens. Education is (by which we mean, of course, that in our view the neutral sociological use of the term education is correctly used as a normative term only when the following conditions are met) the development of virtuous character[20] in the sense of a character that exhibits socially desirable attitudes and behavioural tendencies, the precise nature of which is to be decided by appeal to the principle of happiness in the light of actual circumstances. A man is educated in so far as he exhibits this virtuous character. He is not educated merely because he has been initiated into a cultural heritage, or because he has acquired a corpus of information, or because he has acquired certain technical skills, or because he has developed a brain capable of shrewd calculation, or even because he has developed 'some kind of cognitive perspective'. But let us be quite clear what we are saying here: first we are not necessarily denying that some or all of these may represent desirable objectives for the educational system, but if they are desirable objectives they will be so, because, for example, 'some kind of cognitive perspective' may contribute to the aim of producing sociable and happy citizens. Secondly it is open to anyone to object that this is simply not what people generally mean by an educated man. This is probably true, and of very little interest. In saying that an educated man is one who exhibits virtuous character, I am, of course, saying that in bringing up children we ought to aim at promoting this virtuous character, and that this is what we ought to understand as education in a normative sense. The substantiation for this claim is to be found in the body of this book.

(b) All children should therefore be trained from an early age to adopt the norms of society.

(c) The precise nature of the education that a child undergoes at a later stage should be decided, in so far as it is possible, by reference to his aptitude and the demands and needs of the society. (The norms, needs and demands of society must, of course, be defined with reference to the claims of Platonic utilitarianism.)

It is clear that these three educational principles will lead to three distinct stages of education that may be defined by reference to their immediate objective: the first stage is primarily concerned with the formation of attitudes, the second stage is primarily concerned with developing aptitude in relation to a specific social role (or groups of social roles), and the third stage is primarily concerned with the probing of moral principles. This must be the order of the three stages, since attitudes are perforce acquired early on, since aptitudes develop gradually, and since the probing of moral principles, besides being a sophisticated practice that requires a certain maturity, cannot take place until the principles are known, and is to be regarded as a specific job or social role (see below). These three stages can, of course, be found in the *Republic*, but we are not committed to Plato's actual divisions of time (for instance, that the third stage should continue until the fiftieth year). What is the best age at which to change the nature of the education provided must be decided by empirical considerations, which cannot be dictated here.

I shall now briefly outline the nature of each of these three stages, thereby to some extent summarising conclusions drawn in previous chapters.

The immediate consequence for education of utilitarianism is that the educational process ought to be concerned to ensure equal happiness; for, if the ideal society is one in which all individuals are equally happy, then clearly it is wrong to manipulate or interfere with people in any way that runs counter to this aim. The happiness of the community at large is dependent on the upbringing of its children.

In view of the nature of happiness, being a feeling brought about by enmeshment between the individual and his situation, it is necessary that there shall be a homogeneous conviction created in respect of such things as affect the whole community, and that such things as an individual should be called upon to experience that are not common to all, the most obvious example of which is his job, should be suited to him. Since attitudes of some sort are inevitably formed very early on in life, and since forming the desired ones from the beginning is obviously more painless than attempting to drive out casually formed and unacceptable attitudes at a later stage, the homogeneous conviction in respect of such things as affect the whole community should be the task essentially of the first stage of education. And naturally this stage must be undergone by all children.

One such thing is the value code of the community or the moral norms. There are two distinct points being made at this juncture:
(a)   A happy community is dependent in part upon the acceptance by the individuals within it of the moral norms that are put into practice in the rules and conventions of their society. This is a purely formal point, arising out of the Platonic analysis of happiness, and one that has validity regardless of one's view of the status of moral norms.

(b)   The norms that ought to be accepted are the Platonic norms: that is to say, the belief or conviction that happiness is the supreme value and that there are no good grounds, *a priori*, for so organising any aspect of community life so as to treat people unequally in respect of happiness. In addition, the belief that the criterion of aptitude, or ability and interest, is the right and proper criterion for the distribution of activities within the community; and, finally, the assumption that freedom is an unhelpful concept, and that freedom is desirable only where and when men have clearly shown themselves able and willing to put the claims of equal happiness before all other claims.

Accordingly we must bring up our children to feel that they ought to be concerned for the equal happiness of all; they must come to feel and to express approval at examples of this code being observed in practice; they must be commended when they show concern for the happiness of others.

At this juncture we are thinking of young children and we are implanting or cultivating attitudes. Strictly speaking we are not propagating doctrines (i.e. Platonism) the truth of which 'is seriously doubted, and on excellent grounds . . . as if they were unquestionably true',[21] because we are not propagating doctrines at all; we are not getting people to believe that certain propositions are true or false; propositions do not have a place in the infant world. The question whether, and in what way, it is true that one ought to promote equal happiness for all men, is a highly specialised and complex question, and children's attitudes are formed, deliberately or by chance, somewhat in advance of any capability of dealing with it.

But in any case, allowing for the argument that there will come a time when these children will attempt to formulate to themselves the substance of the attitudes they hold in some such statement as 'one ought to promote the equal happiness of all', so that in the long run we *are* effectively propagating a doctrine as if it were unquestionably true, there are two possible replies, either of which may be made and may be the more appropriate depending upon the position adopted by the objector, but the former of which is the one that I should choose to give.

(a) We are indeed in the long run effectively propagating a doctrine as it if were unquestionably true, because in our judgment it is unquestionably true, and we have given our reasons for that judgment. We have *not* claimed that its truth can be established in the same manner as one would establish the truth of an empirical proposition, merely that it is true, and that its truth is established by all the proof the case admits of.

(b) If the reader/objector takes the view, like Russell, that ultimate moral propositions not only cannot be proven true in a manner similar to that involved in proving an empirical proposition true, but cannot meaningfully be said to be proven true at all, so that, whatever the value of my arguments above, the truth of the proposition 'one ought to promote the equal happiness of all' is essentially undiscoverable, I reply: in so far as it were true that ultimate moral propositions were unprovable, it would be quite acceptable to inculcate values nonetheless. Either ultimate moral principles can in principle be known to be true, in which case we necessarily teach what we believe we know to be true, just as we teach children certain scientific laws as true, even though one day the laws may be invalidated, and even though some of the children will never be able to understand the reasoning that, at the moment, convinces us of their truth—or the world is such that, in principle, we could establish the truth or falsity of all empirical propositions, but could never establish the truth or falsity of ultimate moral propositions, in which case, in insisting on promulgating certain injunctions as if they were true, we are not teaching what is false, but are merely promoting belief in something that, according to the argument, can only be believed in or not believed in. If the claim that 'one ought to X' is merely man's way of expressing his pro-attitude to X, then all we *can* be doing in fostering commitment to this injunction is fostering taste.

Assuming that the former defence is the one chosen (the claim that the proposition in question is true), it has been conceded that the inculcation of belief is this proposition, with the express intention that it shall remain, and in the knowledge that we shall not necessarily be encouraging all children ultimately to examine the arguments behind the injunction, constitutes, on most definitions, indoctrination; but it has been argued that indoctrination, on such definitions, is justifiable. Some individuals will later be encouraged to probe the arguments that lie behind the proposition, that is to say some individuals will later specialise in the field of moral philosophy, just as others will specialise in the field of geology, and probe the arguments that lie behind certain geological propositions. But the individuals who undertake the specific task of probing the field of moral philosophy will be, in practice, a limited number: the aim of promoting enmeshment will prevent us from encouraging those whose *lack of interest* or whose lack of ability in the matter would lead merely to a loss of faith in the proposition, rather than a reasoned rejection of it, to undertake the task. Some individuals, probably many, will imbibe the proposition's contents at an early age and be allowed to continue in adult life in unquestioning acceptance of the proposition's truth.

We may call this process, which is the essential business of the first stage of education, 'socialisation', but by this term I mean to refer not only to the inculcation of those Platonic moral norms and such specific injunctions as follow from them, but also to the inculcation of certain social norms, which it may be agreed are ultimately conventional and arbitrary. For instance a society may adopt the social norm that one does not undress in public. We may suppose that it might just as well have adopted the opposite norm, that one does undress in public, rather as the Eskimoes offer their wives to guests for intimate kissing sessions, whereas we do not. Or the hypothetical society in question might have adopted a norm such that it was a matter of indifference whether one undressed in public or not. Such a norm, whichever variant is selected, is morally neutral; although reasons might be given for preferring one to another (the climate, for instance), we do not regard any one as necessarily more rationally justifiable than another. The value of such a norm is entirely dependent on its being universally recognised and accepted, for only thus is enmeshment assured. If I am brought up to disapprove of the idea of somebody stripping naked in the Albert Hall, it is necessary for my happiness, however trivially so, that I shall not be subjected to such a sight. The promotion of such a sight upsets the situation with which my character is enmeshed and therefore diminishes my happiness. More simply, I am indignant, outraged or shocked, which concepts are incompatible with the concept of happiness. But equally, of course, the man who is motivated to undress in public needs to do so for his happiness. We have to avoid situations in which such conflict arises, if we are to ensure the happiness of all, and therefore we must see to it that such social norms as are opted for by society are successfully and universally inculcated. This is not, of course, to say that we should adopt as many positive social norms as possible, merely that when we do opt for one it should be generally imbibed.

Since the primary object of this stage of education is the formation of attitude and behavioural tendency, it is possible that we should seek to start it considerably earlier than the present age at which children are obliged to go to school and perhaps extend it for longer. But such suggestions are now dependent for their resolution on empirical data, which it is beyond the scope of this book to provide.

The imbibement of the moral and conventional norms, the acquisition of a sense of brotherhood and an attitude of tolerance, the adherence to such notions as impartiality, dependability and honesty, will, of course, be achieved symbolically at this stage. One does not, for instance, try to reason with the child that there are no relevant criteria for discriminating between people in respect of happiness, because such reasoning would be meaningless to the child. Instead one fosters the attitude of impartiality by example; and to this end material in books, on television, etc. should be censored, not only with the negative purpose of deleting the undesirable, but with the positive purpose of promoting the desirable, until such time, if ever, as evidence is forthcoming to discredit the assumption that books, films, etc. have a direct effect on the developing mind.

At a later stage it is the task of education to apply itself to role formation or the equipping of the individual for a social function that is both desirable and available. The necessity for this has been shown in our analysis of happiness. If we wish to ensure the enmeshment of the individual we cannot leave the business of his finding a role, whether as dustman or doctor, to some form of chance such as competition or the law of supply and demand.

There is an advertisement for a certain make of bed that admonishes us to take some trouble over our choice of bed since we spend a third of our life in it. It seems extraordinary that when we spend considerably more of our life in a job, it still seems necessary to exhort educationalists to come down from the clouds and do something about preparing children for a job.

Plato offers us the eminently rational criterion of aptitude, by which is meant both interest in doing X and the ability to do X, for allotting individuals to roles. The slight obscurity, already noted, in his view of the relative weight to be attached to hereditary and environmental factors in the formation of aptitude is not of critical importance to us. In view of the conflicting claims made by psychologists about the degree to which intelligence is an innate factor and the extent to which it is determined by heredity, we must in any case proceed by hypothesis.

Whenever a child does display a marked aptitude for a specific role, this, according to Plato, is a relevant criterion for developing that aptitude in the child, provided that it is a socially desirable role. Clearly there is room for equivocation on the question of what roles are socially desirable, but we may say that any role that promotes the smooth and happy running of the community is desirable; once the roles that are essential to the happiness of the community have been filled, other roles, provided they are not antipathetic to the happiness of the community, constitute socially desirable roles. We cannot lay down a long list of roles that are necessarily necessary to the happiness of the community, because it follows from the fact elucidated in our analysis of happiness that there are no necessary conditions for happiness, that what roles are socially desirable will vary from community to community. But in our society, for instance, because it is greatly dependent on mobility, bus-driving and train-driving are socially desirable roles.

The reason that aptitude for a desirable role is a relevant criterion for developing that aptitude is once again tied up with enmeshment. Aptitude includes interest, and, if a child has an interest in X, to cater to that interest is to promote enmeshment, whereas to ignore it or curb it is to promote at least temporary frustration. Sometimes, particularly during the years of development, immediate frustration for the individual will be necessary in his or the community's long-term happiness interest, but where the child has an interest in train-driving, and the community has a need for train-drivers, there is no good reason not to develop the child's interest. Aptitude also involves ability, and potential ability at X is obviously, in the absence of any other considerations, a relevant reason for developing that ability in X rather than trying to foster an interest in Y or Z, on the assumption that X, Y and Z are all socially desirable roles that need to be filled. This is particularly clear in the reverse situation. Ought implies can, and therefore when an individual displays a marked lack of aptitude for certain types of role, as for instance, to take an extreme example, in the case of educationally subnormal children who lack the ability to engage in any academic roles, that is a relevant criterion for trying to foster different aptitudes.

But, and this is the crucial point, in so far as a child does not display any particular aptitude and is not obviously debarred from the possibility of acquiring any aptitude, it is the task of education to create an aptitude for some socially desirable role.

If we assume, purely for the sake of a pointed example, that we are faced with a group of children who appear to be equally capable of developing any aptitude, and that society happens to have need for biologists, house agents and dustmen in equal proportion, then, since there is no relevant criterion for deciding which children shall have which aptitude developed, the decision must be arbitrary. But the decision must be made, because, if it is not, one effectively condemns some children to develop an aptitude for one thing, only to find no possibility of fulfilling that aptitude in later life, and, instead, to be forced to work in a role for which they have no aptitude.

If it be argued that arbitrarily deciding to educate an individual to be a dustman rather than, say, a biologist is unfair on him, we reply that it is only an example of obnoxious discrimination on the supposition that it is worse to be a dustman than a biologist. But would the liberal-democrat want to assert that being a dustman was inherently inferior or worse than being a biologist? Or would he rather point to our society and argue that it is a worse job inasmuch as it is less satisfying and worse paid? The argument that it is less satisfying is absurd in the face of a proposal to make sure that dustmen are satisfied being dustmen. The argument that it is worse paid fails to achieve its object also: for, if it is worse paid, it is so, however we decide to allocate the role. Faced with roles that are agreed to be relatively undesirable because less well paid, the obvious solution is the political one, which Plato today would certainly advocate, of paying an equal wage for these roles. But, until that time comes, the question of how they should be distributed must be decided without reference to the rate of pay. The liberal-democratic view that distribution of roles should essentially be decided by merit and free choice has been rejected precisely because it necessarily leads to a measure of dissatisfaction amongst those who find that, in practice, they have no choice and the worst job.

However, in fact the situation will not be as extreme as that envisaged above. Although it is unlikely that any individual will leap from the womb with a fully fledged aptitude for the role of house agent, it is certainly likely that by the end of the first stage of education, which, except for the emphasis on socialisation, has been as free as possible, in order to let the child display such embryonic interests and types of ability as he has, it will be possible to make a broad division between those whose potential aptitude is likely to be academic and those whose potential aptitude is likely to be practical. This division corresponds to Plato's division between the third group and the combined group of guardians and future rulers, and we must understand such aptitudes as that for being a house agent as coming under the wing of academics, while the practical will include such trades as that of electrician or motor mechanic.

Once this division has been made the cultivation of more specific aptitudes in either group will proceed gradually, as a spiral between observed interests and abilities and reinforcement by the educational machine. In practice we may expect to see some individuals developing clear and specific aptitudes at this stage. But for the rest the school must make it the major part of its task, during the second half of this stage, to bring the various social roles and what they involve home to the child, and, when some specific interest is shown, to develop the corresponding ability.

The view that education ought to involve socialisation in the sense outlined and a close attention to future social role will probably offend both the Left educational wing, who may fear type-casting for the workers, and the Right who will without doubt argue that this is all very well, but it is not education.

But to say that this is not education, to argue, for instance, that education involves the promotion of a certain cultural heritage, is simply to put forward the view that we ought to promote the study of a certain cultural heritage amongst our children. The onus is clearly on those who believe this, to set out the arguments leading to that injunction, and to discredit the arguments above that lead to the Platonic conclusion. And the same procedure may and must be adopted in the face of any other prescriptive analysis of education.

The widely held view that education is primarily about developing rationality likewise needs to be considered with caution, though here it is important to know precisely what is meant by rationality. If we understand the term rationality to pick out such procedural qualities as impartiality, consistency, coherence, relevance and a refusal to countenance fallacious argument, then Plato would agree with his critics that rationality is everywhere preferable to irrationality. We should therefore discourage reasoning of the type 'Hitler is undesirable; Hitler inspired a totalitarian regime; therefore all totalitarian regimes are undesirable'.

But this is not the same as saying that we ought to encourage all people to enquire into and satisfy for themselves the rational foundations of all beliefs that they have. Some beliefs, such as moral beliefs, will be better left unquestioned by those people whose abilities are limited in this field to the extent that they will merely become confused by attempting to question them or (more disastrous from the point of view of the harmony of the whole community), that they will actually come out with different beliefs that are in fact not rationally justifiable, but for the adoption of which they will agitate: they will then be unenmeshed with the society as it is and the overall stability of the state will be under pressure.

In recognising the claims of rationality, then, one is committed to avoiding the promotion of beliefs that involve partiality, incoherence, inconsistency or irrelevance, and one must require that when people indulge in reasoning they shall be impartial, coherent, consistent and relevant. But nothing here suggests that people ought to be necessarily encouraged to search for a rational justification for every belief they hold. A man's rationality is judged by the extent to which, *if* he reasons, he avoids partiality and so on, and not by the extent to which he tries to reason about things. Our desire is to implant rational beliefs and attitudes and behavioural tendencies in people, where there is a choice between rational and irrational, and not that each individual should be his own philosopher.

But if one takes rationality to be equivalent to autonomy, so that the aim of promoting rationality may be identified with the aim of promoting the active process of reasoning and 'awakening of self-criticism and critical thought',[22] and argues that this is what education necessarily involves, then one is doing no more than arguing that children ought to be brought to question and challenge all assumptions with which they might come into contact. Such a view requires a substantiation, which we have argued is lacking, and would need to show either that the claims of equal happiness are not overriding, or that the argument suggesting that in practice the policy involved in such a view leads to a lack of enmeshment is empirically false. In short all *a priori* assumptions about the nature of education have to be discarded, or else the Platonic politico-ethical philosophy has to be discredited.

However, the fact that the view that education is essentially about the dissemination of culture or about critical analysis is rejected, does not mean that the Platonist is hostile to either culture or critical thought. It is simply that he welcomes them and positively encourages them only in so far as they contribute, long-term or short-term, to a happy and justly organised society. The fact that it may be extremely difficult in practice to calculate whether and to what extent certain cultural studies in education do contribute to happiness does not, of course, invalidate the procedure.

In so far as the role of each individual in our society is likely to involve considerably increased leisure in the future, we clearly have to educate with a view to that leisure, and for many children the development of an interest in various cultural pursuits, will seem the most worthwhile way to prepare for that leisure and the course of action most suited to their interests and abilities. The Platonic utilitarian differs from those who see education as essentially concerned with the transmission of culture, in that he would promote cultural *oeuvres* only in so far as the study of them contributes indirectly to the promotion of happiness or in so far as they provide a source of satisfaction and are not anti-social in their content, and not because they are deemed to be inherently worthy in some other non-moral sense. This is because it follows from all that has been said that expressions such as 'valuable in itself', which are often applied to works of art or the study thereof, can only be interpreted to mean 'valuable in that it directly provides a source of pleasure'. Nothing is valuable in any respect whatsoever that does not either directly, by providing pleasure or satisfaction, or indirectly, by contributing to means that may serve the end, promote a balance of happiness over misery.

In so far as any degree of intelligence is needed for the appreciation of such works, that, of course, provides a relevant criterion in respect of deciding which pupils should be initiated into the culture in question, just as it may provide a good reason for the study of such works, since the promotion of intelligence may contribute to the promotion of happiness (though clearly such a claim requires considerably more elucidation and empirical backing than it has ever yet, to my knowledge, received: one would like to know in respect of claims for the increased sensitivity, awareness and intelligence that are sometimes made for the study of literature whether there is actually any evidence that people who study literature are more sensitive, aware and intelligent people in some general sense. If all that is meant is that, by definition people who appreciate, say *Othello*, are aware of and sensitive to the dimensions of the play and can talk about it intelligently, it would seem to be a separate question as to whether they necessarily transpose these qualities to other spheres of their life). But because Plato, consistently with his utilitarian position, does not evaluate works of art, except by assessment of their tendency to promote moral behaviour or to contribute to the demands of morality, he would not, and rightly would not, share the apparent hostility of some educationalists to less subtle and less complex material such as detective novels and pop music. Such material indeed, provided that it gives pleasure and does not promote socially undesirable attitudes, would be eminently suitable for those unable to cope with the cultural heritage.

The Platonic utilitarian view of the place of culture in education is thus to be carefully distinguished from that of men such as G. H. Bantock. Bantock, as I understand him, would claim (a) that there is a cultural heritage, which has 'inherent value' apart from its effects in producing pleasure, otherwise contributing to happiness, or promoting morally desirable behaviour, and (b) that although a distinct culture may be necessary for the majority, that culture cannot consist of detective novels and pop music—'the ephemeral offerings of railway bookstalls'[23] and 'piped commercial culture'[24]— since these products are inherently valueless.

Although Bantock refers to the use of literature for presenting moral norms to a sophisticated minority, and remarks that 'fundamentally, great literature affords us the means of moral and perceptual growth',[25] it must be remembered that he is 'propounding a doctrine of self-realisation in terms of that excellence which is proper to a human being'.[26] Consequently, although from a utilitarian point of view detective novels and pop music may be admirable, because they may inculcate desirable norms, and although Bantock himself sees the need to approach many via 'affective' methods rather than rational argument, he is unable to accept the use of the products of the industrial culture as educative material, and, conversely, is able to claim that some books are of greater importance than others, even if they do not do any more to promote belief in desirable norms, 'because they represent a more deliberate, refined and sophisticated exploitation of human potentiality—as poetry is superior to pushpin'.[27] All we can say here is that, quantity of pleasure being equal, poetry is not superior to pushpin, while conceding that it may well be better for those who can to study poetry than play pushpin at school, since the study of poetry may well contribute both directly and indirectly considerably more to the maintenance and promotion of happiness. (My cautious phrasing in the above is not due to any doubt that this is so, but merely to the fact that we do not have sufficient evidence to assert boldly that it is the case.)

Similarly rationality in both the senses outlined above will be promoted. Rationality in the sense of the display of impartiality, objectivity, relevance and coherence, will at all times be required of all children, in so far as they are engaged in the task of reasoning about any stage of their work, or indeed more generally of their life. An obvious area in which such a display of rationality may be called upon is when consideration is given to such material as we have just been considering (i.e. pop music, detective novels), and it will be all the more reasonable for us to hope that children will discuss this material rationally in so far as we have suited the material to the aptitude of the child.

But what there should not be at this stage is any deliberate attempt to foster rationality, in that other peculiar sense of critical enquiry, into all matters. Of course there will be critical enquiry into various aspects of the educational experiences to which children are subject. But to encourage critical enquiry into the workings of a car engine, for instance, in order to arrive at a greater understanding of that engine, is not the same thing as encouraging critical enquiry into all manner of subjects for the sake of promoting a tendency to critical enquiry.

The secondary stage of Platonic education is clearly distinct from the ideal of a liberal-education as pioneered by such men as Hirst, notwithstanding the fact that in an important article Hirst sees liberal education as originally a Greek ideal.[28]

It is in fact Plato who first clearly puts an emphasis on the pursuit of knowledge as desirable, and Hirst may well have him in mind. Nonetheless it is quite wrong, as the previous chapters should have made clear, to see Plato as the advocate of liberal-education in Hirst's sense of the term. It is true that both Plato and Aristotle, the latter considerably more than the former, tend to talk as if the pursuit of knowledge is the essential good for man, on the grounds that a rational mind is man's distinctive feature and hence must be connected with man's distinctive good. But, of course, as Hirst rightly points out, Plato (or, as he says, the Greeks) is committed to the view that the mind can come 'to know the essential nature of things and can apprehend what is ultimately real and immutable'. On these terms we need not dispute that the pursuit of knowledge is desirable for man. However, despite the hints in Plato's writing that the reasoning faculty is the divine element in man, it is absolutely clear that he does not see the activity of the pursuit of knowledge as necessarily desirable for man. He does not advocate it for all men. He is anxious only that some shall engage in the activity in order to find the truth.

Hirst explicates what he means by 'liberal-education' very clearly. A 'liberal-education' is not defined as the antithesis of a specialised education; it is not initiation into a broad range of subjects. Rather it is initiation into the various forms of knowledge with which man is familiar. It is coming to understand the distinctive features of such things as historical reasoning, mathematical reasoning and religious reasoning, not necessarily so that in each sphere the individual will become an expert (e.g. an expert historian, an expert mathematician). The object is that the individual should understand and recognise the manner of historical enquiry or of the pursuit of mathematical knowledge. 'It is the coming to look at things in a certain way that is being aimed at ... it is the ability to recognise empirical assertions or aesthetic judgements for what they are'.[30] And the key feature of a liberal-education is that it is comprehensive: we are concerned with 'the range of knowledge as a whole'.[31]

The members of the largest group of citizens in the Republic evidently do not receive such a liberal-education. But nor, probably, do the philosopher-kings; for although they go through a curriculum that involves, for instance, an awareness of an experience in mathematical knowledge, there is no evidence that active steps will be taken to initiate them into, say, the form of knowledge associated with 'literature and the fine arts'[32] as Hirst would understand that knowledge.

Now it is to be stressed both that, apparently, on Hirst's view a liberal-education must be concerned with all forms of knowledge and that this education is the 'ultimate form of education',[33] which, I take it, means that this is the sort of education we ought to be giving and that other considerations are subordinate to it (though not, therefore, necessarily, unimportant). The sort of education that we are led to demand by considering present conditions in the light of Platonic principles is not hostile to liberal-education in itself. The Platonist, like Hirst, may be critical of 'the narrow minded boffin' and 'the arts man, blank in his incomprehension of the scientific outlook'[34] up to a point. But whereas Hirst would presumably scorn such people as unworthily educated, the Platonist would worry only that in our society the narrow minded boffin is expected to, is called upon to and expects to consider, discuss and pass judgment on matters where his acquaintance with scientific knowledge is largely irrelevant. Thus he makes moral judgments without being familiar with any of the distinctive features of moral knowledge. If a man may be familiar with all forms of knowledge, and competent in the handling of them, the Platonist will not object. But, that having been said, he takes issue with the idea that liberal-education is the best education.

First, while conceding Hirst's point that the suggestion that not all individuals could profitably undergo such an education is backed to a considerable extent by the mere fact that not enough effort has yet gone into experimentation to establish the contrary, he feels entitled to remain sceptical about the practical likelihood of all men displaying competence in the intricacies of all forms of knowledge. Secondly, and this of course is the point of interest to us, he holds that happiness is the supreme moral principle and that the happiness of both individuals and community is promoted by an education concerned to equip the individual for a particular social role. This consideration does not preclude a liberal-education, but it requires that emphasis (and time) be given to this end rather than to concern for a liberal-education. And the Platonist also holds that happiness as the ultimate end does not necessitate familiarity with all, or indeed any specific, forms of knowledge.

The question therefore is whether any justification can be given of the claim that a liberal-education is the ultimate education. The answer is evidently that it cannot, for in a sense we have been arguing this point throughout the above chapters in which it was established that happiness is the supreme principle. Nonetheless we should briefly note Hirst's attempt at justification.

His argument is that the concept 'mind' and the concept 'knowledge' are so related that 'the achievement of knowledge is necessarily the development of mind'.[35] This we may accept. The question now, therefore, is ought the development of mind or the achievement of knowledge to override all other considerations? We recognise at once that we are on familiar ground. We are told that to ask for justification of this is 'a peculiar question' and that 'to ask for a justification of the pursuit of rational knowledge itself presupposes some form of commitment to what one is seeking to justify'.[36] But once again we must say that this argument will not serve to establish 'the ultimate significance' of a liberal-education. In seeking the justification, one is committed only to the notion that propositions, opinions or whatever, should be based on sound reasoning. One is not necessarily committed to the view that each individual who believes a proposition to be true or who holds an opinion should be able to give an account of those reasons. Still less is one committed to the view that all people ought to pursue knowledge of all kinds.

Of course on Hirst's analysis it is by definition true that the more forms of knowledge with which one is familiar the more extended or developed is one's mind. But no argument has been forthcoming to establish that there is an ultimate obligation on mankind to develop or extend the mind. The Platonist will not accept, and no reasoning establishes that he should, that the unreflective peasant, whose beliefs are true according to the reasoning of those who do indulge in reasoning about these beliefs, whatever they are, but who does not himself reason about them, and who, perhaps, is totally unacquainted with certain forms of knowledge, such as mathematical or artistic, is a less worthy or a less perfect human being. One cannot help but suspect that behind the emphasis on mind-development of some philosophers, is lurking a species of naturalism: man is a rational animal, therefore he ought to be a rational animal, therefore the more he practices rational enquiry the better he is. But it hardly need be said that the premiss does not lead to the conclusion.

If we want people to examine and arrive at their own moral beliefs, then it goes without saying that we shall require them to be familiar with that, and in fact other, forms of knowledge. But the Platonist does not want this. He wants to ensure happiness. Beneath that ultimate objective he will approve of initiation into various forms of knowledge precisely and only in so far as awareness of various forms of knowledge on the part of a given individual contributes to happiness. The provision of a liberal-education for all could only be justified as the best education if it could be established that the active pursuit of all forms of knowledge by all individuals was more important than the happiness of those same individuals.

I pass over in silence certain problems that I find inherent in Hirst's thesis—most particularly his actual classification of the forms of knowledge and his criteria for classification—preferring to stress my main point that initiation into such logically distinct forms of knowledge as there are (and I do not dispute that there are some) is a desirable educational objective only if such an initiation will contribute to happiness, and not for its own sake or because it is one with the development of mind. Prima facie, since to understand and distinguish between various forms of knowledge is to avoid error, it is difficult to see how such understanding could not contribute to the happiness of the community. But of course, while endorsing Hirst's objective as a desirable educational objective, the manner of my justification of this objective, besides being acceptable in a way that Hirst's is not, leaves open the possibility that for practical reasons it may be better not to attempt to provide a liberal-education for all. If, for whatever reason, there are individuals whose initiation into what Hirst calls the moral form of knowledge (which I should prefer to regard as an aspect of the philosophical form of knowledge), for example, leads them merely to an ill-informed sceptical relativism, then it would be better that they had not experienced the initiation. And again, if a liberal-education has to take the place of vocational training, then it would be better for some that it should not do so.

It is to be presumed that if the socialisation of stage 1 has been effective, and if it has led to a greater degree of enmeshment in our secondary stage children, than our own society can boast at the moment, there will be very little impetus towards critical analysis of the norms of society. This fact, which is entirely as we planned, nonetheless leads us into our third and final educational stage.

It has been conceded throughout this book, that, although I believe that Plato's moral philosophy commands assent and have tried to show why this is so, nonetheless the status of ultimate moral principles is peculiar, and one cannot claim to have proved that X ought to be done in the same way that one can claim to be able to prove that George Gissing wrote *Demos*.[37] However confident one may be, however convincing one may be, one appreciates the liberal-democratic point that the search for truth never ends. Therefore we do not want to suppress all further enquiry. We welcome critical thought directed to examining the rationale behind our way of life.

But questioning the status and validity of value judgments is not a secondary school option. It is reserved, and it alone is reserved, for a third stage.

Critics of Plato have made a fundamental error in thinking that, if it is the case that absolute knowledge is not possible in the sphere of morality in the same way as it is in the sphere of medicine, it therefore follows that there can be no experts in ethics. There can, of course, be experts in ethics, but they will not be judged by reference to possession of an absolute body of knowledge. They will be judged as Plato wanted to judge them: first and foremost they must be people who have studied in depth the business of philosophy, for it patently *is* a field, as distinct as any other, with its own language, its own techniques, and its own way of proceeding; it also has its own library which one would be rash to simply ignore. The fact that my neighbour can make moral judgments which one may despair of ultimately disproving, no more makes him an expert in ethics than the fact that I can make aesthetic judgments, which others may despair of ultimately disproving, would make me an artistic expert.

Secondly in order to undergo a philosophical training with profit a certain degree of intelligence would seem to be required, and a positive interest in pursuing the truth. This combination constitutes the aptitude which we regard as necessary to any social role. Thirdly, although the specific degree of intelligence necessary to constitute an aptitude, and the manner of determining that degree, may be difficult to establish, a steady commitment to rationality, in the Platonic sense of impartiality, coherence, relevance, etc. is required.

The moral norms, then, involved in the socialisation process are continually scrutinised by those whose inclination, talents and training have made them most adept at this particular skill, and who have a fundamental concern for the well-being of their fellow citizens. But so long as these philosopher-kings remain convinced of a certain code, the educational machine will continue to inculcate adherence and commitment to that code.

It may, finally, be objected that, since we are dealing with a representative democracy in which the citizens are called upon to give an expression of their opinions that has a real effect on the community, it is absurd to resist the liberal-democratic plea for the development of critical thought *per se*. Thus Crossman argues that 'our purpose as educationalists today is to train up an electorate capable of understanding the issues on which they are called to vote, not experts on economics and politics, but men and women imbued with sound political judgement'.[38]

This is a most interesting statement, because it presupposes that there is such a thing as sound political judgment, in a sense other than mere knowledge of empirical data, and a way of judging it, which supposition is incompatible with the liberal-democratic opposition to the notion of philosopher-kings and what is referred to as Plato's dogmatism.

However as far as Platonism is concerned this purpose is served. For sound political judgment, according to Plato, is only possible within the framework of a moral philosophy that places the principle of happiness on a pinnacle. By ensuring that our citizens observe that principle and by encouraging impartiality, coherence and relevance at all times, we have done our best, allowing for the individual's incapacity to be rational at times, and subject to the dissemination of the factual data necessary for any political decision, to ensure that political decisions will be, as we see it, sound.

But what would sound judgment involve for a liberal-democrat? One can only refer to judgment as sound within an agreed framework, whether that framework be proven or merely assumed. Presumably for Crossman sound judgment would have to fall within the framework of what he calls 'liberal ideas', namely the principles of equality, freedom, self-government and happiness. To this there are two devastating objections: first, it has been argued that liberal-democratic commitment to a principle of freedom does not constitute sound judgment, since the nature of that commitment is incoherent. And secondly, inasmuch as these principles in practice clash and yet are deemed to be of equal weight, 'sound judgment' in a given situation could issue forth in quite contradictory decisions. The emphasis on the purpose of training up citizens with sound judgment, within the liberal-democratic framework, is thus, in practice, useless.

Unless the liberal-democrats are prepared boldly to assert that the claims of happiness are actually subordinate to the claims of freedom, which they nowhere explicitly do, then, the more political power that is given to all citizens and the more freedom that is conceded to the adult population, the more necessary it becomes to inculcate the idea of equal happiness for all. If people do not subserve this ideal, it does not require much imagination to see that, in the name of freedom, the claims of the principle of happiness will go to the wall.

3 Conclusion

At this point one might easily pass over into a more rigorous consideration of practical and detailed educational proposals, although in most cases one would also need to draw upon other disciplines for empirical data. Such issues as the move towards comprehensivisation, integrated curricula, free schools versus more traditional schools, deschooling, the appropriate ages for educational divisions, specialisation, selection or the content of the curriculum, all require some specialised empirical knowledge, particularly psychological and sociological data, before they can be finally and satisfactorily answered. This is not the place, therefore, to go into such matters: there are already far too many easy solutions being offered by educationalists whose fluency is not matched by competence in the various disciplines that they casually embrace.

But the need for empirical data in finally resolving certain educational problems does not seem to be in danger of being overlooked at the present time. It is still the need for an adequate philosophy, and in particular for a coherent value structure, that needs stressing. Educational theorists continue very often to write and talk as if to establish facts were sufficient to answer questions and settle disputes; as if, for instance, to establish that the abolition of grammar schools would involve a decline in academic achievement were sufficient to settle that grammar schools ought not to be abolished, or, conversely, that to establish that comprehensivisation will contribute to a greater social homogenity were sufficient to settle that the move towards comprehensives is desirable. To proceed thus is to indulge in Popper's habit of making 'demands'; and yet it is surely clear that one must attempt to *justify* demands, and not merely make them. Any problem that is going to be settled in terms of a convincing prescription is dependent equally upon the justification of value assumptions and factual data. That is to say no more than that one cannot derive ought simply from is. Nor is there any good reason to be misled by the logical-positivists and the pygmy army of conceptual analysts who followed in their wake, whose semantic sparring has nearly killed philosophy and whose dogmatic ethical nihilism is primarily responsible for the widespread assumption that what is good is what grabs your fancy, into thinking that value assumptions are beyond assessment.

There is a simply truth that we have to face up to: given that as a matter of fact we live in a society where different people appear to make very different value judgments in specific instances, if value judgments are ultimately beyond assessment, there is not ultimately a great deal of point in pursuing even empirical research in education. To know that because of factors A, B and C, Z is the appropriate means to the end X, is only of significance in so far as X is desired as an end. If it were, without qualification, the case that 'ends' could not be assessed or evaluated, then, since any 'end' would be as acceptable as any other, it would not actually matter what means we adopted or even whether we knew what end specific means would serve.

This ridiculous conclusion would not, of course, be acceptable to any liberal-democrat, notwithstanding their occasional remarks to the effect that 'ends' cannot be reasoned about. But their compromise solution falls heavily between all available stools: they propose or demand various ends—happiness, truth, self-realisation, etc. These ends cannot, on their own admission, be shown to be ends that ought to be adopted, nor, according to them, is there any means of deciding between the claims of these various ends. And yet, for the most part, particularly in educational philosophy, we complacently and unquestioningly work on their assumptions. For most, if not all, of the educational jargon currently thrown into the debate—autonomy, self-realisation, growth-theory, indoctrination, censorship, equality of opportunity—presupposes for its prescriptive analysis a liberal-democratic framework with particular reference to a principle of freedom. This almost universal assumption of a single framework must be depressing for a society that objects to tradition and wishes to promote a critical ability that is the antithesis of the acceptance of wants, tastes and prejudices as given facts, and for those like Popper, who are praeternaturally obsessed with fear of 'dogmatic self-satisfaction and massive intellectual complacency'.[39]

As I approach the end of this book let me state unequivocally my central points:

(a)   Practical directives in education are dependent, amongst other things, on value judgments.

(b)   There is only one coherent value system, and that is one that places the principle of happiness as supreme.

(c)   Educational philosophy, as she is practised, tends by and large to analyse concepts while formally fighting shy of the need to evaluate; but one cannot analyse normative terms without reference to evaluation. A veil is drawn over this difficulty in the form of a multiplicity of moral ends.

(d)   Amongst these 'ends' is freedom, which, alas, is permanently in conflict with other ends. We are therefore enjoined by the liberal-democrats to take 'a little of Manfred, but not very much of him'. But this will not do at all.

Even if the principle of freedom could be explained and justified as meaning *more* than that reasons that draw on (other) ultimate principles must be given for interfering with people's activities, the possibility of which we incidentally reject, the liberal-democrats' frequent demands that we ought to override the claims of freedom, as for instance when compulsory education is advocated, are quite inconsistent with their equally frequent assertion that the principle of freedom is of equal weight to other ultimate principles, or, more simply, with other demands in the name of freedom. The formula to the effect that the individual's freedom must never be interfered with, except where not to do so would infringe the freedom of others, cannot remove this contradiction until it is adequately explained what constitutes an infringement of the freedom of others; and we do not see how this can be explained without reference to some such term as 'harm', which can only be understood as dependent on the principle of happiness.

Liberal-democratic inconsistency is thus evidenced in the way in which they proceed; they are mistaken in their view that value judgments cannot be assessed; they have removed from their reach any grounds for criticising any view that makes any one of their principles supreme: that is their dilemma. The resolution of the dilemma is to be found in an admission (that is implicit very often in their actual procedure) that the principle of happiness is supreme.

Once the framework of liberal-democratic theory is jolted all the concepts that derive their favourable connotations from it have to seek to defend themselves as best they may. It becomes once again an open question whether indoctrination, defined in any of the proposed ways, is necessarily undesirable, whether censorship differs in any significant way from any other form of positive manipulation or control, and whether one must want even the least interested and least adept mind to attempt to reason out for itself problems that are perhaps insoluble. One may even hope to give the liberal-democrats a helping hand in giving a positive justification for many of the peremptory demands that they wanted to make.

There have been references recently to 'the undifferentiated mush of our educational theory'[40] and to 'our largely haphazard, hand to mouth procedures dictated too often by expediency and political considerations rather than by philosophic principles'.[41] Crossman even confesses that he finds it 'quite impossible to discuss education with a man who sacrifices everything to logical consistency'.[42] The prime reason for this 'mush', this many coloured dress,[43] is liberal-democratic philosophy and the conflicting demands that it is necessarily capable of producing.

The 'mush' must therefore be lived with, unless Plato was right and a knock-down blow can be delivered to the notion that it makes sense to refer to man's right to freedom, undefined, and without reference to a higher principle of happiness.

Notes

1 Dearden, 'Happiness and education', p. 95.
2 Quoted by Dearden from the Scottish Report of 1946 on primary education.
3 Dearden, 'Happiness and education', p. 96.
4 Wilson, P. S., 'Child-centred education' in the *Proceedings of the Philosophy of Education Society of Great Britain*, vol. III, January, 1969.
5 472 E. Cf. 502 C.
6 412 B, 581 C.
7 536 D. 424. *Laws*, 765, 643. *Protagoras*, 325.
8 Popper, op. cit., p. 52.
9 E.g. the contributors to Hollins, op. cit. See Introduction p. xii.
10 E.g. Wilson, J., in Hollins, op. cit. and Dearden, R. F., in *The Philosophy of Primary Education*.
11 E.g. A. MacIntyre in Hollins, op. cit.
12 Anderson, J., quoted by MacIntyre in Hollins, op. cit., p. 18.
13 Crossman, op. cit., p. 75.
14 Popper, op. cit., p. 131.
15 Ibid., p. 111.
16 Russell, B., *On Education*, Allen & Unwin, London, 1960, p. 122.
17 Russell, *Education and the Social Order*, p. 26.
18 Ibid., p. 144.
19 Ibid.
20 'That which makes a man eagerly pursue the ideal perfection of citizenship . . . is the only training to be characterised as education'. *Laws*, 644.
21 Dearden, R. F., in Peters, R. S., ed., *Perspectives on Plowden*, Routledge & Kegan Paul, London, 1969, p. 27.
22 Popper, op. cit., p. 131.
23 Bantock, G. H., *Culture, Industrialisation and Education*, Routledge & Kegan Paul, London, 1968, p. 15.
24 Bantock, G. H., *Education in an Industrial Society*, Faber, London, 1963, p. 77.
25 Ibid., p. 167.
26 Ibid., p. 131.
27 Ibid., p. 201.
28 Hirst, P. H., 'Liberal education and the nature of knowledge' in Dearden, Hirst and Peters, op. cit., p. 391ff.
29 Ibid., p. 392.
30 Ibid., p. 409.
31 Ibid., p. 408.
32 Ibid.
33 Ibid., p. 404.
34 Hirst, P. H., 'Logic of the curriculum', *Journal of Curriculum Studies*, vol. I, 1968–9, p. 146.
35 Hirst, 'Liberal education and the nature of knowledge', p. 400.
36 Ibid., p. 403.
37 Gissing, G., *Demos*, J. M. Dent, London, 1915.

38 Crossman, op. cit., p. 101.
39 Popper, op. cit., p. 130.
40 Peters, R. S., quoted by Morrish, I., *Disciplines of Education*, Allen & Unwin, London, 1967.
41 Winn, C. and Jacks, M. L., *Aristotle*, Methuen, London, 1967, p. 9.
42 Crossman, op. cit., p. 104.
43 557 C.

Select bibliography

BAMBROUGH, J. R. (ed.), *Plato, Popper and Politics*, Heffer, 1967.

BANTOCK, G. H., *Education in an Industrial Society*, Faber & Faber, 1963.
Freedom and Authority in Education, Faber & Faber, 1970.

BENN, S. I., and PETERS, R. S., *Social Principles and the Democratic State*, Allen &
Unwin, 1959.

CORBETT, P., *Ideologies*, Hutchinson, 1965.

COWAN, J. L., *Pleasure and Pain*, Macmillan, 1968.

CROMBIE, I. M., *An Examination of Plato's Doctrines*, 2 vols, Routledge &
Kegan Paul, 1962.

CROSS, R., and WOOZLEY, A. D., *Plato's Republic: A Philosophical Commentary*,
Macmillan, 1964.

CROSSMAN, R. H. S., *Plato Today*, Allen & Unwin, 1963.

DEARDEN, R. F., *The Philosophy of Primary Education: an Introduction*, Routledge
& Kegan Paul, 1968.

DEARDEN, R. F., HIRST, P. H., and PETERS, R. S. (eds), *Education and the
Development of Reason*, Routledge & Kegan Paul, 1972.

ELIOT, T. S., *Notes towards the Definition of Culture*, Faber & Faber, 1962.

D'ENTREVES, A. P., *Natural Law*, Hutchinson, 1951.

FEINBERG, J. (ed.), *Moral Concepts*, Oxford University Press, 1969.

FOOT, P. (ed.), *Theories of Ethics*, Oxford University Press, 1967.

FROMM, E., *Fear of Freedom*, Routledge & Kegan Paul, 1960.

GARFORTH, F. W., *Education and Social Purpose*, Oldbourne, 1962.

GOULDNER, A. W., *Enter Plato: Classical Greece and the Origins of Social Theory*,
Routledge & Kegan Paul, 1967.

GRUBE, G. M. A., *Plato's Thought*, Methuen, 1970.

HART, H. L. A., *The Concept of Law*, Oxford University Press, 1961.

HUDSON, W. D., *Modern Moral Philosophy*, Macmillan, 1970.

JOSHI, N., *Political Ideals of Plato*, Manaktalas, Bombay, 1965.

KEMP, J., *Ethical Naturalism*, Macmillan, 1970.

LEVINSON, R. B., *In Defense of Plato*, Russell & Russell, New York, 1953.

PETERS, R. S., *Ethics and Education*, Allen & Unwin, 1966.

PETERS, R. S. (ed.), *The Concept of Education*, Routledge & Kegan Paul, 1967.

POPPER, K. R., *The Open Society and its Enemies*, 2 vols, Routledge & Kegan
Paul, 1966.

QUINTON, A. (ed.), *Political Philosophy*, Oxford University Press, 1967.

RANKIN, H. D., *Plato and the Individual*, Methuen, 1964.

RUSSELL, B., *On Education*, Allen & Unwin, 1932.
Education and the Social Order, Allen & Unwin, 1967.

SCHNEEWIND, J. B. (ed.), *Mill: Modern Studies in Philosophy*, Macmillan, 1968.

SIDGWICK, H., *The Methods of Ethics*, Macmillan, 1963.

WARNOCK, M. (ed.), *Mill: Utilitarianism*, Fontana, 1962.

WILD, J. D., *Plato's Modern Enemies and the Theory of Natural Law*, University of Chicago Press, 1953.

Index

Index

Liberal-democratic philosophy,
—*cont.*

and equality, 8, 11, 14, 107, 140,
144, 149, 152, 155–6, 158–9, 167
and freedom, 8, 10, 11, 14, 70,
73, 101, 105, 129, 135, 136,
156, 158, 166–7, 196, 198–9
and happiness, 8, 11, 14, 47, 67–9,
89, 94, 106–7, 128, 129, 136,
166–7
individual/beliefs examination,
122, 123–4
and indoctrination, 8, 76, 114,
118, 119, 122, 128
meritocracy, 158, 186
Plato, criticisms of, 2–7, 8, 14, 45,
46–7, 95, 106, 164, 166
and ultimate moral principles, 8–
10, 12–14, 45, 47, 105–6, 113,
118, 125, 126–7
and value judgments, 12–14, 197–
198
(*see also* Crossman, Popper, and
Russell)
Liberal education, 191–4
Liberty, 101
excessive, 36–7
Literature, 110, 189, 190
Lodge, R., 23
Logical positivists, 44, 197

Mabbot, J. D., *The State and the
Citizen*, 101, 102
Mass media, 110, 111, 184, 189, 190
Meritocracy, 158–9
Mill, J. S., 77, 80, 91, 97, 103, 175
analysis of his position, 91–3
community interests, 99
and freedom, 95, 99
of speech, 111, 112
'great things', 97–8
and happiness, 76–7, 80, 90–1, 95,
97
and pleasures, 172
self- and other–regarding actions,
96
utilitarianism, 43, 46, 90, 96, 97,
98
On Liberty, 95, 96, 97, 137 n.4

Misery, 144
and poverty, 74
and unhappiness, 55, 107
Moral discourse, 89–91
Moral laws, 46
Moral propositions, 6, 18, 44, 122,
125, 180
Moral relativism, 45, 72, 73
Music, 22–3
censorship (Plato), 110

Naturalist fallacy, 45, 47, 91, 102,
168 n.43
Nazism, an ideology, 118
Neill, A. S., 169, 170, 173
Nettleship, R. L., knowledge of
eternal truth, 33

Pain, absolute and relative, 59
Peters, R. S., *Ethics and Education*, 89,
107
Philosopher, the, defined by Plato,
29–30
Philosopher-kings
education, 31, 33, 34, 192
and freedom, 99
and intellectual enquiry, 111, 113,
124, 126, 195
and moral knowledge, 43, 44, 47
qualities demanded of, 125, 164,
175
and the State, 7, 29, 31, 43, 145,
174
Pindar, *pseudos gluku*, 139 n.70
Plamenatz, J., and the open society,
16 n.34
Plato, 2, 4, 6–7, 41–3 and *passim*
beauty, 29–30
Cave saga, 31, 32
education (*see* education)
environmental influences, 25, 148,
164, 165
equality, 35, 40–2, 144, 160–2
eugenics, 28, 108–9, 147, 164,
165, 174
freedom, 2, 35, 36, 95, 97, 100–1,
107–8
Good, idea of, 30, 31, 35, 38 n.23,
39 n.25, 41

208

Plato,—*cont.*
  happiness (*see* Happiness)
  individualism, 34, 113
  indoctrination, 101, 127–8, 129–
    130, 133
  justice, just man, just society, 3,
    13, 17, 18, 27–9, 42, 163–7
  Myth of Er, 37
  myth
    of mother earth, 132–3
    of rulership, 129, 133, 147
  political power, 165, 174, 175
  social roles, society (*see* Social
    roles)
  and the soul, 27–9, 37, 67
  and the State (*see* State)
  Theory of Forms (Ideas), 29, 41–2
  totalitarianism, 36, 49, 69
  tribalism, 101
  utilitarianism (*see* Utilitarianism)
  wealth, 26, 35, 38 n.4, 65, 66,
    150, 162–3, 166
  and the whole, 44–50
Pleasure, 172, 190
  and the Good, 31, 40
  and happiness, 54, 75 n.11, 81
Politics, 101, 196
  and education, 176, 187
  election by popular vote, 151,
    168 n.27
  and equality, 159
  and power, 165, 174, 175
Popper, K. R., 44, 102, 103
  criticism of Crossman, 69, 177
  and equality, 140, 141, 142, 144,
    158
  and freedom, 16 n.35, 103, 105,
    106, 136, 177–8
  indoctrination, 177–8
  liberal-democratic Platonic
    criticism, 1–2, 4–7, 13, 21, 23,
    36, 47, 49, 130, 135
  censorship, 110, 112
  education, 132, 135, 136, 176
  equality, 140, 144, 150
  happiness, 49, 69, 70, 72, 73
  sexual freedom, 109
  The Open Society and its Enemies, 4–
    7, 13, 21, 23, 45, 73

Power, equal distribution, 150, 164,
  167
Progressive educationists, 10, 169
Psychological harm, 96
  restraint, 96–7

Rankin, H. D., and social roles, 148,
  149
Rationality, 36, 105, 163, 188
  divine element in man, 37, 191
  an educational aim, 113, 187–8,
    190
  and individual beliefs, 123, 188
  rules of discourse, 141
  and search for moral principles,
    124–7
Romanticism, and the individual,
  134
Rubinstein, D., and Stoneman, C.,
  and educational roles, 155,
    168 n.29
Russell, B., 3, 45, 144
  educational theories, 110–11, 119,
    178
  and happiness, 67–8, 178
  and justice, 150, 164, 165
  liberal-democratic Platonic
    criticism, 1–3, 10, 13, 36, 49,
    119, 130, 144, 163, 164
  Education and the Social Order, 10–
    11, 44, 119, 178
Ryle, G., *Mind*, 76

Science, 5, 174
Self-determination, 135, 136
Self-development, 96
  an educational objective, 1, 113,
    135
Sexual desire, 66, 78, 108–9, 147, 174
Shaw, Bernard, 'knowing your
  place', 69
Shorey, P., 21, 33
Social roles, 180
  and equality of opportunity, 153f.
  in an open society, 74
  self-perpetuating groups, 149
  women and, 28
Social roles, Plato and
  distribution by aptitude and
    ability, 27, 67, 69–70, 145–50,

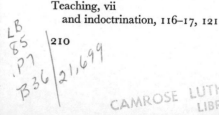